COMPUTER NETWORKS
A SYSTEMS APPROACH

COMPUTER NETWORKS
A SYSTEMS APPROACH

VOLUME 1

Victor Garcia Perdomo

Kruger Brentt
Publishers
2025

Kruger Brentt Publishers UK. LTD.

Company Number 9728962

Regd. Office: 68 St Margarets Road, Edgware, Middlesex HA8 9UU

© 2025 AUTHOR

ISBN: 978-1-78715-301-1 (Vol. 1)

For information on all our publications visit our website at http://krugerbrentt.com/

PREFACE

"Computer Networks: A Systems Approach" is a comprehensive exploration into the principles, protocols, and technologies that underpin modern computer networks. This book serves as an essential resource for students, educators, and professionals seeking to understand the fundamentals of computer networking and its practical applications in today's interconnected world.

Computer networks form the backbone of our digital infrastructure, enabling communication and data exchange between devices, systems, and users across the globe. From local area networks (LANs) and wide area networks (WANs) to the Internet and beyond, computer networks play a crucial role in facilitating information sharing, collaboration, and innovation in virtually every aspect of modern life.

As editors of this volume, we have endeavored to compile a diverse array of perspectives, methodologies, and case studies from leading experts and practitioners in the field of computer networking. Through a blend of theoretical foundations, practical insights, and real-world examples, this book covers a wide range of topics, including network architecture, protocols, routing, switching, security, and emerging trends such as software-defined networking (SDN) and network function virtualization (NFV).

Our overarching goal in presenting this book is to provide readers with a comprehensive and up-to-date resource that fosters a deeper understanding of computer networking principles and practices. By offering clear explanations, illustrative examples, and practical advice, we aim to empower students, educators, and professionals to design, deploy, and manage robust and reliable computer networks that meet the needs of today's digital society.

We extend our sincere gratitude to all the contributors who have generously shared their expertise, experiences, and insights in the field of computer networks. It is our hope that this book will serve as a valuable reference and guide for readers as they navigate the complexities of modern networking and contribute to the advancement of networked systems and technologies.

Victor Garcia Perdomo

CONTENTS

Contents

Contents

CHAPTER-1

ESTABLISHING A NETWORK INFRASTRUCTURE

INTRODUCTION: AN OVERVIEW

If you desire to construct a computer network with the capability to expand on a worldwide scale and facilitate a wide range of applications such as teleconferencing, video on demand, electronic commerce, distributed computing, and digital libraries, then consider the following. Which technologies are now accessible and suitable as the foundational components, and what software architecture would you create to seamlessly incorporate these components into a functional communication service? The primary objective of this book is to provide a comprehensive description of the various building materials and demonstrate their application in the construction of a network from its foundation.

Prior to delving into the intricacies of computer network design, it is imperative that we establish a clear and unanimous definition of what constitutes a computer network. Previously, the term "network" referred to the collection of sequential connections utilized to connect unintelligent terminals to mainframe computers. Additional significant networks encompass the telephony network and the cable television network utilized for the distribution of video signals. These networks share two primary characteristics: they are designed to handle a certain type of data (such as keystrokes, speech, or video) and they usually connect to devices that are specifically built for that purpose (such as terminals, hand receivers, and television sets).

What sets apart a computer network from other sorts of networks? The primary attribute of a computer network that holds the utmost significance is its universality. Computer networks are predominantly constructed using versatile programmable hardware, and they are not specifically tailored for a particular use such as telephony or television broadcasting. Instead, they possess the capability to transport many forms of information and provide extensive support for a broad and continuously expanding array of applications. Modern computer networks have largely replaced the functions that were formerly carried out by dedicated networks. This chapter examines common applications of computer networks and explores the necessary considerations for a network designer aiming to enable these applications.

After comprehending the requirements, what is the next course of action? Fortunately, we will not be constructing the inaugural network. Previous pioneers, particularly the group of scholars who developed the Internet, have paved the way for us. We will utilize the vast reservoir of knowledge accumulated from the Internet to inform our design process. This expertise is manifested in a network design that discerns the accessible hardware and software elements and demonstrates how they might be organized to constitute a comprehensive network system.

It is crucial to comprehend not only the construction of networks, but also their operation and management, as well as the development of network applications. The majority of individuals today possess computer networks in their residences, workplaces, and occasionally even in their vehicles, thus managing networks is no longer limited to a select few experts. Due to the widespread use of smartphones, a larger number of individuals from this generation are now creating networked applications compared to previous times. It is necessary to take into account networks from several viewpoints, including those of builders, operators, and application developers.

This chapter aims to achieve four objectives that will enable us to develop a thorough comprehension of the process of constructing, managing, and coding a network. At first, it analyzes the specific requirements that different applications and diverse groups of persons place on the network. Moreover, it introduces the notion of a network architecture, which forms the foundation for the rest of the book. Moreover, it offers a range of essential elements involved in the implementation of computer networks. Ultimately, it determines the fundamental metrics used to evaluate the effectiveness of computer networks.

1.1 Applications

The Internet is commonly experienced by individuals through many applications such as the World Wide Web, email, social networking platforms, streaming services for music or movies, videoconferencing, instant messaging, and file-sharing. In other words, we engage with the Internet in the capacity of network users. The largest demographic of those that engage with the Internet in any capacity is comprised of internet users, although there are several other significant groups as well.

There is a cohort of individuals who make applications, which has experienced significant growth in recent years due to the emergence of strong programming platforms and the proliferation of smartphones. These advancements have provided new avenues for rapid application development and access to a wide consumer base.

Additionally, there are individuals that oversee or administer networks, which is primarily a behind-the-scenes role. However, it is a crucial and frequently intricate responsibility. Due to the increasing frequency of home networks, an increasing number of individuals are also becoming network operators, even if it is just to a limited extent.

Lastly, there are individuals who conceive and construct the devices and protocols that collectively constitute the Internet. The ultimate demographic that this textbook, as well as others of its kind, aims to reach is the customary audience, and it will remain our primary area of concentration. Nevertheless, in this book, we shall also take into account the viewpoints of application developers and network operators.

By taking into account various viewpoints, we may enhance our comprehension of the varied criteria that a network must fulfill. Application developers can enhance the performance of their apps by gaining a comprehensive understanding of the underlying technology and its interaction with the applications. Prior to delving into the process of constructing a network, it is essential to thoroughly examine the various sorts of applications that modern networks provide.

1.1.1 Classes of Applications

The World Wide Web is the Internet application that propelled the Internet from a relatively unknown instrument primarily utilized by scientists and engineers to the widely popular phenomenon it is today. The Internet has become an immensely influential platform, to the extent that some individuals mistakenly equate it with the Web. However, it is important to note that the Web is not a singular application.

The Web, in its fundamental state, offers a user-friendly and instinctively uncomplicated interface. Users navigate between pages containing textual and graphical elements, selecting objects of interest to access additional information, which is displayed on a new page. It is widely known that each chosen object on a page is associated with an identifier that determines the next page or object to be viewed. A Uniform Resource Locator (URL) is an identifier that allows for the identification of all the accessible items that may be shown through a web browser. As an illustration, http://www.cs.princeton.edu/~llp/index.html is the URL for a page providing information about one of this book's authors: the string http indicates that the Hypertext Transfer Protocol (HTTP) should be used to download the page, www.cs.princeton.edu is the name of the machine that serves the page, and /~llp/index.html uniquely identifies Larry's home page at this site.

Many web users are unaware that clicking on a single URL might result in the exchange of over a dozen messages over the Internet. This number can increase significantly if the web page has numerous embedded objects. This message exchange consists of six messages to translate the server name (www.cs.princeton.edu) into its Internet Protocol (IP) address (128.112.136.35), three messages to establish a Transmission Control Protocol (TCP) connection between your browser and this server, four messages for your browser to send the HTTP "GET" request and for the server to respond with the requested page (with both sides acknowledging receipt of the message), and four messages to terminate the TCP connection. However, this does not encompass the vast number of messages transmitted between Internet nodes on a daily basis solely for the purpose of acknowledging their presence and readiness to provide web pages, convert names into addresses, and route messages to their final destination. Another widespread application class of the Internet is the delivery of "streaming" audio and video. Services such as video on demand and Internet radio use this technology. While we frequently start at a website to initiate a streaming session, the delivery of audio and video has some important differences from fetching a simple web page of text and images. For example, you often don't want to download an entire video file—a process that might take a few minutes—before watching the first scene. Streaming audio and video implies a more timely transfer of messages from sender to receiver, and the receiver displays the video or plays the audio pretty much as it arrives.

It is important to understand that streaming apps differ from the usual distribution of text, graphics, and images in that humans ingest audio and video streams continuously. Any interruptions, such as skipped sounds or halted video, are not tolerated. In contrast, a conventional (non-streaming) page can be transmitted and consumed in fragments. This disparity impacts the manner in which the network facilitates these distinct categories of applications.

Another variant of the application class is real-time audio and video. Streaming applications have looser time limitations compared to these applications. When utilizing a voice-over-IP application like Skype or a videoconferencing application, it is crucial for the participants to engage in timely exchanges. When a person at one end gestures, then that action must be displayed at the other end as quickly as possible.[1]

When an individual attempts to interject, the person being interrupted must promptly perceive this and make a decision whether to permit the interruption or continue speaking despite the interrupter. An excessive amount of latency in this particular context renders the system inoperable. In contrast, video on demand services are considered satisfactory even if there is a delay of several seconds between the user initiating the movie and the first image being presented. Interactive apps typically involve bidirectional audio and/or video streams, whereas streaming applications primarily transmit video or audio in a unidirectional manner.

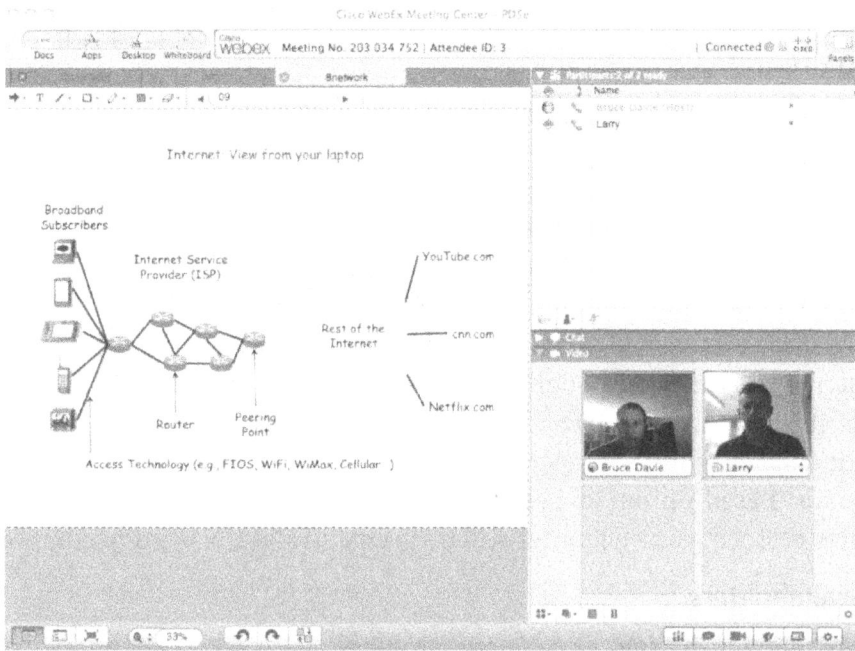

Figure 1. A multimedia application including videoconferencing.

Internet-based videoconferencing solutions have been in existence since the early 1990s, but their popularity has surged in recent years, with numerous commercial products available. Figure 1 illustrates an example of such a system. Similar to the complexity involved in downloading a web page, video apps also require more than what is first apparent. Network and protocol designers must address challenges such as optimizing video content for low bandwidth networks and ensuring that video and audio remain synchronized and delivered on time to provide a satisfactory user experience. Later in the book, we will examine these and various other topics pertaining to multimedia applications.

While these are only two instances, the act of retrieving online pages and engaging in a videoconference exemplify the range of possibilities for developing applications on the Internet and provide a glimpse into the intricate nature of its design. In subsequent sections of the book, we will establish a comprehensive classification system for different types of applications. This taxonomy will serve as a framework to inform our analysis of crucial design choices involved in the construction, management, and utilization of networks. The book finishes by reviewing these two particular applications, along with several others that exemplify the wide range of possibilities on the current Internet.

Currently, this brief overview of a few common applications will be sufficient to allow us to begin examining the challenges that need to be tackled in order to construct a network that can accommodate a wide range of applications.

1.2 Requirements

Our objective is to comprehensively comprehend the process of constructing a computer network starting from its foundation. To achieve this objective, we will adopt a methodological approach that involves beginning with fundamental concepts and thereafter posing the types of inquiries that would naturally arise when constructing a real network. Throughout the process, we will employ current protocols to demonstrate different design options, but we will not blindly adhere to these established artifacts. Instead, we will explore the rationale behind the design of networks. Although it may be tempting to simply grasp the current methods, it is crucial to acknowledge the fundamental principles because networks are continually evolving with technological advancements and the creation of new applications. Based on our experience, once you grasp the basic concepts, any unfamiliar protocol you encounter will be pretty straightforward to comprehend.

1.2.1 Stakeholders

⊙ As previously said, a student studying networks can adopt multiple viewpoints. During the initial publication of this book, the vast majority of individuals did not have any means of accessing the Internet. The few who did were able to do so either at their workplace, at a university, or through a dial-up modem connection at home. The number of popular programs is extremely limited. Therefore, similar to the majority of books during that period, our book centered on the viewpoint of an individual who would create networking equipment and protocols. Our primary objective remains centered on this viewpoint, with the expectation that upon completing this book, you will possess the knowledge and skills necessary to develop networking equipment and protocols for future applications.

⊙ Additionally, we aim to include the viewpoints of two other stakeholders: developers of networked applications and network managers or operators. Let us see how these three stakeholders could outline their demands for a network: An application programmer would list the services that his or her application needs: for example, a guarantee that each message the application sends will be delivered without error within a certain amount of time or the ability to switch gracefully among different connections to the network as the user moves around.

⊙ A network operator would list the characteristics of a system that is easy to administer and manage: for example, in which faults can be easily isolated, new devices can be added to the network and configured correctly, and it is easy to account for usage.

⊙ A network designer would list the properties of a cost-effective design: for example, that network resources are efficiently utilized and fairly allocated to different users. Issues of performance are also likely to be important.

This section attempts to distill the requirements of different stakeholders into a high-level introduction to the major considerations that drive network design and, in doing so, identify the challenges addressed throughout the rest of this book.

1.2.2 Scalable Connectivity

First and foremost, a network must facilitate the connection between a group of computers. Occasionally, it suffices to construct a restricted network that exclusively links a small number of chosen machines. Indeed, due to concerns regarding privacy and security, numerous private (business) networks aim to restrict the number of workstations that are linked. On the other hand, the Internet, being a prime example, is specifically designed to expand in a manner that enables it to potentially link all the computers worldwide. Scaling refers to the ability of a system to accommodate growth without any limitations on its size. This book tackles the issue of scalability by taking inspiration from the Internet.

In order to gain a comprehensive understanding of connectivity requirements, it is necessary to closely examine the manner in which computers are interconnected within a network. Connectivity manifests itself at various levels. At its most basic level, a network can comprise of two or more computers that are physically linked by a physical media, such as a coaxial cable or an optical fiber. A physical media that connects computers is commonly referred to as a link, and the computers it connects are often called nodes. (In certain cases, a node may refer to a hardware component that is more specialized than a computer. However, for the purpose of this article, we will not consider this distinction.) Figure 2 demonstrates that physical linkages can be either point-to-point, connecting only two nodes, or multiple-access, allowing more than two nodes to share a single physical link. Wireless links, such as those facilitated by cellular networks and Wi-Fi networks, are a significant category of multiple-access links. Multiple-access links are inherently constrained in terms of both their geographical coverage and the number of nodes they may connect. Therefore, they frequently employ the last mile, which links end consumers to the rest of the network.

If computer networks were limited to situations in which all nodes are directly connected to each other over a common physical medium, then either networks would be very limited in the number of computers they could connect, or the number of wires coming out of the back of each node would quickly become both unmanageable and very expensive. Fortunately, connectivity between two nodes does not necessarily imply a direct physical connection between them—indirect connectivity may be achieved among a set of cooperating nodes. Consider the following two examples of how a collection of computers can be indirectly connected.

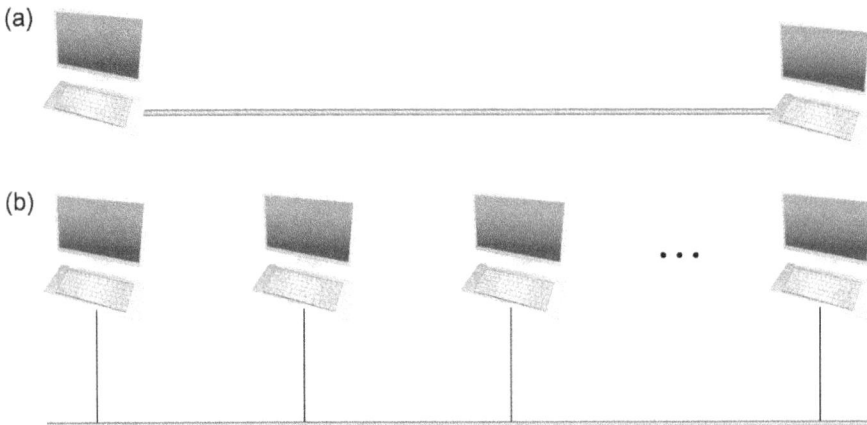

Figure 2. Direct links: (a) point-to-point; (b) multiple-access.

Figure 3 shows a set of nodes, each of which is attached to one or more point-to-point links. Those nodes that are attached to at least two links run software that forwards data received on one link out on another. If organized in a systematic way, these forwarding nodes form a switched network. There are numerous types of switched networks, of which the two most common are circuit switched and packet switched. The former is most notably employed by the telephone system, while the latter is used for the overwhelming majority of computer networks and will be the focus of this book. (Circuit switching is, however, making a bit of a comeback in the optical networking realm, which turns out to be important as demand for network capacity constantly grows.) The important feature of packet-switched networks is that the nodes in such a network send discrete blocks of data to each other. Think of these blocks of data as corresponding to some piece of application data such as a file, a piece of email, or an image. We call each block of data either a packet or a message, and for now we use these terms interchangeably.

Packet-switched networks typically use a strategy called store-and-forward. As the name suggests, each node in a store-and-forward network first receives a complete packet over some link, stores the packet in its internal memory, and then forwards the complete packet to the next node. In contrast, a circuit-switched network first establishes a dedicated circuit across a sequence of links and then allows the source node to send a stream of bits across this circuit to a destination node. The major reason for using packet switching rather than circuit switching in a computer network is efficiency, discussed in the next subsection.

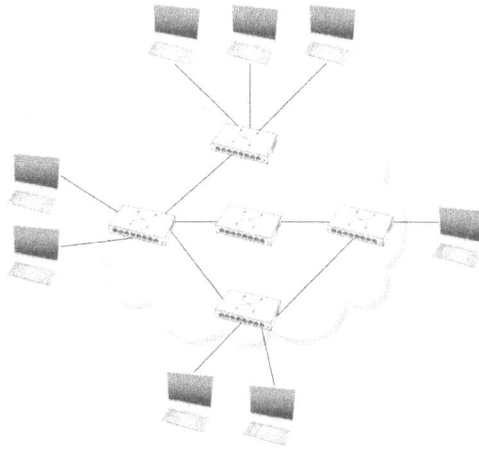

Figure 3. Switched network.

The cloud in Figure 3 distinguishes between the nodes on the inside that implement the network (they are commonly called switches, and their primary function is to store and forward packets) and the nodes on the outside of the cloud that use the network (they are traditionally called hosts, and they support users and run application programs). Also note that the cloud is one of the most important icons of computer networking. In general, we use a cloud to denote any type of network, whether it is a single point-to-point link, a multiple-access link, or a switched network. Thus, whenever you see a cloud used in a figure, you can think of it as a placeholder for any of the networking technologies covered in this book.[1]

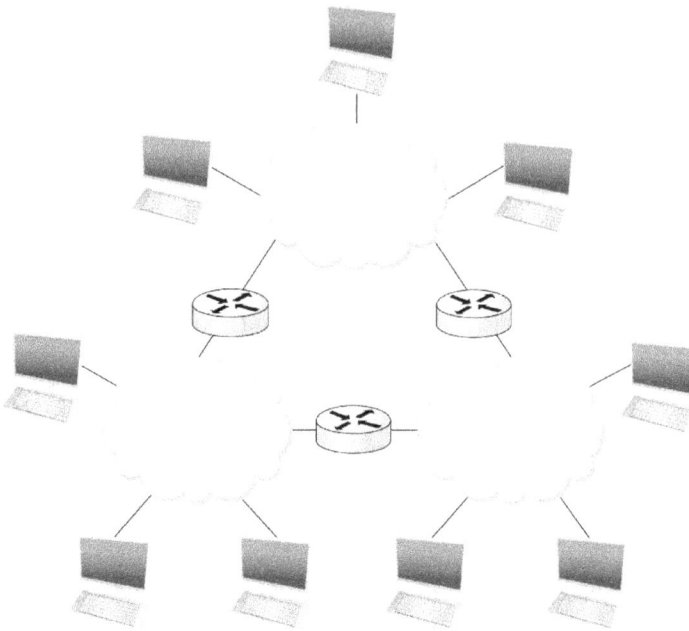

Figure 4. Interconnection of networks.

Figure 4 illustrates another method of indirectly connecting a group of computers. In this scenario, a collection of autonomous networks (clouds) are linked together to create an internetwork, commonly referred to as the internet. We adhere to the Internet's standard of denoting a generic internetwork of networks as a lowercase "i" internet, while the specific TCP/IP Internet that we utilize on a daily basis is referred to as the capital "I" Internet. A node that is interconnected with two or more networks is generally referred to as a router or gateway. It performs a similar function as a switch by transmitting messages from one network to another. It is important to understand that an internet can be considered as a distinct type of network, implying that an internet can be constructed by combining multiple internets. Therefore, we can construct networks of any size by recursively joining clouds to create larger clouds. The notion that interconnecting vastly disparate networks was the pivotal innovation of the Internet can be reasonably contended. The successful expansion of the Internet to a global scale, encompassing billions of nodes, can be attributed to the astute design choices made by the early Internet architects, which we will delve into at a later point.Just because a set of hosts are directly or indirectly connected to each other does not mean that we have succeeded in providing host-to-host connectivity. The final requirement is that each node must be able to say which of the other nodes on the network it wants to communicate with. This is done by assigning an address to each node. An address is a byte string that identifies a node; that is, the network can use a node's address to distinguish it from the other nodes connected to the network. When a source node wants the network to deliver a message to a certain destination node, it specifies the address of the destination node. If the sending and receiving nodes are not directly connected, then the switches and routers of the network use this address to decide how to forward the message toward the destination. The process of determining systematically how to forward messages toward the destination node based on its address is called routing.

This brief introduction to addressing and routing has presumed that the source node wants to send a message to a single destination node (unicast). While this is the most common scenario, it is also possible that the source node might want to broadcast a message to all the nodes on the network. Or, a source node might want to send a message to some subset of the other nodes but not all of them, a situation called multicast. Thus, in addition to node-specific addresses, another requirement of a network is that it supports multicast and broadcast addresses.

Key Takeaway

The key concept to grasp from this talk is that a network can be defined recursively as a collection of two or more nodes linked together physically, or as a collection of two or more networks linked together by a node. Put simply, a network can be formed by layering networks, with the lowest level being the network that is actually implemented using a physical medium. One of the main difficulties in establishing network connectivity is determining a unique address for each node that can be accessed on the network, whether it is a logical or physical address. Additionally, these addresses are used to correctly route messages to the intended target node(s).

1.2.3 Cost-Effective Resource Sharing

This book specifically centers on packet-switched networks, as previously mentioned. This part elucidates the primary necessity of computer networks, which is efficiency, and hence directs us towards the preferred approach of packet switching.

In a network with nested networks, it is feasible for any two hosts to communicate with each other by transmitting messages through a series of links and nodes. Naturally, our goal is not limited to supporting a single pair of communicating hosts. We aim to enable all pairs of hosts to exchange messages. The topic at hand is how multiple hosts may effectively share the network, particularly when they desire simultaneous usage. In addition to the existing challenge, how can multiple hosts concurrently access the same link?

In order to comprehend the manner in which hosts distribute a network, it is necessary to present the fundamental notion of multiplexing. This term refers to the sharing of a system resource among several users. Multiplexing can be understood by comparing it to a timesharing computer system, where a single physical processor is divided across numerous jobs, giving each job the illusion of having its own dedicated processor. In the same way, data transmitted by several users can be combined and transmitted over the physical links that form a network.

To understand the functionality, let's examine the basic network depicted in Figure 5. In this network, three hosts on the left side (S1-S3) are transmitting data to three hosts on the right side (R1-R3). They accomplish this by utilizing a switched network that consists of a single physical link. (To simplify, let's assume that host S1 is transmitting data to host R1, and so forth.) In this scenario, switch 1 combines three data streams, each associated with a pair of hosts, onto a single physical link. Switch 2 then separates the combined data streams back into their original individual flows. Please be aware that we deliberately refrain from providing precise details regarding the specific definition of a "flow of data". For the purpose of this explanation, let's imagine that each host on the left side has a substantial amount of data that it wants to transmit to its corresponding host on the right side.

Multiple flows can be multiplexed onto a single physical link using various ways. A widely used technique is synchronous time-division multiplexing (STDM).

The concept of STDM involves dividing time into uniform intervals and allowing each flow to transmit its data via the physical link in a sequential manner. Put simply, data is communicated from S1 to R1 during time quantum 1, from S2 to R2 during time quantum 2, and from S3 to R3 during quantum 3. At this juncture, the initial flow (S1 to R1) is allowed to proceed once more, and the cycle continues. Another technique that can be used is frequency-division multiplexing (FDM). Frequency Division Multiplexing (FDM) involves transmitting each flow over the physical link using a distinct frequency, similar to how signals for multiple TV stations are carried at separate frequencies over the airways or on a coaxial cable TV link.

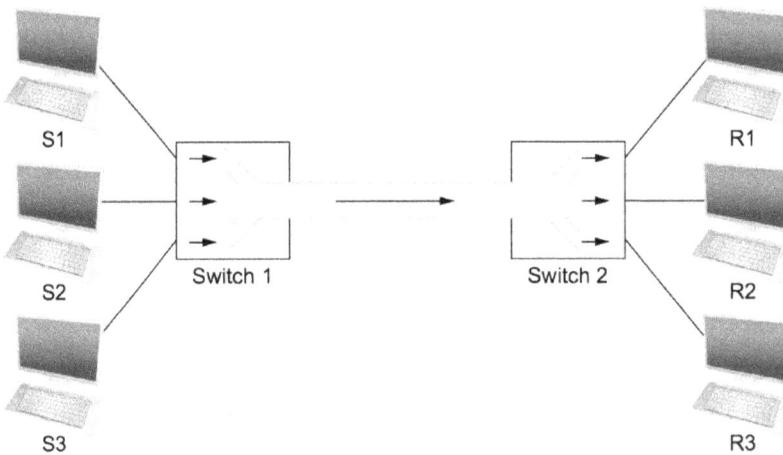

Figure 5. Multiplexing multiple logical flows over a single physical link.

While STDM and FDM are easy to comprehend, they have two inherent limitations. If one of the flows (host pairs) does not have any data to communicate, its portion of the physical link, known as its time quantum or frequency, will remain unused, even if one of the other flows has data to broadcast. As an illustration, S3 had to patiently wait its turn after S1 and S2 in the above paragraph, even if S1 and S2 had no data to transmit. In computer communication, the duration of idle time for a link can be significant. For instance, consider the substantial amount of time spent viewing a web page, during which the link remains idle, in contrast to the relatively shorter time spent fetching the page. Furthermore, both STDM and FDM are constrained by the requirement that the maximum number of flows must be predetermined and unchanging. Modifying the size of the quantum or including extra quanta in the case of STDM, or introducing new frequencies in the case of FDM, is not feasible.

The method of multiplexing that specifically targets these limitations, and that we extensively utilize in this book, is referred to as statistical multiplexing. Despite its misleading moniker, statistical multiplexing is a straightforward subject that revolves around two fundamental notions. Initially, the system operates similarly to STDM, where the physical link is shared over time. This means that data from one flow is transferred over the physical link first, followed by data from another flow, and so forth. Unlike Synchronous Time Division Multiplexing (STDM), data is broadcast from each flow in response to a specific request, rather than being sent during a prearranged time interval. Therefore, if there is just one flow with data to transmit, it can do so immediately without waiting for its allocated time interval and without seeing the unused time intervals assigned to other flows. The effectiveness of packet switching is derived from the avoidance of idle time.

As currently described, statistical multiplexing lacks a means to guarantee that all flows will eventually have the opportunity to transmit over the physical link. Essentially, once a flow initiates the transmission of data, it is necessary to provide a mechanism to restrict the transmission in order to allow other flows to take their turn. In order to address this requirement, statistical multiplexing establishes a maximum limit on the size of the data block that each flow is allowed to send at any given time. A packet, which is a small block of data, is used to differentiate it from the potentially enormous message that an application software may need to send. Due to the imposed limitations on packet size in a packet-switched network, it is possible for a host to be unable to transmit an entire message in a single packet. The source may require the communication to be divided into many packets, while the receiver must then reassemble the packets to reconstruct the original message.

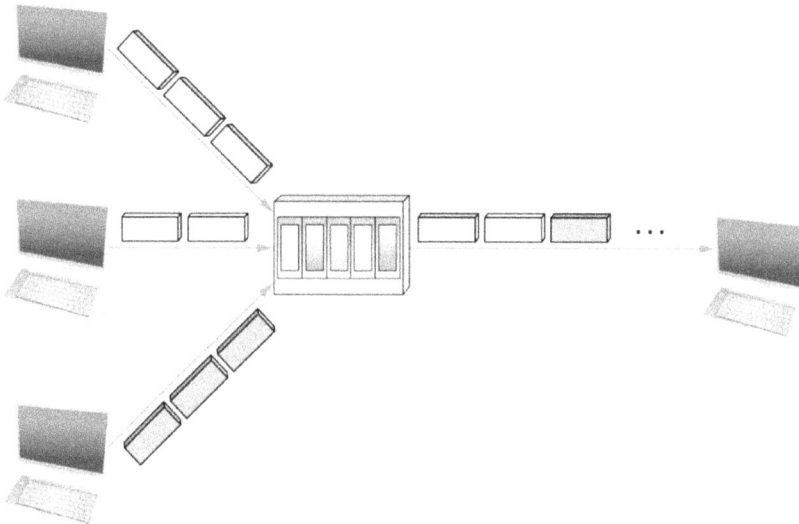

Figure 6. A switch multiplexing packets from multiple sources onto one shared link.

In other words, each flow sends a sequence of packets over the physical link, with a decision made on a packet-by-packet basis as to which flow's packet to send next. Notice that, if only one flow has data to send, then it can send a sequence of packets back-to-back; however, should more than one of the flows have data to send, then their packets are interleaved on the link. Figure 6 depicts a switch multiplexing packets from multiple sources onto a single shared link.

The decision as to which packet to send next on a shared link can be made in a number of different ways. For example, in a network consisting of switches interconnected by links such as the one in Figure 5, the decision would be made by the switch that transmits packets onto the shared link. (As we will see later, not all packet-switched networks actually involve switches, and they may use other mechanisms to determine whose packet goes onto the link next.) Each switch in a packet-switched network makes this decision independently, on a packet-by-packet basis. One of the issues that faces a network designer is how to make this decision in a fair manner. For example, a switch could be designed to service packets on a first-in, first-out (FIFO) basis. Another approach would be to transmit the packets from each of the different flows that are currently sending data through the switch in a round-robin manner. This might be done to ensure that certain flows receive a particular share of the link's bandwidth or that they never have their packets delayed in the switch for more than a certain length of time. A network that attempts to allocate bandwidth to particular flows is sometimes said to support quality of service (QoS).

Also, notice in Figure 6 that since the switch has to multiplex three incoming packet streams onto one outgoing link, it is possible that the switch will receive packets faster than the shared link can accommodate. In this case, the switch is forced to buffer these packets in its memory. Should a switch receive packets faster than it can send them for an extended period of time, then the switch will eventually run out of buffer space, and some packets will have to be dropped. When a switch is operating in this state, it is said to be congested.

Key Takeaway

The bottom line is that statistical multiplexing defines a cost-effective way for multiple users (e.g., host-to-host flows of data) to share network resources (links and nodes) in a fine-grained manner. It defines the packet as the granularity with which the links of the network are allocated to different flows, with each switch able to schedule the use of the physical links it is connected to on a per-packet basis. Fairly allocating link capacity to different flows and dealing with congestion when it occurs are the key challenges of statistical multiplexing.

1.2.4 Support for Common Services

The preceding discourse centered on the difficulties associated with offering economical connectivity among a cluster of hosts, nevertheless it is excessively reductionist to perceive a computer network as merely transmitting packets among an assemblage of computers. A network can be better understood as a mechanism that enables a group of application programs, which are spread across multiple computers, to exchange information. Put simply, a computer network must have the capability for application programs on connected hosts to communicate effectively. From the standpoint of the application developer, the network should facilitate their work.

When two application programs require communication, several intricate processes must occur beyond the basic act of transmitting a message from one host to another. An alternative approach would include integrating all the intricate functionality into every application software by the application designers. Nevertheless, considering that numerous apps want shared services, it is far more rational to develop these shared services once and allow application designers to construct their applications utilizing these services. The task for a network designer is to determine the appropriate collection of shared services. The objective is to conceal the intricacy of the network from the application while avoiding excessive limitations on the application designer.

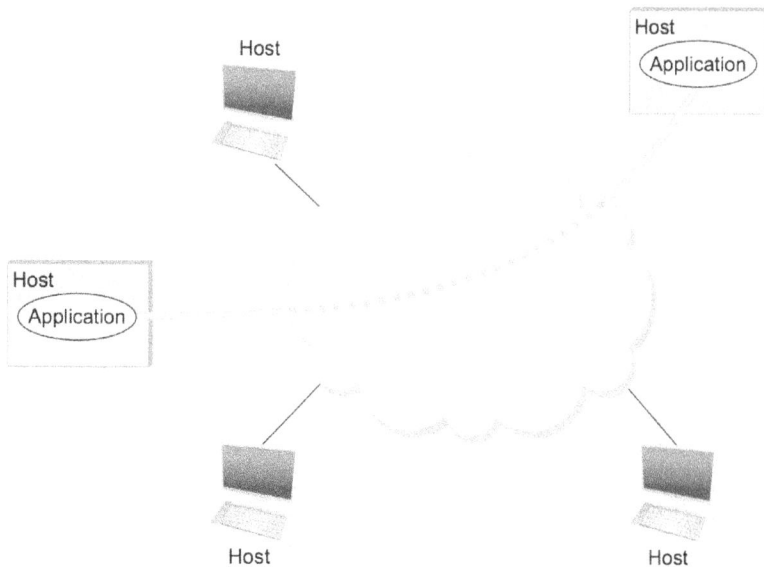

Figure 7. Processes communicating over an abstract channel.

From an intuitive perspective, we perceive the network as a means of establishing logical channels via which application-level processes can interact with one another. Each channel is designed to offer the specific services needed by the corresponding application. Put simply, similar to how we use a cloud to symbolize the connection between a group of computers, we now perceive a channel as the link between two processes. Figure 7 depicts a duo of application-level processes engaging in communication through a logical channel, which is built on top of a cloud that interconnects a group of hosts. The channel can be conceptualized as a conduit that links two applications, enabling a sending application to transmit data from one end and anticipate the network to transport that data to the receiving application at the other end of the conduit.

Similar to other abstractions, logical process-to-process channels are constructed using a set of physical host-to-host channels. Layering is the fundamental concept of network architectures that will be further explained in the following section.

The task at hand is to identify the specific features and capabilities that the channels need to offer to application programs. For instance, does the application necessitate an assurance that messages transmitted across the channel are successfully delivered, or is it satisfactory if certain messages do not reach their destination? Is it imperative for messages to be received by the recipient process in the exact sequence they were sent, or does the receiver disregard the order in which messages arrive? Is it necessary for the network to guarantee that no unauthorized individuals can intercept communications on the channel, or is privacy not a priority? Typically, a network offers a range of channels, and each application chooses the most suitable type based on its requirements. The subsequent portion of this section demonstrates the cognitive processes involved in delineating valuable channels.

IDENTIFY COMMON COMMUNICATION PATTERNS

The process of designing abstract channels begins with comprehending the communication requirements of a representative assortment of applications. Next, the common communication requirements are extracted and subsequently integrated into the network by including the necessary functionality.

An example of an early application that can be used on any network is a file access software such as the File Transfer Protocol (FTP) or Network File System (NFS). The communication aspect of remote file access is characterized by two processes: one process that initiates a request to read or write a file, and another process that fulfills this request. While the specifics may differ, such as whether entire files are transferred or only individual blocks of the file are accessed at a time, these variations do not change the fundamental nature of the remote file access communication. The process responsible for requesting access to the file is referred to as the client, while the process responsible for facilitating access to the file is known as the server.

The process of reading a file entails the client transmitting a concise request message to a server, and the server reciprocating with a substantial message that encompasses the data within the file. In the context of writing data, the process operates in a reverse manner. The client transmits a substantial message containing the data to be written to the server, and in response, the server provides a concise message to acknowledge that the data has been successfully written to the disk.

A digital library is a more advanced and complex application compared to file transfer, yet, it necessitates similar communication services. One example is the Association for Computing Machinery (ACM), which manages a vast digital collection of computer scientific literature accessible at http://portal.acm.org/dl.cfm

This library offers an extensive array of search and navigation functionalities to assist users in locating desired materials. However, its primary function is to fulfill user requests for files, such as electronic versions of journal articles. Using file access, a digital library, and the two video applications described in the introduction (videoconferencing and video on demand) as a representative sample, we might decide to provide the following two types of channels: request/reply channels and message stream channels. The request/reply channel would be used by the file transfer and digital library applications. It would guarantee that every message sent by one side is received by the other side and that only one copy of each message is delivered. The request/reply channel might also protect the privacy and integrity of the data that flows over it, so that unauthorized parties cannot read or modify the data being exchanged between the client and server processes.

The message stream channel could be used by both the video on demand and videoconferencing applications, provided it is parameterized to support both one-way and two-way traffic and to support different delay properties. The message stream channel might not need to guarantee that all messages are delivered, since a video application can operate adequately even if some video frames are not received. It would, however, need to ensure that those messages that are delivered arrive in the same order in which they were sent, to avoid displaying frames out of sequence. Like the request/reply channel, the message stream channel might want to ensure the privacy and integrity of the video data. Finally, the message stream channel might need to support multicast, so that multiple parties can participate in the teleconference.

While it is common for a network designer to strive for the smallest number of abstract channel types that can serve the largest number of applications, there is a danger in trying to get away with too few channel abstractions. Simply stated, if you have a hammer, then everything looks like a nail. For example, if all you have are message stream and request/reply channels, then it is tempting to use them for the next application that comes along, even if neither type provides exactly the semantics needed by the application. Thus, network designers will probably be inventing new types of channels—and adding options to existing channels—for as long as application programmers are inventing new applications.

Also note that independent of exactly what functionality a given channel provides, there is the question of where that functionality is implemented. In many cases, it is easiest to view the host-to-host connectivity of the underlying network as simply providing a bit pipe, with any high-level communication semantics provided at the end hosts. The advantage of this approach is that it keeps the switches in the middle of the network as simple as possible—they simply forward packets—but it requires the end hosts to take on much of the burden of supporting semantically rich process-to-process channels. The alternative is to push additional functionality onto the switches, thereby allowing the end hosts to be "dumb" devices (e.g., telephone handsets). We will see this question of how various network services are partitioned between the packet switches and the end hosts (devices) as a recurring issue in network design.

RELIABLE MESSAGE DELIVERY

As suggested by the examples just considered, reliable message delivery is one of the most important functions that a network can provide. It is difficult to determine how to provide this reliability, however, without first understanding how networks can fail. The first thing to recognize is that computer networks do not exist in a perfect world. Machines crash and later are rebooted, fibers are cut, electrical interference corrupts bits in the data being transmitted, switches run out of buffer space, and, as if these sorts of physical problems aren't enough to worry about, the software that manages the hardware may contain bugs and sometimes forwards packets into oblivion. Thus, a major requirement of a network is to recover from certain kinds of failures, so that application programs don't have to deal with them or even be aware of them.

There are three general classes of failure that network designers have to worry about. First, as a packet is transmitted over a physical link, bit errors may be introduced into the data; that is, a 1 is turned into a 0 or vice versa. Sometimes single bits are corrupted, but more often than not a burst error occurs—several consecutive bits are corrupted. Bit errors typically occur because outside forces, such as lightning strikes, power surges, and microwave ovens, interfere with the transmission of data. The good news is that such bit errors are fairly rare, affecting on average only one out of every 10^6 to 10^7 bits on a typical copper-based cable and one out of every 10^{12} to 10^{14} bits on a typical optical fiber. As we will see, there are techniques that detect these bit errors with high probability. Once detected, it is sometimes possible to correct for such errors—if we know which bit or bits are corrupted, we can simply flip them—while in other cases the damage is so bad that it is necessary to discard the entire packet. In such a case, the sender may be expected to retransmit the packet.

The second class of failure is at the packet, rather than the bit, level; that is, a complete packet is lost by the network. One reason this can happen is that the packet contains an uncorrectable bit error and therefore has to be discarded. A more likely reason, however, is that one of the nodes that has to handle the packet—for example, a switch that is forwarding it from one link to another—is so overloaded that it has no place to store the packet and therefore is forced to drop it. This is the problem of congestion just discussed. Less commonly, the software running on one of the nodes that handles the packet makes a mistake. For example, it might incorrectly forward a packet out on the wrong link, so that the packet never finds its way to the ultimate destination. As we will see, one of the main difficulties in dealing with lost packets is distinguishing between a packet that is indeed lost and one that is merely late in arriving at the destination.

The third class of failure is at the node and link level; that is, a physical link is cut, or the computer it is connected to crashes. This can be caused by software that crashes, a power failure, or a reckless backhoe operator. Failures due to misconfiguration of a network device are also common. While any of these failures can eventually be corrected, they can have a dramatic effect on the network for an extended period of time. However, they need not totally disable the network. In a packet-switched network, for example, it is sometimes possible to route around a failed node or link. One of the difficulties in dealing with this third class of failure is distinguishing between a failed computer and one that is merely slow or, in the case of a link, between one that has been cut and one that is very flaky and therefore introducing a high number of bit errors.

Key Takeaway

The key idea to take away from this discussion is that defining useful channels involves both understanding the applications' requirements and recognizing the limitations of the underlying technology. The challenge is to fill in the gap between what the application expects and what the underlying technology can provide. This is sometimes called the semantic gap.

1.2.5 Manageability

A final requirement, which seems to be neglected or left till last all too often (as we do here), is that networks need to be managed. Managing a network includes upgrading equipment as the network grows to carry more traffic or reach more users, troubleshooting the network when things go wrong or performance isn't as desired, and adding new features in support of new applications. Network management has historically been a human-intensive aspect of networking, and while it is unlikely we'll get people entirely out of the loop, it is increasingly being addressed by automation and self-healing designs.

This requirement is partly related to the issue of scalability discussed above— as the Internet has scaled up to support billions of users and at least hundreds of millions of hosts, the challenges of keeping the whole thing running correctly and correctly configuring new devices as they are added have become increasingly problematic. Configuring a single router in a network is often a task for a trained expert; configuring thousands of routers and figuring out why a network of such a size is not behaving as expected can become a task beyond any single human. This is why automation is becoming so important.

One way to make a network easier to manage is to avoid change. Once the network is working, simply do not touch it! This mindset exposes the fundamental tension between stability and feature velocity: the rate at which new capabilities are introduced into the network. Favoring stability is the approach the telecommunications industry (not to mention University system administrators and corporate IT departments) adopted for many years, making it one of the most slow moving and risk averse industries you will find anywhere. But the recent explosion of the cloud has changed that dynamic, making it necessary to bring stability and feature velocity more into balance. The impact of the cloud on the network is a topic that comes up over and over throughout the book, and one we pay particular attention to in the Perspectives section at the end of each chapter. For now, suffice it to say that managing a rapidly evolving network is arguably the central challenge in networking today.

1.3 Architecture

The preceding section outlined a comprehensive set of prerequisites for network architecture. A computer network must offer inclusive, economical, equitable, and resilient connection for a considerable number of computers. In addition to this, networks are not static and must adapt to changes in both the underlying technologies they rely on and the demands placed on them by application programs. In addition, networks need to be capable of being controlled by individuals with different levels of expertise. Creating a network that fulfills these needs is a challenging endeavor.

In order to address this intricacy, network designers have devised comprehensive frameworks, sometimes referred to as network architectures, which provide guidance for the design and implementation of networks. This section provides a more precise definition of a network architecture by introducing the fundamental concepts that are universally applicable to all network designs. Additionally, it presents two highly cited architectures, namely the OSI (or 7-layer) architecture and the Internet architecture..

1.3.1 Layering and Protocols

Abstraction is the act of concealing the intricate workings of a system by establishing a clearly defined interface. It serves as the primary method employed by system designers to effectively handle complexity. An abstraction is a concept that involves creating a model to represent a key aspect of a system. This model is then encapsulated in an object, which provides an interface for other components of the system to interact with. The implementation details of the object are hidden from the users of the object. The task at hand is to discern abstractions that may both offer a valuable service in numerous scenarios and be effectively executed within the system's infrastructure. In the last section, we introduced the concept of a channel to simplify the network's complexity for application writers. This abstraction allows applications to interact with the network without having to deal with its intricacies.

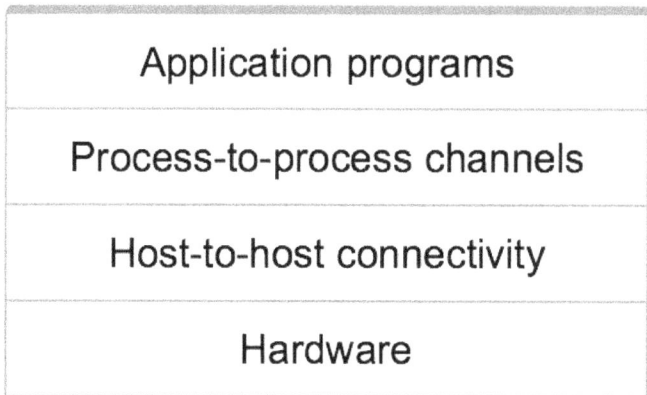

Application programs
Process-to-process channels
Host-to-host connectivity
Hardware

Figure 8. Example of a layered network system.

Abstractions naturally lead to layering, especially in network systems. The general idea is that you start with the services offered by the underlying hardware and then add a sequence of layers, each providing a higher (more abstract) level of service. The services provided at the high layers are implemented in terms of the services provided by the low layers. Drawing on the discussion of requirements given in the previous section, for example, we might imagine a simple network as having two layers of abstraction sandwiched between the application program and the underlying hardware, as illustrated in Figure 8. The layer immediately above the hardware in this case might provide host-to-host connectivity, abstracting away the fact that there may be an arbitrarily complex network topology between any two hosts. The next layer up builds on the available host-to-host communication service and provides support for process-to-process channels, abstracting away the fact that the network occasionally loses messages, for example.

Layering provides two useful features. First, it decomposes the problem of building a network into more manageable components. Rather than implementing a monolithic piece of software that does everything you will ever want, you can implement several layers, each of which solves one part of the problem. Second, it provides a more modular design. If you decide that you want to add some new service, you may only need to modify the functionality at one layer, reusing the functions provided at all the other layers.

Thinking of a system as a linear sequence of layers is an oversimplification, however. Many times there are multiple abstractions provided at any given level of the system, each providing a different service to the higher layers but building on the same low-level abstractions. To see this, consider the two types of channels discussed in the previous section. One provides a request/reply service and one supports a message stream service. These two channels might be alternative offerings at some level of a multilevel networking system, as illustrated in Figure 9.

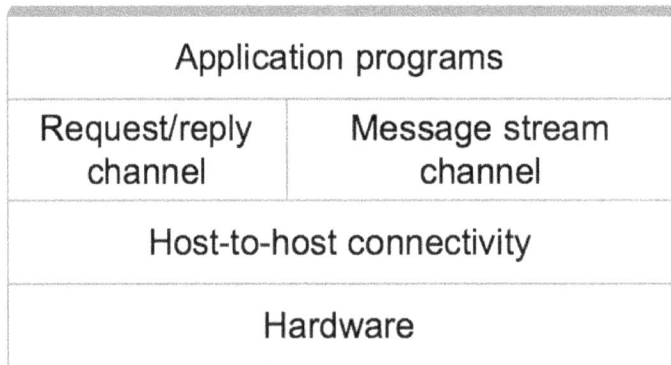

Application programs	
Request/reply channel	Message stream channel
Host-to-host connectivity	
Hardware	

Figure 9. Layered system with alternative abstractions available at a given layer.

Using this discussion of layering as a foundation, we are now ready to discuss the architecture of a network more precisely. For starters, the abstract objects that make up the layers of a network system are called protocols. That is, a protocol provides a communication service that higher-level objects (such as application processes, or perhaps higher-level protocols) use to exchange messages. For example, we could imagine a network that supports a request/reply protocol and a message stream protocol, corresponding to the request/reply and message stream channels discussed above.

Each protocol defines two different interfaces. First, it defines a service interface to the other objects on the same computer that want to use its communication services. This service interface defines the operations that local objects can perform on the protocol. For example, a request/reply protocol would support operations by which an application can send and receive messages. An implementation of the HTTP protocol could support an operation to fetch a page of hypertext from a remote server. An application such as a web browser would invoke such an operation whenever the browser needs to obtain a new page (e.g., when the user clicks on a link in the currently displayed page).

Furthermore, a protocol establishes a peer interface with its corresponding peer on a different system. The second interface specifies the structure and significance of messages that are shared between protocol peers in order to execute the communication service. This would govern the manner in which a request/reply protocol on one system establishes communication with its counterpart on another machine. For instance, in the context of HTTP, the protocol specification provides a thorough description of the structure of a GET command, the permissible arguments that might accompany the operation, and the expected response from a web server upon receiving such a query.

In essence, a protocol establishes a communication service that it offers locally (the service interface), together with a set of regulations dictating the messages that the protocol shares with its counterpart(s) to execute this service (the peer interface). Figure 10 depicts this condition.

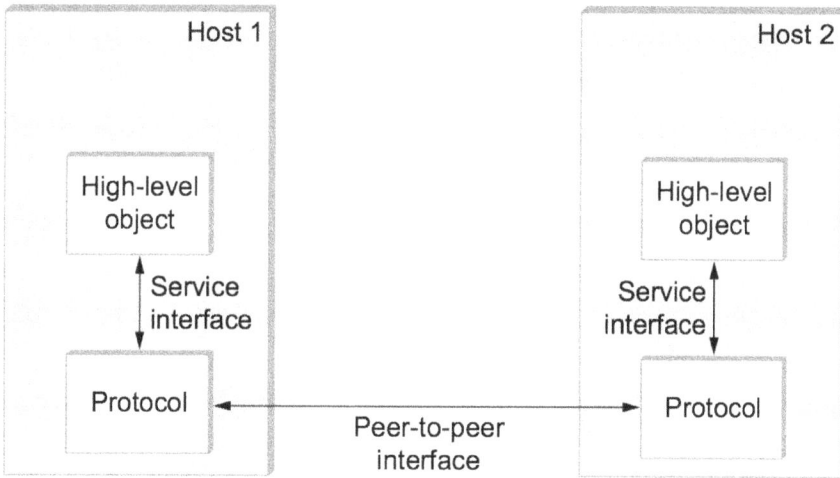

Figure 10. Service interfaces and peer interfaces.

Except at the hardware level, where peers directly communicate with each other over a physical medium, peer-to-peer communication is indirect—each protocol communicates with its peer by passing messages to some lower-level protocol, which in turn delivers the message to its peer. In addition, there are potentially more than one protocol at any given level, each providing a different communication service. We therefore represent the suite of protocols that make up a network system with a protocol graph. The nodes of the graph correspond to protocols, and the edges represent a depends on relation. For example, Figure 11 illustrates a protocol graph for the hypothetical layered system we have been discussing—protocols RRP (Request/Reply Protocol) and MSP (Message Stream Protocol) implement two different types of process-to-process channels, and both depend on the Host-to-Host Protocol (HHP) which provides a host-to-host connectivity service.

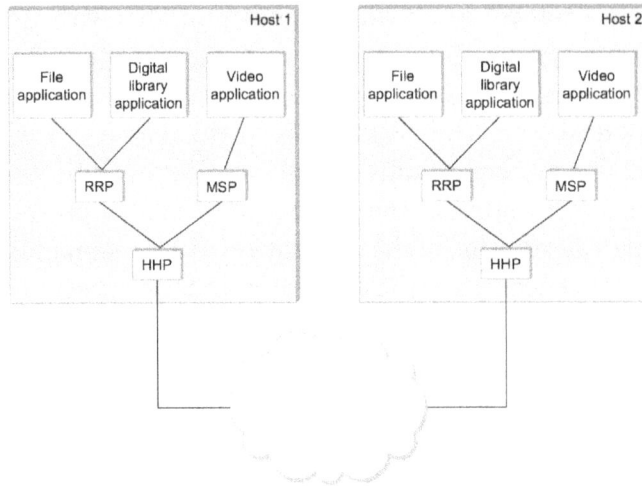

Figure 11. Example of a protocol graph.

In this example, suppose that the file access program on host 1 wants to send a message to its peer on host 2 using the communication service offered by RRP. In this case, the file application asks RRP to send the message on its behalf. To communicate with its peer, RRP invokes the services of HHP, which in turn transmits the message to its peer on the other machine. Once the message has arrived at the instance of HHP on host 2, HHP passes the message up to RRP, which in turn delivers the message to the file application. In this particular case, the application is said to employ the services of the protocol stack RRP/HHP.

Note that the term protocol is used in two different ways. Sometimes it refers to the abstract interfaces—that is, the operations defined by the service interface and the form and meaning of messages exchanged between peers, and sometimes it refers to the module that actually implements these two interfaces. To distinguish between the interfaces and the module that implements these interfaces, we generally refer to the former as a protocol specification. Specifications are generally expressed using a combination of prose, pseudocode, state transition diagrams, pictures of packet formats, and other abstract notations. It should be the case that a given protocol can be implemented in different ways by different programmers, as long as each adheres to the specification. The challenge is ensuring that two different implementations of the same specification can successfully exchange messages. Two or more protocol modules that do accurately implement a protocol specification are said to interoperate with each other.

We can imagine many different protocols and protocol graphs that satisfy the communication requirements of a collection of applications. Fortunately, there exist standardization bodies, such as the Internet Engineering Task Force (IETF) and the International Standards Organization (ISO), that establish policies for a particular protocol graph. We call the set of rules governing the form and content of a protocol graph a network architecture. Although beyond the scope of this book, standardization bodies have established well-defined procedures for introducing, validating, and finally approving protocols in their respective architectures. We briefly describe the architectures defined by the IETF and ISO shortly, but first there are two additional things we need to explain about the mechanics of protocol layering.

1.3.2 Encapsulation

Examine the scenario depicted in Figure 11, where an application software delivers a message to its peer by transmitting the message to RRP. From RRP's standpoint, the application provides it with a message that consists of a sequence of bytes without any interpretation. The RRP protocol is indifferent to the nature of these bytes, whether they represent an array of integers, an email message, a digital image, or any other data. Its sole responsibility is to transmit them to its counterpart. Nevertheless, RRP is required to transmit control information to its counterpart, including instructions on how to process the message upon receipt. RRP achieves this by appending a header to the message. In general, a header is a compact data structure, often ranging from a few bytes to a few dozen bytes, which facilitates communication between peers. Headers, as the name implies, are typically appended at the beginning of a message. Occasionally, the control information for peer-to-peer communication is transmitted at the conclusion of the message, in which instance it is referred to as a trailer. The protocol specification defines the precise format of the header attached by RRP. The remaining portion of the message, which refers to the data being transmitted on behalf of the application, is sometimes referred to as the message's body or payload. The application's data is enclosed within the newly generated message via RRP, demonstrating encapsulation.

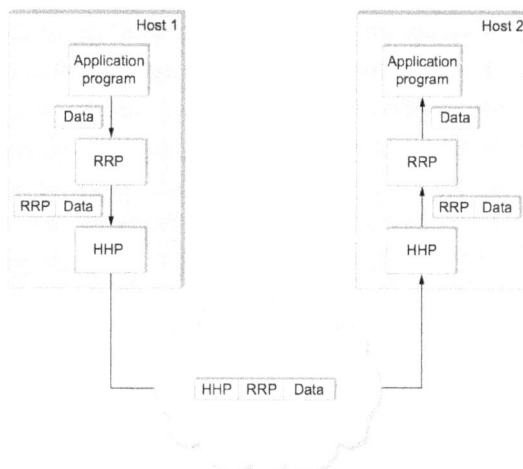

Figure 12. High-level messages are encapsulated inside of low-level messages.

This process of encapsulation is then repeated at each level of the protocol graph; for example, HHP encapsulates RRP's message by attaching a header of its own. If we now assume that HHP sends the message to its peer over some network, then when the message arrives at the destination host, it is processed in the opposite order: HHP first interprets the HHP header at the front of the message (i.e., takes whatever action is appropriate given the contents of the header) and passes the body of the message (but not the HHP header) up to RRP, which takes whatever action is indicated by the RRP header that its peer attached and passes the body of the message (but not the RRP header) up to the application program. The message passed up from RRP to the application on host 2 is exactly the same message as the application passed down to RRP on host 1; the application does not see any of the headers that have been attached to it to implement the lower-level communication services. This whole process is illustrated in Figure 12. Note that in this example, nodes in the network (e.g., switches and routers) may inspect the HHP header at the front of the message.

When we refer to a low-level protocol as not interpreting the message provided by a high-level protocol, we are indicating that it lacks the ability to derive any significance from the information within the message. Occasionally, the low-level protocol may apply basic alterations to the provided data, such as compression or encryption. In this scenario, the protocol is modifying the complete content of the message, which includes the data of the original application as well as all the headers added to that data by higher-level protocols.

1.3.3 Multiplexing and Demultiplexing

Packet switching involves the multiplexing of several data flows across a single physical channel. This concept is applicable throughout the entire protocol graph, not limited to switching nodes. Figure 11 illustrates the concept of RRP as a logical communication channel. It involves the multiplexing of messages from two distinct applications at the source host and their subsequent demultiplexing at the destination host to the respective programs.

In practical terms, this implies that the header attached to RRP messages includes an identity that indicates the application to which the message belongs. This identification is referred to as RRP's demultiplexing key, or simply demux key. At the originating host, the Resource Reservation Protocol (RRP) includes the suitable demultiplexing key in its header. Upon arrival at the destination host, the message is received by RRP, which removes its header, analyzes the demux key, and then separates the message into the appropriate application.

RRP is not the only protocol that supports multiplexing; almost every protocol incorporates this feature. For instance, HHP possesses its own demultiplexing key to ascertain which messages should be forwarded to RRP and which should be forwarded to MSP. Nevertheless, there is a lack of consensus among protocols, including those within a single network architecture, regarding the precise definition of a demux key. Certain protocols have an 8-bit field, limiting their capacity to accommodate just 256 high-level protocols. In contrast, other protocols employ 16- or 32-bit fields. Furthermore, certain protocols feature a solitary demultiplexing field in their header, whereas others incorporate a dual demultiplexing field. In the former scenario, a single demux key is utilized for communication on both ends, whereas in the later scenario, each side employs a distinct key to identify the high-level protocol (or application program) to which the message is intended to be sent.

1.3.4 OSI Model

The ISO was one of the first organizations to formally define a common way to connect computers. Their architecture, called the Open Systems Interconnection (OSI) architecture and illustrated in Figure 13, defines a partitioning of network functionality into seven layers, where one or more protocols implement the functionality assigned to a given layer. In this sense, the schematic given in Figure 13 is not a protocol graph, per se, but rather a reference model for a protocol graph. It is often referred to as the 7-layer model. While there is no OSI-based network running today, the terminology it defined is still widely used, so it is still worth a cursory look.

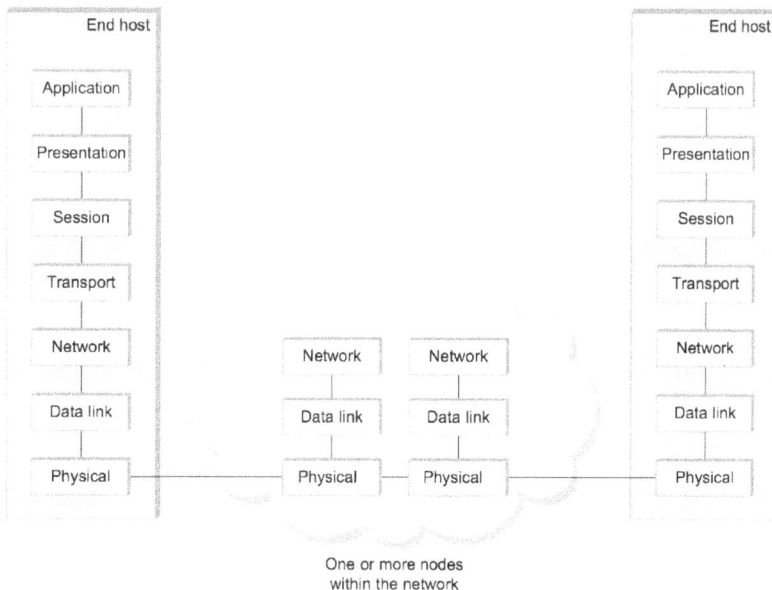

Figure 13. The OSI 7-layer model.

The physical layer is responsible for transmitting raw bits via a communications network, starting at the bottom and working up. The data connection layer assembles a sequence of bits into a bigger unit known as a frame. Network adapters, in conjunction with device drivers functioning in the node's operating system, generally carry out the data link layer. Consequently, hosts receive frames rather than raw bits. The network layer is responsible for the process of routing between nodes in a packet-switched network. At this level, the data sent between nodes is commonly referred to as a packet, but it is essentially equivalent to a frame. All network nodes, including switches within the network and hosts connecting to the external of the network, implement the lower three levels. The transport layer is responsible for establishing a communication link between processes. In this context, the term "message" is typically used to refer to the unit of data that is transmitted, as opposed to being referred to as a packet or a frame. The transport layer and higher layers are normally confined to the end hosts and do not operate on the intermediate switches or routers.Skipping ahead to the top (seventh) layer and working our way back down, we find the application layer. Application layer protocols include things like the Hypertext Transfer Protocol (HTTP), which is the basis of the World Wide Web and is what enables web browsers to request pages from web servers. Below that, the presentation layer is concerned with the format of data exchanged between peers—for example, whether an integer is 16, 32, or 64 bits long, whether the most significant byte is transmitted first or last, or how a video stream is formatted. Finally, the session layer provides a name space that is used to tie together the potentially different transport streams that are part of a single application. For example, it might manage an audio stream and a video stream that are being combined in a teleconferencing application.

1.3.5 Internet Architecture

Figure 14 illustrates the Internet architecture, often known as the TCP/IP architecture, named after its two primary protocols. Figure 15 provides an alternative depiction. The Internet architecture developed from the experiences gained with the ARPANET, a previous packet-switched network. The Advanced Research Projects Agency (ARPA), a research and development funding agency of the U.S. Department of Defense, provided money for both the Internet and the ARPANET. Prior to the development of the OSI architecture, both the Internet and ARPANET were in existence, and the knowledge acquired from their construction significantly impacted the OSI reference model.

While the 7-layer OSI model can, with some imagination, be applied to the Internet, a simpler stack is often used instead. At the lowest level is a wide variety of network protocols, denoted NET1, NET2, and so on. In practice, these protocols are implemented by a combination of hardware (e.g., a network adaptor) and software (e.g., a network device driver). For example, you might find Ethernet or wireless protocols (such as the 802.11 Wi-Fi standards) at this layer. (These protocols in turn may actually involve several sublayers, but the Internet architecture does not presume anything about them.) The next layer consists of a single protocol—the Internet Protocol (IP). This is the protocol that supports the interconnection of multiple networking technologies into a single, logical internetwork. The layer on top of IP contains two main protocols—the Transmission Control Protocol (TCP) and the User Datagram Protocol (UDP). TCP and UDP provide alternative logical channels to application programs: TCP provides a reliable byte-stream channel, and UDP provides an unreliable datagram delivery channel (datagram may be thought of as a synonym for message). In the language of the Internet, TCP and UDP are sometimes called end-to-end protocols, although it is equally correct to refer to them as transport protocols.

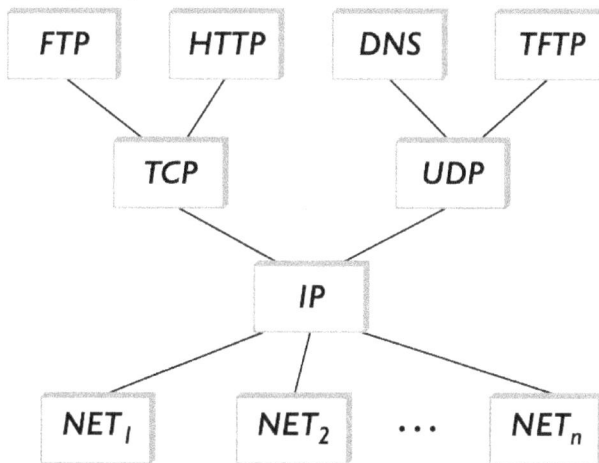

Figure 14. Internet protocol graph.

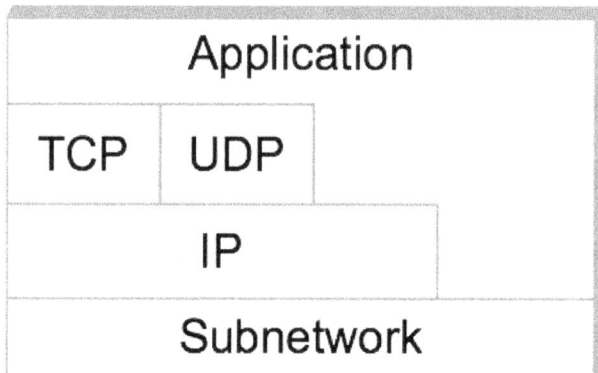

Figure 15. Alternative view of the Internet architecture. The "subnetwork" layer was historically referred to as the "network" layer and is now often referred to as "Layer 2" (influenced by the OSI model).

Running above the transport layer is a range of application protocols, such as HTTP, FTP, Telnet (remote login), and the Simple Mail Transfer Protocol (SMTP), that enable the interoperation of popular applications. To understand the difference between an application layer protocol and an application, think of all the different

World Wide Web browsers that are or have been available (e.g., Firefox, Chrome, Safari, Netscape, Mosaic, Internet Explorer). There is a similarly large number of different implementations of web servers. The reason that you can use any one of these application programs to access a particular site on the Web is that they all conform to the same application layer protocol: HTTP. Confusingly, the same term sometimes applies to both an application and the application layer protocol that it uses (e.g., FTP is often used as the name of an application that implements the FTP protocol).

Most people who work actively in the networking field are familiar with both the Internet architecture and the 7-layer OSI architecture, and there is general agreement on how the layers map between architectures. The Internet's application layer is considered to be at layer 7, its transport layer is layer 4, the IP (internetworking or just network) layer is layer 3, and the link or subnet layer below IP is layer 2.

IETF and Standardization

Although we call it the "Internet architecture" rather than the "IETF architecture," it's fair to say that the IETF is the primary standardization body responsible for its definition, as well as the specification of many of its protocols, such as TCP, UDP, IP, DNS, and BGP. But the Internet architecture also embraces many protocols defined by other organizations, including IEEE's 802.11 ethernet and Wi-Fi standards, W3C's HTTP/HTML web specifications, 3GPP's 4G and 5G cellular networks standards, and ITU-T's H.232 video encoding standards, to name a few.

In addition to defining architectures and specifying protocols, there are yet other organizations that support the larger goal of interoperability. One example is the IANA (Internet Assigned Numbers Authority), which as its name implies, is responsible for handing out the unique identifiers needed to make the protocols work. IANA, in turn, is a department within the ICANN (Internet Corporation for Assigned Names and Numbers), a non-profit organization that's responsible for the overall stewardship of the Internet.

The Internet architecture has three features that are worth highlighting. First, as best illustrated by Figure 15, the Internet architecture does not imply strict layering. The application is free to bypass the defined transport layers and to directly use IP or one of the underlying networks. In fact, programmers are free to define new channel abstractions or applications that run on top of any of the existing protocols.

Furthermore, upon careful examination of the protocol graph depicted in Figure 14, one can observe an hourglass configuration, characterized by a broad upper section, a slender middle section, and a broad lower section. This shape embodies the fundamental ideology of the architecture. Essentially, IP acts as the central element of the architecture by establishing a standardized approach for transmitting packets over a diverse range of networks. There can be an unlimited number of transport protocols above IP, each providing a distinct channel abstraction to application programs. Hence, the matter of transmitting messages between hosts is quite distinct from the matter of offering a functional process-to-process communication service. Under the Internet Protocol (IP), the structure permits an unlimited number of diverse network technologies, including Ethernet, wireless, and single point-to-point connections. A final attribute of the Internet architecture (or more accurately, of the IETF culture) is that in order for a new protocol to be officially included in the architecture, there must be both a protocol specification and at least one (and preferably two) representative implementations of the specification. The existence of working implementations is required for standards to be adopted by the IETF. This cultural assumption of the design community helps to ensure that the architecture's protocols can be efficiently implemented. Perhaps the value the Internet culture places on working software is best exemplified by a quote on T-shirts commonly worn at IETF meetings:

We reject kings, presidents, and voting. We believe in rough consensus and running code. (David Clark)

Key Takeaway

Of these three attributes of the Internet architecture, the hourglass design philosophy is important enough to bear repeating. The hourglass's narrow waist represents a minimal and carefully chosen set of global capabilities that allows both higher-level applications and lower-level communication technologies to coexist, share capabilities, and evolve rapidly. The narrow-waisted model is critical to the Internet's ability to adapt to new user demands and changing technologies.

1.4 Software

Network architectures and protocol specifications are essential things, but a good blueprint is not enough to explain the phenomenal success of the Internet: The number of computers connected to the Internet has grown exponentially for over three decades (although precise numbers are hard to come by). The number of users of the Internet was estimated to be around 4.1 billion by the end of 2018—roughly half of the world's population.

What explains the success of the Internet? There are certainly many contributing factors (including a good architecture), but one thing that has made the Internet such a runaway success is the fact that so much of its functionality is provided by software running on general-purpose computers. The significance of this is that new functionality can be added readily with "just a small matter of programming." As a result, new applications and services have been showing up at an incredible pace.

A related factor is the massive increase in computing power available in commodity machines. Although computer networks have always been capable in principle of transporting any kind of information, such as digital voice samples, digitized images, and so on, this potential was not particularly interesting if the computers sending and receiving that data were too slow to do anything useful with the information. Virtually all of today's computers are capable of playing back digitized audio and video at a speed and resolution that are quite usable.

In the years since the first edition of this book appeared, the writing of networked applications has become a mainstream activity and not a job just for a few specialists. Many factors have played into this, including better tools to make the job easier and the opening up of new markets such as applications for smartphones.

The point to note is that knowing how to implement network software is an essential part of understanding computer networks, and while the odds are you will not be tasked to implement a low-level protocol like IP, there is a good chance you will find reason to implement an application-level protocol—the elusive "killer app" that will lead to unimaginable fame and fortune. To get you started, this section introduces some of the issues involved in implementing a network application on top of the Internet. Typically, such programs are simultaneously an application (i.e., designed to interact with users) and a protocol (i.e., communicates with peers across the network).

1.4.1 Socket API

The place to start when implementing a network application is the interface exported by the network. Since most network protocols are in software (especially those high in the protocol stack), and nearly all computer systems implement their network protocols as part of the operating system, when we refer to the interface "exported by the network," we are generally referring to the interface that the OS provides to its networking subsystem. This interface is often called the network application programming interface (API).

Although each operating system is free to define its own network API (and most have), over time certain of these APIs have become widely supported; that is, they have been ported to operating systems other than their native system. This is what has happened with the socket interface originally provided by the Berkeley distribution of Unix, which is now supported in virtually all popular operating systems, and is the foundation of language-specific interfaces, such as the Java or Python socket library. We use Linux and C for all code examples in this book, Linux because it is open source and C because it remains the language of choice for network internals. (C also has the advantage of exposing all the low-level details, which is helpful in understanding the underlying ideas.)

SOCKETS ENABLED APPLICATION EXPLOSION

It is hard to overstate the importance of the Socket API. It defines the demarcation point between the applications running on top of the Internet, and the details of how the Internet is implemented. As a consequence of Sockets providing a well-defined and stable interface, writing Internet applications exploded into a multi-billion dollar industry. Starting from the humble beginnings of the client/ server paradigm and a handful of simple application programs like email, file transfer, and remote login, everyone now has access to an never-ending supply of cloud applications from their smartphones.

This section lays the foundation by revisiting the simplicity of a client program opening a socket so it can exchange messages with a server program, but today a rich software ecosystem is layered on top of the Socket API. This layer includes a plethora of cloud-based tools that lower the barrier for implementing scalable applications. We return to the interplay between the cloud and the network in every chapter, starting with the Perspective section at the end of Chapter 1.

Before describing the socket interface, it is important to keep two concerns separate in your mind. Each protocol provides a certain set of services, and the API provides a syntax by which those services can be invoked on a particular computer system. The implementation is then responsible for mapping the tangible set of operations and objects defined by the API onto the abstract set of services defined by the protocol. If you have done a good job of defining the interface, then it will be possible to use the syntax of the interface to invoke the services of many different protocols. Such generality was certainly a goal of the socket interface, although it's far from perfect.

The main abstraction of the socket interface, not surprisingly, is the socket. A good way to think of a socket is as the point where a local application process attaches to the network. The interface defines operations for creating a socket, attaching the socket to the network, sending/receiving messages through the socket, and closing the socket. To simplify the discussion, we will limit ourselves to showing how sockets are used with TCP.

The first step is to create a socket, which is done with the following operation: intsocket(int domain, int type, int protocol);

The reason that this operation takes three arguments is that the socket interface was designed to be general enough to support any underlying protocol suite. Specifically, the domain argument specifies the protocol family that is going to be used: PF_INET denotes the Internet family, PF_UNIX denotes the Unix pipe facility, and PF_PACKET denotes direct access to the network interface (i.e., it bypasses the TCP/IP protocol stack). The type argument indicates the semantics of the communication. SOCK_STREAM is used to denote a byte stream. SOCK_DGRAM is an alternative that denotes a message-oriented service, such as that provided by UDP. The protocol argument identifies the specific protocol that is going to be used. In our case, this argument is UNSPEC because the combination of PF_INET and SOCK_STREAM implies TCP. Finally, the return value from socket is a handle for the newly created socket—that is, an identifier by which we can refer to the socket in the future. It is given as an argument to subsequent operations on this socket.

The next step depends on whether you are a client or a server. On a server machine, the application process performs a passive open—the server says that it is prepared to accept connections, but it does not actually establish a connection. The server does this by invoking the following three operations:

- int bind(int socket, struct sockaddr *address, int addr_len);
- int listen(int socket, int backlog);
- int accept(int socket, struct sockaddr *address, int *addr_len);

The bind operation, as its name suggests, binds the newly created socket to the specified address. This is the network address of the local participant—the server. Note that, when used with the Internet protocols, address is a data structure that includes both the IP address of the server and a TCP port number. Ports are used to indirectly identify processes. They are a form of demux keys. The port number is usually some well-known number specific to the service being offered; for example, web servers commonly accept connections on port 80.

The listen operation then defines how many connections can be pending on the specified socket. Finally, the accept operation carries out the passive open. It is a blocking operation that does not return until a remote participant has established a connection, and when it does complete it returns a new socket that corresponds to this just-established connection, and the address argument contains the remote participant's address. Note that when accept returns, the original socket that was given as an argument still exists and still corresponds to the passive open; it is used in future invocations of accept.

On the client machine, the application process performs an active open; that is, it says who it wants to communicate with by invoking the following single operation:

- int connect(int socket, struct sockaddr *address, int addr_len);

This operation does not return until TCP has successfully established a connection, at which time the application is free to begin sending data. In this case, address contains the remote participant's address. In practice, the client usually specifies only the remote participant's address and lets the system fill in the local information. Whereas a server usually listens for messages on a well-known port, a client typically does not care which port it uses for itself; the OS simply selects an unused one.

Once a connection is established, the application processes invoke the following two operations to send and receive data:

- ⦿ int send (int socket, char *message, int msg_len, int flags);
- ⦿ int recv (int socket, char *buffer, int buf_len, int flags);

The first operation sends the given message over the specified socket, while the second operation receives a message from the specified socket into the given buffer. Both operations take a set of flags that control certain details of the operation.

1.4.2 Example Client/Server

We now show the implementation of a simple client/server program that uses the socket interface to send messages over a TCP connection. The program also uses other Linux networking utilities, which we introduce as we go. Our application allows a user on one machine to type in and send text to a user on another machine. It is a simplified version of the Linux talk program, which is similar to the program at the core of instant messaging applications.

Client

We start with the client side, which takes the name of the remote machine as an argument. It calls the Linux utility to translate this name into the remote host's IP address. The next step is to construct the address data structure (sin) expected by the socket interface. Notice that this data structure specifies that we'll be using the socket to connect to the Internet (AF_INET). In our example, we use TCP port 5432 as the well-known server port; this happens to be a port that has not been assigned to any other Internet service. The final step in setting up the connection is to call socket and connect. Once the operation returns, the connection is established and the client program enters its main loop, which reads text from standard input and sends it over the socket.

```
#include <stdio.h>
#include <sys/types.h>
#include <sys/socket.h>
#include <netinet/in.h>
```

```
#include <netdb.h>
#include <stdlib.h>
#include <unistd.h>
#include <string.h>
#define SERVER_PORT 5432
#define MAX_LINE 256
int
main(int argc, char * argv[])
{
  FILE *fp;
  struct hostent *hp;
  struct sockaddr_in sin;
  char *host;
  char buf[MAX_LINE];
  int s;
  int len;

  if (argc==2) {
   host = argv[1];
  }
  else {
   fprintf(stderr, "usage: simplex-talk host\n");
   exit(1);
  }

  /* translate host name into peer's IP address */
  hp = gethostbyname(host);
  if (!hp) {
   fprintf(stderr, "simplex-talk: unknown host: %s\n", host);
   exit(1);
  }
```

```
/* build address data structure */
bzero((char *)&sin, sizeof(sin));
sin.sin_family = AF_INET;
bcopy(hp->h_addr, (char *)&sin.sin_addr, hp->h_length);
sin.sin_port = htons(SERVER_PORT);

/* active open */
if ((s = socket(PF_INET, SOCK_STREAM, 0)) < 0) {
  perror("simplex-talk: socket");
  exit(1);
}
if (connect(s, (struct sockaddr *)&sin, sizeof(sin)) < 0)
{
  perror("simplex-talk: connect");
  close(s);
  exit(1);
}
/* main loop: get and send lines of text */
while (fgets(buf, sizeof(buf), stdin)) {
  buf[MAX_LINE-1] = '\0';
  len = strlen(buf) + 1;
  send(s, buf, len, 0);
}
}
```

Server

The server is equally simple. It first constructs the address data structure by filling in its own port number (SERVER_PORT). By not specifying an IP address, the application program is willing to accept connections on any of the local host's IP addresses. Next, the server performs the preliminary steps involved in a passive open; it creates the socket, binds it to the local address, and sets the maximum number of pending connections to be allowed. Finally, the main loop waits for a remote host to try to connect, and when one does, it receives and prints out the characters that arrive on the connection.

```
#include <stdio.h>
#include <sys/types.h>
#include <sys/socket.h>
#include <netinet/in.h>
#include <netdb.h>
#include <stdlib.h>
#include <unistd.h>
#include <string.h>

#define SERVER_PORT  5432
#define MAX_PENDING  5
#define MAX_LINE     256

int
main()
{
  struct sockaddr_in sin;
  char buf[MAX_LINE];
  int buf_len, addr_len;
  int s, new_s;

  /* build address data structure */
  bzero((char *)&sin, sizeof(sin));
  sin.sin_family = AF_INET;
  sin.sin_addr.s_addr = INADDR_ANY;
  sin.sin_port = htons(SERVER_PORT);

  /* setup passive open */
  if ((s = socket(PF_INET, SOCK_STREAM, 0)) < 0) {
```

```
    perror("simplex-talk: socket");
    exit(1);
  }
  if ((bind(s, (struct sockaddr *)&sin, sizeof(sin))) < 0) {
    perror("simplex-talk: bind");
    exit(1);
  }
  listen(s, MAX_PENDING);

  /* wait for connection, then receive and print text */
  while(1) {
    if ((new_s = accept(s, (struct sockaddr *)&sin, &addr_len)) < 0) {
      perror("simplex-talk: accept");
      exit(1);
    }
    while (buf_len = recv(new_s, buf, sizeof(buf), 0))
      fputs(buf, stdout);
    close(new_s);
  }
}
```

PreviousNext

1.5 Performance

So far, our main attention has been on the functional elements of networks. Similar to any computer system, computer networks are likewise anticipated to exhibit optimal performance. The efficiency of network data delivery directly impacts the effectiveness of distributed computing. Although the traditional programming principle of "prioritize correctness before optimizing for speed" still holds true, in the field of networking, it is frequently essential to specifically focus on designing for optimal performance. Consequently, it is crucial to comprehend the diverse elements that influence network efficiency.

1.5.1 Bandwidth and Latency

Network performance is measured in two fundamental ways: bandwidth (also called throughput) and latency (also called delay). The bandwidth of a network is given by the number of bits that can be transmitted over the network in a certain period of time. For example, a network might have a bandwidth of 10 million bits/second (Mbps), meaning that it is able to deliver 10 million bits every second. It is sometimes useful to think of bandwidth in terms of how long it takes to transmit each bit of data. On a 10-Mbps network, for example, it takes 0.1 microsecond (μs) to transmit each bit.

Bandwidth and throughput are subtly different terms. First of all, bandwidth is literally a measure of the width of a frequency band. For example, legacy voice-grade telephone lines supported a frequency band ranging from 300 to 3300 Hz; it was said to have a bandwidth of 3300 Hz - 300 Hz = 3000 Hz. If you see the word bandwidth used in a situation in which it is being measured in hertz, then it probably refers to the range of signals that can be accommodated.

When we talk about the bandwidth of a communication link, we normally refer to the number of bits per second that can be transmitted on the link. This is also sometimes called the data rate. We might say that the bandwidth of an Ethernet link is 10 Mbps. A useful distinction can also be made, however, between the maximum data rate that is available on the link and the number of bits per second that we can actually transmit over the link in practice. We tend to use the word throughput to refer to the measured performance of a system. Thus, because of various inefficiencies of implementation, a pair of nodes connected by a link with a bandwidth of 10 Mbps might achieve a throughput of only 2 Mbps. This would mean that an application on one host could send data to the other host at 2 Mbps.

Finally, we often talk about the bandwidth requirements of an application. This is the number of bits per second that it needs to transmit over the network to perform acceptably. For some applications, this might be "whatever I can get"; for others, it might be some fixed number (preferably not more than the available link bandwidth); and for others, it might be a number that varies with time. We will provide more on this topic later in this section.

While you can talk about the bandwidth of the network as a whole, sometimes you want to be more precise, focusing, for example, on the bandwidth of a single physical link or of a logical process-to-process channel. At the physical level, bandwidth is constantly improving, with no end in sight. Intuitively, if you think of a second of time as a distance you could measure with a ruler and bandwidth as how many bits fit in that distance, then you can think of each bit as a pulse of some width. For example, each bit on a 1-Mbps link is 1 μs wide, while each bit on a 2-Mbps link is 0.5 μs wide, as illustrated in Figure 16. The more sophisticated the transmitting and receiving technology, the narrower each bit can become and, thus, the higher the bandwidth. For logical process-to-process channels, bandwidth is also influenced by other factors, including how many times the software that implements the channel has to handle, and possibly transform, each bit of data.

(a)

1 second

(b)

1 second

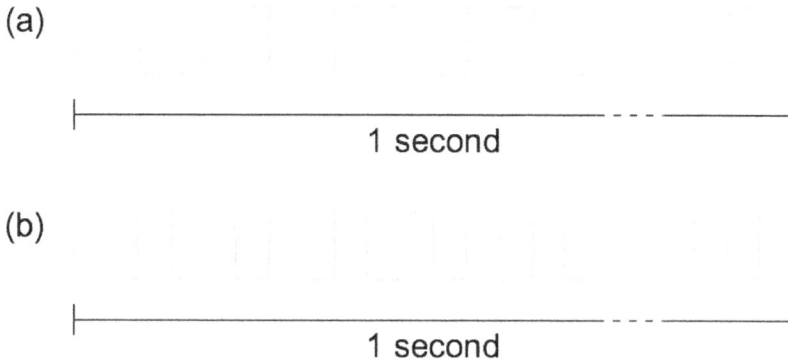

Figure 16. Bits transmitted at a particular bandwidth can be regarded as having some width: (a) bits transmitted at 1 Mbps (each bit is 1 microsecond wide); (b) bits transmitted at 2 Mbps (each bit is 0.5 microseconds wide).

The second performance metric, latency, corresponds to how long it takes a message to travel from one end of a network to the other. (As with bandwidth, we could be focused on the latency of a single link or an end-to-end channel.) Latency is measured strictly in terms of time. For example, a transcontinental network might have a latency of 24 milliseconds (ms); that is, it takes a message 24 ms to travel from one coast of North America to the other. There are many situations in which it is more important to know how long it takes to send a message from one end of a network to the other and back, rather than the one-way latency. We call this the round-trip time (RTT) of the network.

We often think of latency as having three components. First, there is the speed-of-light propagation delay. This delay occurs because nothing, including a bit on a wire, can travel faster than the speed of light. If you know the distance between two points, you can calculate the speed-of-light latency, although you have to be careful because light travels across different media at different speeds: It travels at 3.0×108 m/s in a vacuum, 2.3×108 m/s in a copper cable, and 2.0×108 m/s in an optical fiber. Second, there is the amount of time it takes to transmit a unit of data. This is a function of the network bandwidth and the size of the packet in which the data is carried. Third, there may be queuing delays inside the network, since packet switches generally need to store packets for some time before forwarding them on an outbound link. So, we could define the total latency as

$$\text{Latency} = \text{Propagation} + \text{Transmit} + \text{Queue}$$

$$\text{Propagation} = \text{Distance/SpeedOfLight}$$

$$\text{Transmit} = \text{Size/Bandwidth}$$

where Distance is the length of the wire over which the data will travel, SpeedOfLight is the effective speed of light over that wire, Size is the size of the packet, and Bandwidth is the bandwidth at which the packet is transmitted. Note that if the message contains only one bit and we are talking about a single link (as opposed to a whole network), then the Transmit and Queue terms are not relevant, and latency corresponds to the propagation delay only.

Bandwidth and latency combine to define the performance characteristics of a given link or channel. Their relative importance, however, depends on the application. For some applications, latency dominates bandwidth. For example, a client that sends a 1-byte message to a server and receives a 1-byte message in return is latency bound. Assuming that no serious computation is involved in preparing the response, the application will perform much differently on a transcontinental channel with a 100-ms RTT than it will on an across-the-room channel with a 1-ms RTT. Whether the channel is 1 Mbps or 100 Mbps is relatively insignificant, however, since the former implies that the time to transmit a byte (Transmit) is 8 μs and the latter implies Transmit = 0.08 μs.

In contrast, consider a digital library program that is being asked to fetch a 25-megabyte (MB) image—the more bandwidth that is available, the faster it will be able to return the image to the user. Here, the bandwidth of the channel dominates performance. To see this, suppose that the channel has a bandwidth of 10 Mbps. It will take 20 seconds to transmit the image ($25 \times 106 \times 8$-bits / (10×106 Mbps = 20 seconds), making it relatively unimportant if the image is on the other side of a 1-ms channel or a 100-ms channel; the difference between a 20.001-second response time and a 20.1-second response time is negligible.

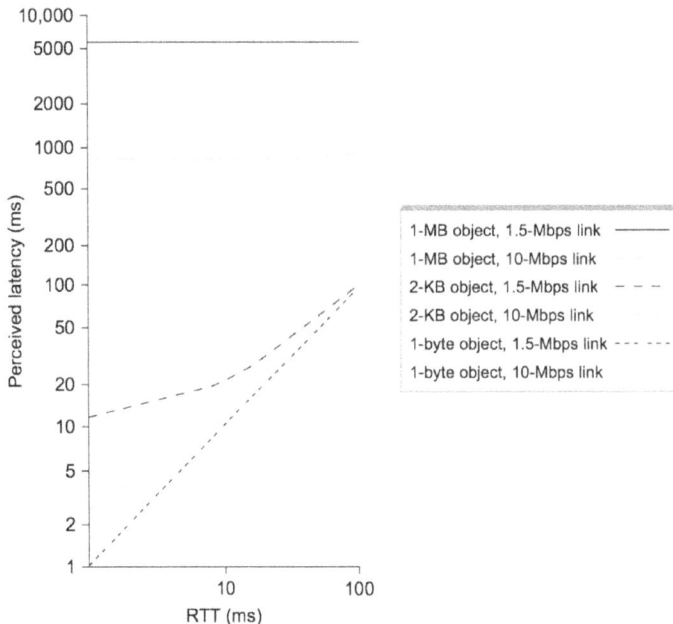

Figure 17. Perceived latency (response time) versus round-trip time for various object sizes and link speeds.

Figure 17 gives you a sense of how latency or bandwidth can dominate performance in different circumstances. The graph shows how long it takes to move objects of various sizes (1 byte, 2 KB, 1 MB) across networks with RTTs ranging from 1 to 100 ms and link speeds of either 1.5 or 10 Mbps. We use logarithmic scales to show relative performance. For a 1-byte object (say, a keystroke), latency remains almost exactly equal to the RTT, so that you cannot distinguish between a 1.5-Mbps network and a 10-Mbps network. For a 2-KB object (say, an email message), the link speed makes quite a difference on a 1-ms RTT network but a negligible difference on a 100-ms RTT network. And for a 1-MB object (say, a digital image), the RTT makes no difference—it is the link speed that dominates performance across the full range of RTT.

Note that throughout this book we use the terms latency and delay in a generic way to denote how long it takes to perform a particular function, such as delivering a message or moving an object. When we are referring to the specific amount of time it takes a signal to propagate from one end of a link to another, we use the term propagation delay. Also, we make it clear in the context of the discussion whether we are referring to the one-way latency or the round-trip time.

As an aside, computers are becoming so fast that when we connect them to networks, it is sometimes useful to think, at least figuratively, in terms of instructions per mile. Consider what happens when a computer that is able to execute 100 billion instructions per second sends a message out on a channel with a 100-ms RTT. (To make the math easier, assume that the message covers a distance of 5000 miles.) If that computer sits idle the full 100 ms waiting for a reply message, then it has forfeited the ability to execute 10 billion instructions, or 2 million instructions per mile. It had better have been worth going over the network to justify this waste.

1.5.2 Delay × Bandwidth Product

It is also useful to talk about the product of these two metrics, often called the delay × bandwidth product. Intuitively, if we think of a channel between a pair of processes as a hollow pipe (see Figure 18), where the latency corresponds to the length of the pipe and the bandwidth gives the diameter of the pipe, then the delay × bandwidth product gives the volume of the pipe—the maximum number of bits that could be in transit through the pipe at any given instant. Said another way, if latency (measured in time) corresponds to the length of the pipe, then given the width of each bit (also measured in time) you can calculate how many bits fit in the pipe. For example, a transcontinental channel with a one-way latency of 50 ms and a bandwidth of 45 Mbps is able to hold

$$50 \times 10\text{-}3 \times 45 \times 106 \text{ bits/sec} = 2.25 \times 106 \text{ bits}$$

or approximately 280 KB of data. In other words, this example channel (pipe) holds as many bytes as the memory of a personal computer from the early 1980s could hold.

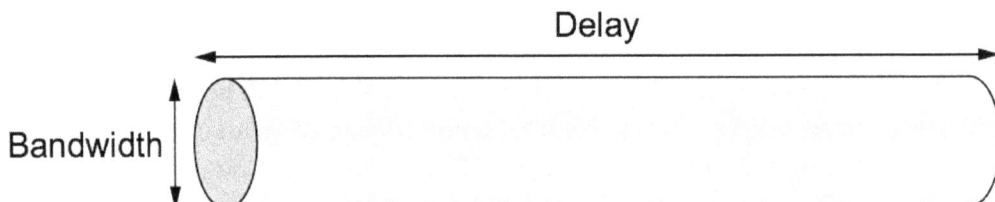

Figure 18. Network as a pipe.

The delay × bandwidth product is important to know when constructing high-performance networks because it corresponds to how many bits the sender must transmit before the first bit arrives at the receiver. If the sender is expecting the receiver to somehow signal that bits are starting to arrive, and it takes another channel latency for this signal to propagate back to the sender, then the sender can send up one RTT × bandwidth worth of data before hearing from the receiver that all is well. The bits in the pipe are said to be "in flight," which means that if the receiver tells the sender to stop transmitting it might receive up to one RTT × bandwidth's worth of data before the sender manages to respond. In our example above, that amount corresponds to 5.5×10^6 bits (671 KB) of data. On the other hand, if the sender does not fill the pipe—i.e., does not send a whole RTT × bandwidth product's worth of data before it stops to wait for a signal—the sender will not fully utilize the network.

Note that most of the time we are interested in the RTT scenario, which we simply refer to as the delay × bandwidth product, without explicitly saying that "delay" is the RTT (i.e., multiply the one-way delay by two). Usually, whether the "delay" in delay × bandwidth means one-way latency or RTT is made clear by the context. Table 1 shows some examples of RTT × bandwidth products for some typical network links.

Table 1. Example delay × bandwidth products.

Link Type	Bandwidth	One-Way Distance	RTT	RTT x Bandwidth
Wireless LAN	54 Mbps	50 m	0.33 µs	18 bits
Satellite	1 Gbps	35,000 km	230 ms	230 Mb
Cross-country fiber	10 Gbps	4,000 km	40 ms	400 Mb

1.5.3 High-Speed Networks

The apparent and ongoing rise in bandwidth prompts network designers to contemplate the implications of having unlimited bandwidth available, or in other words, the effects on network architecture when bandwidth becomes infinite.

Although high-speed networks bring a dramatic change in the bandwidth available to applications, in many respects their impact on how we think about networking comes in what does not change as bandwidth increases: the speed of light. To quote Scotty from Star Trek, "Ye cannae change the laws of physics." In other words, "high speed" does not mean that latency improves at the same rate as bandwidth; the transcontinental RTT of a 1-Gbps link is the same 100 ms as it is for a 1-Mbps link.

To appreciate the significance of ever-increasing bandwidth in the face of fixed latency, consider what is required to transmit a 1-MB file over a 1-Mbps network versus over a 1-Gbps network, both of which have an RTT of 100 ms. In the case of the 1-Mbps network, it takes 80 round-trip times to transmit the file; during each RTT, 1.25% of the file is sent. In contrast, the same 1-MB file doesn't even come close to filling 1 RTT's worth of the 1-Gbps link, which has a delay × bandwidth product of 12.5 MB.

Figure 19 illustrates the difference between the two networks. In effect, the 1-MB file looks like a stream of data that needs to be transmitted across a 1-Mbps network, while it looks like a single packet on a 1-Gbps network. To help drive this point home, consider that a 1-MB file is to a 1-Gbps network what a 1-KB packet is to a 1-Mbps network.

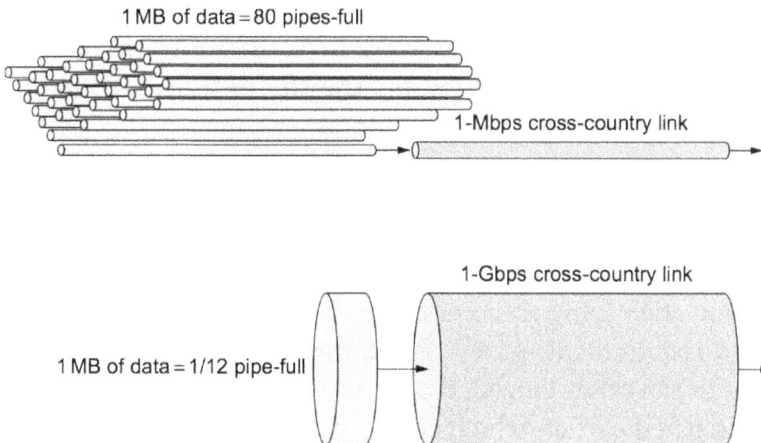

Figure 19. Relationship between bandwidth and latency. A 1-MB file would fill the 1-Mbps link 80 times but only fill 1/12th of a 1-Gbps link.

Another way to think about the situation is that more data can be transmitted during each RTT on a high-speed network, so much so that a single RTT becomes a significant amount of time. Thus, while you wouldn't think twice about the difference between a file transfer taking 101 RTTs rather than 100 RTTs (a relative difference of only 1%), suddenly the difference between 1 RTT and 2 RTTs is significant—a 100% increase. In other words, latency, rather than throughput, starts to dominate our thinking about network design.

Perhaps the best way to understand the relationship between throughput and latency is to return to basics. The effective end-to-end throughput that can be achieved over a network is given by the simple relationship

$$\text{Throughput} = \text{TransferSize} / \text{TransferTime}$$

where TransferTime includes not only the elements of one-way identified earlier in this section, but also any additional time spent requesting or setting up the transfer. Generally, we represent this relationship as

$$\text{TransferTime} = \text{RTT} + 1/\text{Bandwidth} \times \text{TransferSize}$$

We use in this calculation to account for a request message being sent across the network and the data being sent back. For example, consider a situation where a user wants to fetch a 1-MB file across a 1-Gbps with a round-trip time of 100 ms. This includes both the transmit time for 1 MB (1 / 1 Gbps × 1 MB = 8 ms) and the 100-ms RTT, for a total transfer time of 108 ms. This means that the effective throughput will be

$$1 \text{ MB} / 108 \text{ ms} = 74.1 \text{ Mbps}$$

not 1 Gbps. Clearly, transferring a larger amount of data will help improve the effective throughput, where in the limit an infinitely large transfer size will cause the effective throughput to approach the network bandwidth. On the other hand, having to endure more than 1 RTT—for example, to retransmit missing packets— will hurt the effective throughput for any transfer of finite size and will be most noticeable for small transfers.

1.5.4 Application Requirements

In this part, we have approached the topic of performance from a network-centric perspective. Specifically, we have focused on the capacity of individual links or channels. The underlying assumption has been that application programs have uncomplicated requirements—they desire the maximum amount of bandwidth that the network can offer. Indeed, the statement holds true for the digital library application discussed earlier, which is retrieving a 250-MB image. The program's speed in returning the image to the user is directly proportional to the amount of available bandwidth.

However, some applications are able to state an upper limit on how much bandwidth they need. Video applications are a prime example. Suppose one wants to stream a video that is one quarter the size of a standard TV screen; that is, it has a resolution of 352 by 240 pixels. If each pixel is represented by 24 bits of information, as would be the case for 24-bit color, then the size of each frame would be (352 × 240 × 24) / 8 = 247.5 KB If the application needs to support a frame rate of 30 frames per second, then it might request a throughput rate of 75 Mbps. The ability of the network to provide more bandwidth is of no interest to such an application because it has only so much data to transmit in a given period of time.

Unfortunately, the situation is not as simple as this example suggests. Because the difference between any two adjacent frames in a video stream is often small, it is possible to compress the video by transmitting only the differences between adjacent frames. Each frame can also be compressed because not all the detail in a picture is readily perceived by a human eye. The compressed video does not flow at a constant rate, but varies with time according to factors such as the amount of action and detail in the picture and the compression algorithm being used. Therefore, it is possible to say what the average bandwidth requirement will be, but the instantaneous rate may be more or less.

The key issue is the time interval over which the average is computed. Suppose that this example video application can be compressed down to the point that it needs only 2 Mbps, on average. If it transmits 1 megabit in a 1-second interval and 3 megabits in the following 1-second interval, then over the 2-second interval it is transmitting at an average rate of 2 Mbps; however, this will be of little consolation to a channel that was engineered to support no more than 2 megabits in any one second. Clearly, just knowing the average bandwidth needs of an application will not always suffice.

Generally, however, it is possible to put an upper bound on how large a burst an application like this is likely to transmit. A burst might be described by some peak rate that is maintained for some period of time. Alternatively, it could be described as the number of bytes that can be sent at the peak rate before reverting to the average rate or some lower rate. If this peak rate is higher than the available channel capacity, then the excess data will have to be buffered somewhere, to be transmitted later. Knowing how big of a burst might be sent allows the network designer to allocate sufficient buffer capacity to hold the burst.

Analogous to the way an application's bandwidth needs can be something other than "all it can get," an application's delay requirements may be more complex than simply "as little delay as possible." In the case of delay, it sometimes doesn't matter so much whether the one-way latency of the network is 100 ms or 500 ms as how much the latency varies from packet to packet. The variation in latency is called jitter.

Consider the situation in which the source sends a packet once every 33 ms, as would be the case for a video application transmitting frames 30 times a second. If the packets arrive at the destination spaced out exactly 33 ms apart, then we can deduce that the delay experienced by each packet in the network was exactly the same. If the spacing between when packets arrive at the destination—sometimes called the inter-packet gap—is variable, however, then the delay experienced by the sequence of packets must have also been variable, and the network is said to have introduced jitter into the packet stream, as shown in Figure 20. Such variation is generally not introduced in a single physical link, but it can happen when packets experience different queuing delays in a multihop packet-switched network. This queuing delay corresponds to the component of latency defined earlier in this section, which varies with time.

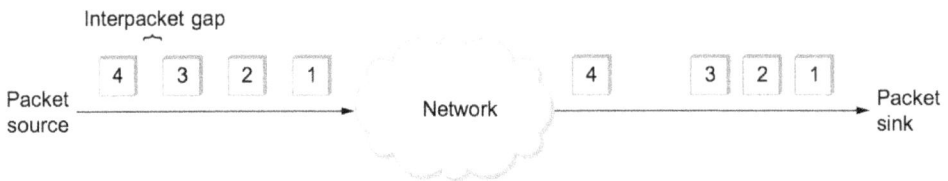

Figure 20. Network-induced jitter.

In order to comprehend the significance of jitter, let us consider a scenario where the packets being transferred over the network consist of video frames. To display these frames on the screen, the receiver must receive a new frame every 33 ms. If a frame is received before its scheduled display time, the receiver can store it until the appropriate time for presentation. Regrettably, in the event that a frame is delayed, the recipient will not receive the required frame in a timely manner to refresh the screen, resulting in a degradation in video quality, specifically a lack of smoothness. It is important to understand that eliminating jitter is not required; rather, it is crucial to accurately assess its severity. The rationale behind this is that if the recipient is aware of the maximum and minimum latency limits that a packet may encounter, it can postpone the initiation of video playback (i.e., showing the first frame) by a sufficient amount of time to guarantee that it will always have a frame available for display when required. The frame is delayed by the receiver and stored in a buffer, which effectively reduces the jitter and creates a smoother output.

PERSPECTIVE: FEATURE VELOCITY

This chapter introduces some of the stakeholders in computer networks—network designers, application developers, end users, and network operators—to help motivate the technical requirements that shape how networks are designed and built. This presumes all design decisions are purely technical, but of course, that's usually not the case. Many other factors, from market forces, to government policy, to ethical considerations, also influence how networks are designed and built. Of these, the marketplace is the most influential, and corresponds to the interplay between network operators (e.g., AT&T, Comcast, Verizon, DT, NTT, China Unicom), network equipment vendors (e.g., Cisco, Juniper, Ericsson, Nokia, Huawei, NEC), application and service providers (e.g., Facebook, Google, Amazon, Microsoft, Apple, Netflix, Spotify), and of course, subscribers and customers (i.e., individuals, but also enterprises and businesses). The lines between these players are not always crisp, with many companies playing multiple roles. The most notable example of this are the large cloud providers, who (a) build their own networking equipment using commodity components, (b) deploy and operate their own networks, and (c) provide end-user services and applications on top of their networks.

When your account for these other factors in the technical design process, you realize there are a couple of implicit assumptions in the textbook version of the story that need to be reevaluated. One is that designing a network is a one-time activity. Build it once and use it forever (modulo hardware upgrades so users can enjoy the benefits of the latest performance improvements). A second is that the job of building the network is largely divorced from the job of operating the network. Neither of these assumptions is quite right.

The network's design is clearly evolving, and we have documented these changes with each new edition of the textbook over the years. Doing that on a timeline measured in years has historically been good enough, but anyone that has downloaded and used the latest smartphone app knows how glacially slow anything measured in years is by today's standards. Designing for evolution has to be part of the decision making process.

On the second point, the companies that build networks are almost always the same ones that operate them. They are collectively known as network operators, and they include the companies listed above. But if we again look to the cloud for inspiration, we see that develop-and-operate isn't true just at the company level, but it is also how the fastest moving cloud companies organize their engineering teams: around the DevOps model. (If you are unfamiliar with DevOps, we recommend you read Site Reliability Engineering: How Google Runs Production Systems to see how it is practiced.)

Computer networks are currently undergoing a significant shift, as network operators strive to both increase the speed of innovation (referred to as feature velocity) and maintain a dependable service (ensuring stability). They are increasingly achieving this by incorporating the most effective methods used by cloud providers. These methods can be summarized into two main themes: (1) utilizing inexpensive hardware and transferring all decision-making processes to software, and (2) implementing flexible engineering processes that eliminate obstacles between development and operations.

This process is occasionally referred to as the "cloudification" or "softwarization" of the network. In the past, the Internet had a strong software ecosystem, but it was mainly confined to the applications that operated on the network, such as those utilizing the Socket API mentioned in Section 1.4. The current development is the application of cloud-inspired engineering approaches to the internal workings of the network. The Software Defined Networks (SDN) approach is revolutionary, not primarily in terms of addressing the core technical challenges of framing, routing, fragmentation/reassembly, packet scheduling, congestion control, security, etc., but in terms of the speed at which the network adapts to accommodate new features.

This transition is of such significance that we revisit it in the Perspective section at the conclusion of every chapter. These conversations will examine the networking sector, which involves both technological and non-technical issues. This demonstrates the significant impact of the Internet on our lives.

Broader Perspective

To continue reading about the cloudification of the Internet, see Perspective: Race to the Edge.

To learn more about DevOps, we recommend: Site Reliability Engineering: How Google Runs Production Systems, 2016.

CHAPTER-2
DIRECT LINKS

PROBLEM: CONNECTING TO A NETWORK

Chapter 1 demonstrated that networks are comprised of links that connect nodes. An essential challenge we encounter is the process of establishing a connection between two nodes. In addition, we implemented the concept of the "cloud" as a way to depict a network without concealing its intricate inner workings. Additionally, we must also tackle the issue of establishing a connection between a host and a cloud. This is essentially the challenge that every Internet Service Provider (ISP) encounters when it seeks to establish a connection with a new customer on its network.

Regardless of whether we aim to create a simple network with only two nodes and one link, or connect the one-billionth host to an already established network such as the Internet, we must address a shared set of concerns. Initially, it is important to acquire a tangible medium via which the link can be established. The medium can take the form of a wire, an optical fiber, or a less tangible medium like air, through which electromagnetic radiation, such as radio waves, can be transferred. It can encompass a limited space, such as an office building, or a vast expanse, such as a transcontinental territory.

However, connecting two nodes with an appropriate medium is merely the initial stage. In order for the nodes to effectively exchange packets and achieve Layer 2 (L2) connectivity, there are five more problems that need to be resolved.

The first step involves the process of encoding bits onto the transmission medium in a manner that allows them to be comprehended by a receiving node. Another important aspect is the process of organizing the series of bits sent over the connection into coherent messages that can be successfully received by the final destination. The issue at hand is known as the framing problem, and the messages sent to the final destinations are commonly referred to as frames (or occasionally packets). Furthermore, due to the occasional corruption of frames during transmission, it becomes imperative to identify these faults and respond accordingly. This issue is sometimes referred to as the error detection problem. The fourth concern pertains to ensuring the perceived trustworthiness of a link, notwithstanding its occasional disruption of frames. In situations when many hosts share a link, such as wireless links, it is required to regulate access to this link. This is the issue pertaining to media access restriction.

While these five concerns, namely encoding, framing, error detection, dependable delivery, and access mediation, can be theoretically examined, they are practical challenges that are tackled through various approaches in diverse networking systems. This chapter examines these matters within the framework of particular network technologies: point-to-point fiber links (with SONET being the most common example); Carrier Sense Multiple Access (CSMA) networks (including classical Ethernet and Wi-Fi as the most well-known examples); fiber-to-the-home (with PON being the prevailing standard); and mobile wireless (where 4G is swiftly evolving into 5G).

The objective of this chapter is to both examine the existing link-level technologies and investigate these five key concerns. We will analyze the necessary requirements for utilizing diverse physical media and connection technologies as fundamental components for the development of resilient and expandable networks.

2.1 Technology Landscape

Prior to addressing the problems presented in the problem statement at the start of this chapter, it is beneficial to first gain an understanding of the various connection technologies involved. This is mostly attributed to the varied settings in which users attempt to establish connections between their devices.

On one side of the spectrum, network operators responsible for constructing worldwide networks must manage connections that stretch across hundreds or thousands of kilometers, linking routers that are the size of refrigerators. On the opposite side of the range, an average user mostly uses links to establish a connection between a computer and the already established Internet. Occasionally, the link may be a wireless connection, such as Wi-Fi, found in a coffee shop. In other cases, it could be an Ethernet connection in an office building or university. Alternatively, it may be a smartphone connected to a cellular network. For a growing number of people, the link is a fiber optic connection provided by an Internet Service Provider (ISP). Additionally, some individuals utilize various types of copper wire or cable for their connection. Fortunately, there are numerous conventional ways employed to ensure the reliability and usefulness of these seemingly unrelated sorts of links to higher tiers in the protocol stack. This chapter explores and analyzes the various strategies.

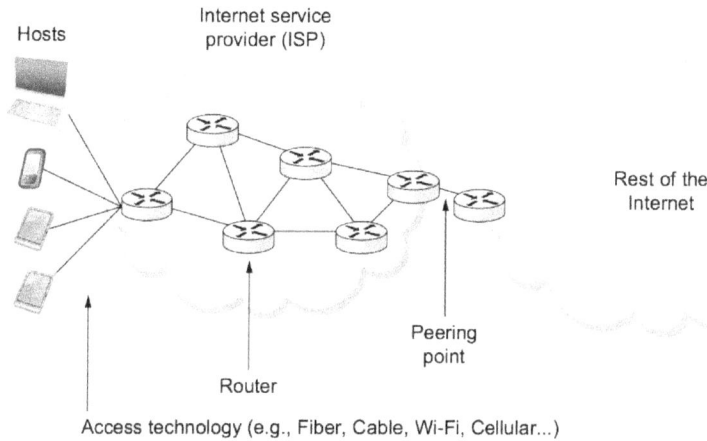

Figure 21. An end-user's view of the Internet.

Figure 21 illustrates various types of links that might be found in today's Internet. On the left, we see a variety of end-user devices ranging from smartphones to tablets to full-fledged computers connected by various means to an ISP. While those links might use different technologies, they all look the same in this picture—a straight line connecting a device to a router. There are links that connect routers together inside the ISP, as well as links that connect the ISP to the "rest of the Internet," which consists of lots of other ISPs and the hosts to which they connect.

These links all look alike not just because we're not very good artists but because part of the role of a network architecture is to provide a common abstraction of something as complex and diverse as a link. The idea is that your laptop or smartphone doesn't have to care what sort of link it is connected to—the only thing that matters is that it has a link to the Internet. Similarly, a router doesn't have to care what sort of link connects it to other routers—it can send a packet on the link with a pretty good expectation that the packet will reach the other end of the link.

How do we make all these different types of links look sufficiently alike to end users and routers? Essentially, we have to deal with all the physical limitations and shortcomings of links that exist in the real world. We sketched out some of these issues in the opening problem statement for this chapter, but before we can discuss these, we need to first introduce some simple physics. All of these links are made of some physical material that can propagate signals, such as radio waves or other sorts of electromagnetic radiation, but what we really want to do is send bits. In the later sections of this chapter, we'll look at how to encode bits for transmission on a physical medium, followed by the other issues mentioned above. By the end of this chapter, we'll understand how to send complete packets over just about any sort of link, no matter what physical medium is involved.

Links can be characterized based on the medium they employ, which usually includes copper wire (such as twisted pair and coaxial) for certain Ethernets and landline phones, optical fiber for fiber-to-the-home connections and long-distance links in the Internet's backbone, or air/free space for wireless links.

The frequency of electromagnetic waves is an essential property that is measured in hertz and indicates how often the waves fluctuate. The wavelength of a wave refers to the distance, usually measured in meters, between two neighboring maxima or minima. The speed of all electromagnetic waves, which varies depending on the medium, may be determined by dividing the speed of light by the frequency of the wave. This calculation yields the wavelength of the wave. We have already seen the example of a voice-grade telephone line, which carries continuous electromagnetic signals ranging between 300 Hz and 3300 Hz; a 300-Hz wave traveling through copper would have a wavelength of

$$\text{SpeedOfLightInCopper} / \text{Frequency}$$

$$= 2/3 \times 3 \times 108 / 300$$

$$= 667 \times 103 \text{ meters}$$

Generally, electromagnetic waves span a much wider range of frequencies, ranging from radio waves, to infrared light, to visible light, to x-rays and gamma rays. Figure 22 depicts the electromagnetic spectrum and shows which media are commonly used to carry which frequency bands.

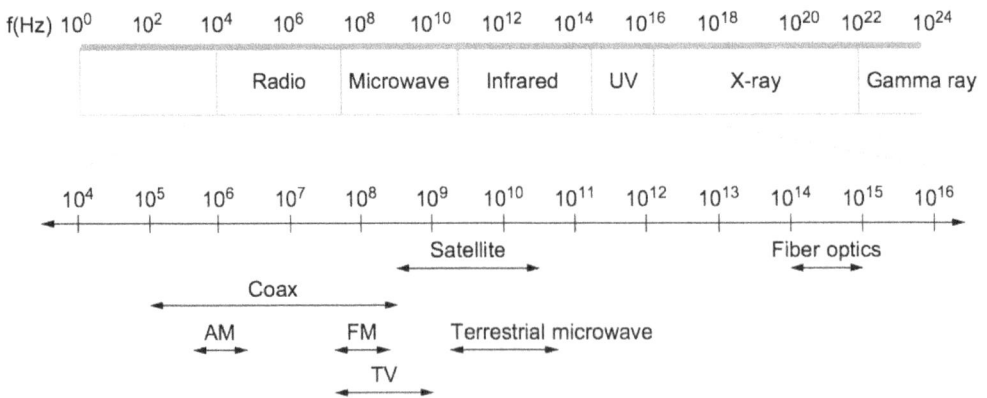

Figure 22. Electromagnetic spectrum.

What Figure 22 doesn't show is where the cellular network fits in. This is a bit complicated because the specific frequency bands that are licensed for cellular networks vary around the world, and even further complicated by the fact that network operators often simultaneously support both old/legacy technologies and new/next-generation technologies, each of which occupies a different frequency band. The high-level summary is that traditional cellular technologies range from 700-MHz to 2400-MHz, with new mid-spectrum allocations now happening at 6-GHz, and millimeter-wave (mmWave) allocations opening above 24-GHz. This mmWave band is likely to become an important part of the 5G mobile network.

So far we understand a link to be a physical medium carrying signals in the form of electromagnetic waves. Such links provide the foundation for transmitting all sorts of information, including the kind of data we are interested in transmitting—binary data (1s and 0s). We say that the binary data is encoded in the signal. The problem of encoding binary data onto electromagnetic signals is a complex topic. To help make the topic more manageable, we can think of it as being divided into two layers. The lower layer is concerned with modulation—varying the frequency, amplitude, or phase of the signal to effect the transmission of information. A simple example of modulation is to vary the power (amplitude) of a single wavelength. Intuitively, this is equivalent to turning a light on and off. Because the issue of modulation is secondary to our discussion of links as a building block for computer networks, we simply assume that it is possible to transmit a pair of distinguishable signals—think of them as a "high" signal and a "low" signal—and we consider only the upper layer, which is concerned with the much simpler problem of encoding binary data onto these two signals. The next section discusses such encodings.

Links can also be categorized based on their usage. Diverse economic and deployment factors typically impact the locations where different types of links are present. The majority of customers access the Internet either through wireless networks found in places like coffee shops, airports, and universities, or through last-mile links supplied by an ISP. This is shown in Figure 21. The various sorts of links are summarized in Table 2. They are often selected due to their cost-effectiveness in reaching a large consumer base. DSL, or Digital Subscriber Line, is an outdated technology that was implemented using the existing twisted pair copper wires used for traditional telephone services. G.Fast is a copper-based technology primarily used in multi-dwelling apartment buildings. On the other hand, PON, or Passive Optical Network, is a more modern technology used to connect homes and businesses using newly installed fiber optic cables.

Table 2. Common services available for the last-mile connection to your home.

Service	Bandwidth
DSL (copper)	up to 100 Mbps
G.Fast (copper)	up to 1 Gbps
PON (optical)	up to 10 Gbps

And of course there is also the mobile or cellular network (also referred to as 4G, but which is rapidly evolving into 5G) that connects our mobile devices to the Internet. This technology can also serve as the sole Internet connection into our homes or offices, but comes with the added benefit of allowing us to maintain Internet connectivity while moving from place to place.

These example technologies are common options for the last-mile connection to your home or business, but they are not sufficient for building a complete network from scratch. To do that, you'll also need some long-distance backbone links to interconnect cities. Modern backbone links are almost exclusively fiber today, and they typically use a technology called SONET (Synchronous Optical Network), which was originally developed to meet the demanding management requirements of telephone carriers.

Finally, in addition to last-mile, backbone, and mobile links, there are the links that you find inside a building or a campus—generally referred to as local area networks (LANs). Ethernet, and its wireless cousin Wi-Fi, are the dominant technologies in this space.

This survey on link kinds is not comprehensive, but it should have provided you with an overview of the various sorts of links that exist and some of the factors contributing to their diversity. In the next sections, we will explore how networking protocols can utilize this variety and provide a unified perspective of the network to higher layers, despite the intricate technical details and economic considerations.

2.2 Encoding

The first step in turning nodes and links into usable building blocks is to understand how to connect them in such a way that bits can be transmitted from one node to the other. As mentioned in the preceding section, signals propagate over physical links. The task, therefore, is to encode the binary data that the source node wants to send into the signals that the links are able to carry and then to decode the signal back into the corresponding binary data at the receiving node. We ignore the details of modulation and assume we are working with two discrete signals: high and low. In practice, these signals might correspond to two different voltages on a copper-based link, two different power levels on an optical link, or two different amplitudes on a radio transmission.

Most of the functions discussed in this chapter are performed by a network adaptor—a piece of hardware that connects a node to a link. The network adaptor contains a signalling component that actually encodes bits into signals at the sending node and decodes signals into bits at the receiving node. Thus, as illustrated in Figure 23, signals travel over a link between two signalling components, and bits flow between network adaptors.

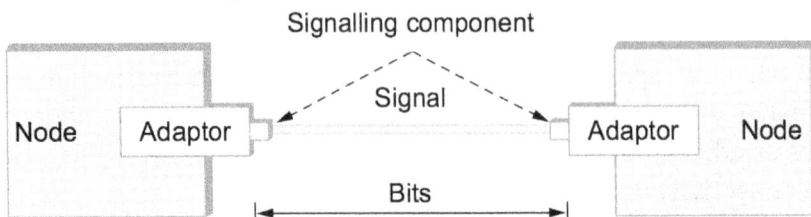

Figure 23. Signals travel between signalling components; bits flow between adaptors.

Let's return to the problem of encoding bits onto signals. The obvious thing to do is to map the data value 1 onto the high signal and the data value 0 onto the low signal. This is exactly the mapping used by an encoding scheme called, cryptically enough, non-return to zero (NRZ). For example, Figure 24 schematically depicts the NRZ-encoded signal (bottom) that corresponds to the transmission of a particular sequence of bits (top).

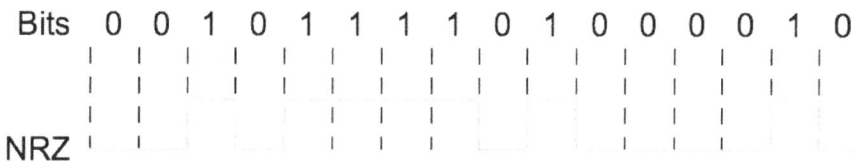

Figure 24. NRZ encoding of a bit stream.

The problem with NRZ is that a sequence of several consecutive 1s means that the signal stays high on the link for an extended period of time; similarly, several consecutive 0s means that the signal stays low for a long time. There are two fundamental problems caused by long strings of 1s or 0s. The first is that it leads to a situation known as baseline wander. Specifically, the receiver keeps an average of the signal it has seen so far and then uses this average to distinguish between low and high signals. Whenever the signal is significantly lower than this average, the receiver concludes that it has just seen a 0; likewise, a signal that is significantly higher than the average is interpreted to be a 1. The problem, of course, is that too many consecutive 1s or 0s cause this average to change, making it more difficult to detect a significant change in the signal.

The second problem is that frequent transitions from high to low and vice versa are necessary to enable clock recovery. Intuitively, the clock recovery problem is that both the encoding and decoding processes are driven by a clock—every clock cycle the sender transmits a bit and the receiver recovers a bit. The sender's and the receiver's clocks have to be precisely synchronized in order for the receiver to recover the same bits the sender transmits. If the receiver's clock is even slightly faster or slower than the sender's clock, then it does not correctly decode the signal. You could imagine sending the clock to the receiver over a separate wire, but this is typically avoided because it makes the cost of cabling twice as high. So, instead, the receiver derives the clock from the received signal—the clock recovery process. Whenever the signal changes, such as on a transition from 1 to 0 or from 0 to 1, then the receiver knows it is at a clock cycle boundary, and it can resynchronize itself. However, a long period of time without such a transition leads to clock drift. Thus, clock recovery depends on having lots of transitions in the signal, no matter what data is being sent.

One approach that addresses this problem, called non-return to zero inverted (NRZI), has the sender make a transition from the current signal to encode a 1 and stay at the current signal to encode a 0. This solves the problem of consecutive 1s, but obviously does nothing for consecutive 0s. NRZI is illustrated in Figure 25. An alternative, called Manchester encoding, does a more explicit job of merging the clock with the signal by transmitting the exclusive OR of the NRZ-encoded data and the clock. (Think of the local clock as an internal signal that alternates from low to high; a low/high pair is considered one clock cycle.) The Manchester encoding is also illustrated in Figure 25. Observe that the Manchester encoding results in 0 being encoded as a low-to-high transition and 1 being encoded as a high-to-low transition. Because both 0s and 1s result in a transition to the signal, the clock can be effectively recovered at the receiver. (There is also a variant of the Manchester encoding, called Differential Manchester, in which a 1 is encoded with the first half of the signal equal to the last half of the previous bit's signal and a 0 is encoded with the first half of the signal opposite to the last half of the previous bit's signal.)

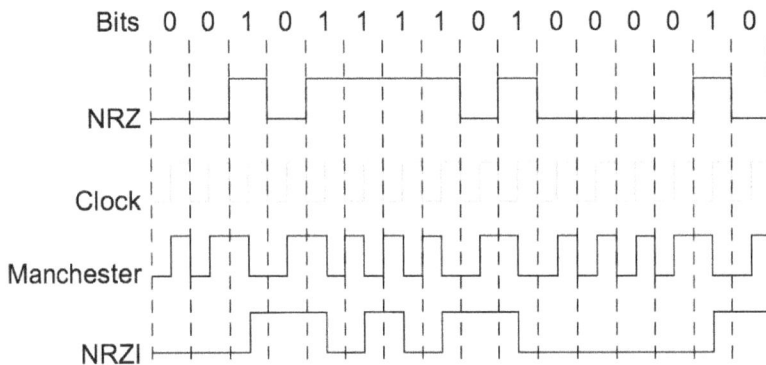

Figure 25. Different encoding strategies.

The problem with the Manchester encoding scheme is that it doubles the rate at which signal transitions are made on the link, which means that the receiver has half the time to detect each pulse of the signal. The rate at which the signal changes is called the link's baud rate. In the case of the Manchester encoding, the bit rate is half the baud rate, so the encoding is considered only 50% efficient. Keep in mind that if the receiver had been able to keep up with the faster baud rate required by the Manchester encoding in Figure 25, then both NRZ and NRZI could have been able to transmit twice as many bits in the same time period.

Note that bit rate isn't necessarily less than or equal to the baud rate, as the Manchester encoding suggests. If the modulation scheme is able to utilize (and recognize) four different signals, as opposed to just two (e.g., "high" and "low"), then it is possible to encode two bits into each clock interval, resulting in a bit rate that is twice the baud rate. Similarly, being able to modulate among eight different signals means being able to transmit three bits per clock interval. In general, it is important to keep in mind we have over-simplified modulation, which is much more sophisticated than transmitting "high" and "low" signals. It is not uncommon to vary a combination of a signal's phase and amplitude, making it possible to encode 16 or even 64 different patterns (often called symbols) during each clock interval. QAM (Quadrature Amplitude Modulation) is widely used example of such a modulation scheme.

A final encoding that we consider, called 4B/5B, attempts to address the inefficiency of the Manchester encoding without suffering from the problem of having extended durations of high or low signals. The idea of 4B/5B is to insert extra bits into the bit stream so as to break up long sequences of 0s or 1s. Specifically, every 4 bits of actual data are encoded in a 5-bit code that is then transmitted to the receiver; hence, the name 4B/5B. The 5-bit codes are selected in such a way that each one has no more than one leading 0 and no more than two trailing 0s. Thus, when sent back-to-back, no pair of 5-bit codes results in more than three consecutive 0s being transmitted. The resulting 5-bit codes are then transmitted using the NRZI encoding, which explains why the code is only concerned about consecutive 0s—NRZI already solves the problem of consecutive 1s. Note that the 4B/5B encoding results in 80% efficiency.

Table 3. 4B/5B encoding.

4-bit Data Symbol	5-bit Code
0000	11110
0001	01001
0010	10100
0011	10101
0100	01010
0101	01011
0110	01110
0111	01111
1000	10010
1001	10011
1010	10110
1011	10111
1100	11010
1101	11011
1110	11100
1111	11101

Table 3 gives the 5-bit codes that correspond to each of the 16 possible 4-bit data symbols. Notice that since 5 bits are enough to encode 32 different codes, and we are using only 16 of these for data, there are 16 codes left over that we can use for other purposes. Of these, code 11111 is used when the line is idle, code 00000 corresponds to when the line is dead, and 00100 is interpreted to mean halt. Of the remaining 13 codes, 7 of them are not valid because they violate the "one leading 0, two trailing 0s," rule, and the other 6 represent various control symbols. Some of the framing protocols described later in this chapter make use of these control symbols.

2.3 Framing

In the next sections, we will explore how networking protocols can utilize this variety and provide a unified perspective of the network to higher layers, despite the intricate technical details and economic considerations.

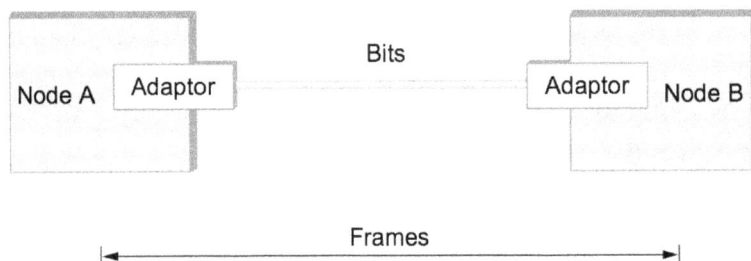

Figure 26. Bits flow between adaptors, frames between hosts.

There are several ways to address the framing problem. This section uses three different protocols to illustrate the various points in the design space. Note that while we discuss framing in the context of point-to-point links, the problem is a fundamental one that must also be addressed in multiple-access networks like Ethernet and Wi-Fi.

2.3.1 Byte-Oriented Protocols (PPP)

One of the most ancient methods of framing, which originated from the connection of terminals to mainframes, involves perceiving each frame as a grouping of bytes (characters) rather than a grouping of bits. Two early instances of byte-oriented protocols are the Binary Synchronous Communication (BISYNC) protocol, created by IBM in the late 1960s, and the Digital Data Communication Message Protocol (DDCMP), which was used in Digital Equipment Corporation's DECNET. (In the past, major computer firms such as IBM and DEC constructed exclusive networks for their clients.) An example of this strategy is the commonly utilized Point-to-Point Protocol (PPP).

Broadly speaking, there are two main methods for byte-oriented framing. One approach is to employ specific symbols called sentinel characters to signify the beginning and end of frames. The concept involves indicating the initiation of a frame by transmitting a distinct SYN (synchronization) signal. The data segment of the frame is occasionally enclosed by two additional special characters: STX (start of text) and ETX (end of text). This approach was employed by BISYNC. The issue with the sentinel approach, however, is that one of the unique characters may occur within the data segment of the frame. To address this issue, the common approach is to "escape" the character by adding a DLE (data-link-escape) character before it wherever it occurs within a frame. Additionally, the DLE character itself is escaped by adding an extra DLE before it in the frame body. (C programmers may see that this is similar to the method of escaping a quote mark with a backslash when it appears within a string.) This method is commonly referred to as character stuffing, as it involves the insertion of additional characters into the data section of the frame.The alternative to detecting the end of a frame with a sentinel value is to include the number of bytes in the frame at the beginning of the frame, in the frame header. DDCMP used this approach. One danger with this approach is that a transmission error could corrupt the count field, in which case the end of the frame would not be correctly detected. (A similar problem exists with the sentinel-based approach if the ETX field becomes corrupted.) Should this happen, the receiver will accumulate as many bytes as the bad count field indicates and then use the error detection field to determine that the frame is bad. This is sometimes called a framing error. The receiver will then wait until it sees the next SYN character to start collecting the bytes that make up the next frame. It is therefore possible that a framing error will cause back-to-back frames to be incorrectly received.

The Point-to-Point Protocol (PPP), which is commonly used to carry Internet Protocol packets over various sorts of point-to-point links, uses sentinels and character stuffing. The format for a PPP frame is given in Figure 27.

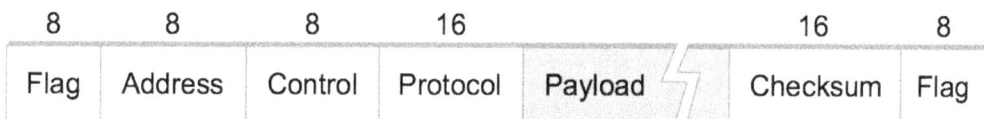

Figure 27. PPP frame format.

This figure is the first of many that you will see in this book that are used to illustrate frame or packet formats, so a few words of explanation are in order. We show a packet as a sequence of labeled fields. Above each field is a number indicating the length of that field in bits. Note that the packets are transmitted beginning with the leftmost field.

The special start-of-text character, denoted as the Flag field is 01111110. The Address and Control fields usually contain default values and so are uninteresting. The (Protocol) field is used for demultiplexing; it identifies the high-level protocol, such as IP. The frame payload size can be negotiated, but it is 1500 bytes by default. The Checksum field is either 2 (by default) or 4 bytes long. Note that despite its common name, this field is actually a CRC and not a checksum (as described in the next section).

The PPP frame format is unusual in that several of the field sizes are negotiated rather than fixed. This negotiation is conducted by a protocol called the Link Control Protocol (LCP). PPP and LCP work in tandem: LCP sends control messages encapsulated in PPP frames—such messages are denoted by an LCP identifier in the PPP (Protocol) field—and then turns around and changes PPP's frame format based on the information contained in those control messages. LCP is also involved in establishing a link between two peers when both sides detect that communication over the link is possible (e.g., when each optical receiver detects an incoming signal from the fiber to which it connects).

2.3.2 Bit-Oriented Protocols (HDLC)

Unlike byte-oriented protocols, a bit-oriented protocol is not concerned with byte boundaries—it simply views the frame as a collection of bits. These bits might come from some character set, such as ASCII; they might be pixel values in an image; or they could be instructions and operands from an executable file. The Synchronous Data Link Control (SDLC) protocol developed by IBM is an example of a bit-oriented protocol; SDLC was later standardized by the ISO as the High-Level Data Link Control (HDLC) protocol. In the following discussion, we use HDLC as an example; its frame format is given in Figure 28.

HDLC denotes both the beginning and the end of a frame with the distinguished bit sequence 01111110. This sequence is also transmitted during any times that the link is idle so that the sender and receiver can keep their clocks synchronized. In this way, both protocols essentially use the sentinel approach. Because this sequence might appear anywhere in the body of the frame—in fact, the bits 01111110 might cross byte boundaries—bit-oriented protocols use the analog of the DLE character, a technique known as bit stuffing.

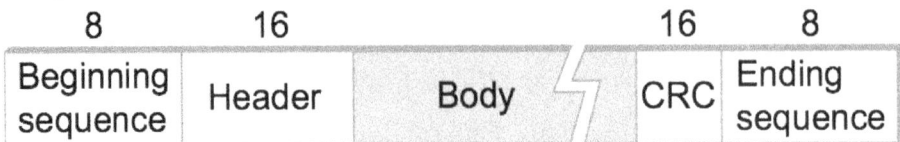

8	16		16	8
Beginning sequence	Header	Body	CRC	Ending sequence

Figure 28. HDLC frame format.

Bit stuffing in the HDLC protocol works as follows. On the sending side, any time five consecutive 1s have been transmitted from the body of the message (i.e., excluding when the sender is trying to transmit the distinguished 01111110 sequence), the sender inserts a 0 before transmitting the next bit. On the receiving side, should five consecutive 1s arrive, the receiver makes its decision based on the next bit it sees (i.e., the bit following the five 1s). If the next bit is a 0, it must have been stuffed, and so the receiver removes it. If the next bit is a 1, then one of two things is true: Either this is the end-of-frame marker or an error has been introduced into the bit stream. By looking at the next bit, the receiver can distinguish between these two cases. If it sees a 0 (i.e., the last 8 bits it has looked at are 01111110), then it is the end-of-frame marker; if it sees a 1 (i.e., the last 8 bits it has looked at are 01111111), then there must have been an error and the whole frame is discarded. In the latter case, the receiver has to wait for the next 01111110 before it can start receiving again, and, as a consequence, there is the potential that the receiver will fail to receive two consecutive frames. Obviously, there are still ways that framing errors can go undetected, such as when an entire spurious end-of-frame pattern is generated by errors, but these failures are relatively unlikely. Robust ways of detecting errors are discussed in a later section.

A notable attribute of both bit stuffing and character stuffing is that the size of a frame is contingent upon the data being transmitted in the payload of the frame. Due to the arbitrary nature of the data delivered in each frame, it is not feasible to ensure that all frames have identical sizes. (To verify this, contemplate the outcome when the final byte of a frame's body is the ETX character.) The subsequent subsection describes a method of framing that guarantees uniform frame sizes.

2.3.3 Clock-Based Framing (SONET)

The Synchronous Optical Network (SONET) standard is a third technique to framing. Due to the absence of a universally recognized generic word, we commonly refer to this strategy as clock-based framing. SONET was initially introduced by Bell Communications Research (Bellcore) and subsequently developed by the American National Standards Institute (ANSI) for the purpose of transmitting digital signals over optical fiber. It has since been universally accepted and implemented by the International Telecommunication Union Telecommunication Standardization Sector (ITU-T). For a significant period of time, SONET has been the prevailing standard for transmitting data via optical networks spanning vast distances.

It is worth noting that the complete specification of SONET is far larger than the content covered in this book. Therefore, the ensuing discourse will specifically address the most significant aspects of the standard. In addition, SONET effectively resolves both the issue of framing and the challenge of encoding. Furthermore, it tackles a crucial issue for phone companies, which is the process of combining numerous low-speed channels into a single high-speed link, known as multiplexing. (SONET's design is mostly influenced by the need for phone companies to efficiently multiplex a large number of 64-kbps channels typically utilized for telephone conversations.) We will first by examining SONET's methodology for framing and thereafter address the remaining concerns.

As with the previously discussed framing schemes, a SONET frame has some special information that tells the receiver where the frame starts and ends;

however, that is about as far as the similarities go. Notably, no bit stuffing is used, so that a frame's length does not depend on the data being sent. So the question to ask is "How does the receiver know where each frame starts and ends?" We consider this question for the lowest-speed SONET link, which is known as STS-1 and runs at 51.84 Mbps. An STS-1 frame is shown in Figure 29. It is arranged as 9 rows of 90 bytes each, and the first 3 bytes of each row are overhead, with the rest being available for data that is being transmitted over the link. The first 2 bytes of the frame contain a special bit pattern, and it is these bytes that enable the receiver to determine where the frame starts. However, since bit stuffing is not used, there is no reason why this pattern will not occasionally turn up in the payload portion of the frame. To guard against this, the receiver looks for the special bit pattern consistently, hoping to see it appearing once every 810 bytes, since each frame is 9 × 90 = 810 bytes long. When the special pattern turns up in the right place enough times, the receiver concludes that it is in sync and can then interpret the frame correctly.

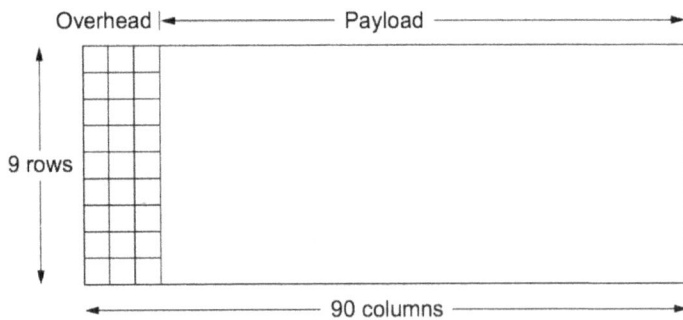

Figure 29. A SONET STS-1 frame.

One of the things we are not describing due to the complexity of SONET is the detailed use of all the other overhead bytes. Part of this complexity can be attributed to the fact that SONET runs across the carrier's optical network, not just over a single link. (Recall that we are glossing over the fact that the carriers implement a network, and we are instead focusing on the fact that we can lease a SONET link from them and then use this link to build our own packet-switched network.) Additional complexity comes from the fact that SONET provides a considerably richer set of services than just data transfer. For example, 64 kbps of a SONET link's capacity is set aside for a voice channel that is used for maintenance.

The overhead bytes of a SONET frame are encoded using NRZ, the simple encoding described in the previous section where 1s are high and 0s are low. However, to ensure that there are plenty of transitions to allow the receiver to recover the sender's clock, the payload bytes are scrambled. This is done by calculating the exclusive OR (XOR) of the data to be transmitted and by the use of a well-known bit pattern. The bit pattern, which is 127 bits long, has plenty of transitions from 1 to 0, so that XORing it with the transmitted data is likely to yield a signal with enough transitions to enable clock recovery.

SONET supports the multiplexing of multiple low-speed links in the following way. A given SONET link runs at one of a finite set of possible rates, ranging from 51.84 Mbps (STS-1) to 39,813,120 Mbps (STS-768).1 Note that all of these rates are integer multiples of STS-1. The significance for framing is that a single SONET frame can contain subframes for multiple lower-rate channels. A second related feature is that each frame is 125 µs long. This means that at STS-1 rates, a SONET frame is 810 bytes long, while at STS-3 rates, each SONET frame is 2430 bytes long. Notice the synergy between these two features: 3 × 810 = 2430, meaning that three STS-1 frames fit exactly in a single STS-3 frame.

Intuitively, the STS-N frame can be thought of as consisting of N STS-1 frames, where the bytes from these frames are interleaved; that is, a byte from the first frame is transmitted, then a byte from the second frame is transmitted, and so on. The reason for interleaving the bytes from each STS-N frame is to ensure that the bytes in each STS-1 frame are evenly paced; that is, bytes show up at the receiver at a smooth 51 Mbps, rather than all bunched up during one particular 1/Nth of the 125-µs interval.

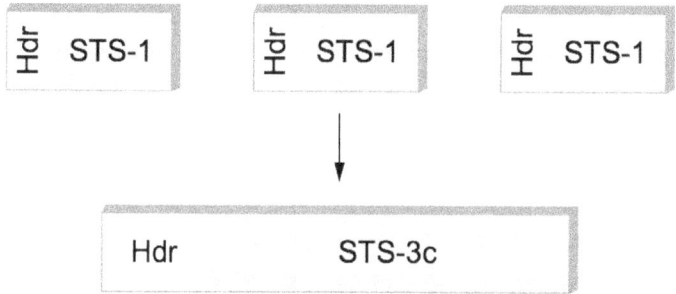

Figure 30. Three STS-1 frames multiplexed onto one STS-3c frame.

Although it is accurate to view an STS-N signal as being used to multiplex N STS-1 frames, the payload from these STS-1 frames can be linked together to form a larger STS-N payload; such a link is denoted STS-Nc (for concatenated). One of the fields in the overhead is used for this purpose. Figure 30 schematically depicts concatenation in the case of three STS-1 frames being concatenated into a single STS-3c frame. The significance of a SONET link being designated as STS-3c rather than STS-3 is that, in the former case, the user of the link can view it as a single 155.25-Mbps pipe, whereas an STS-3 should really be viewed as three 51.84-Mbps links that happen to share a fiber.

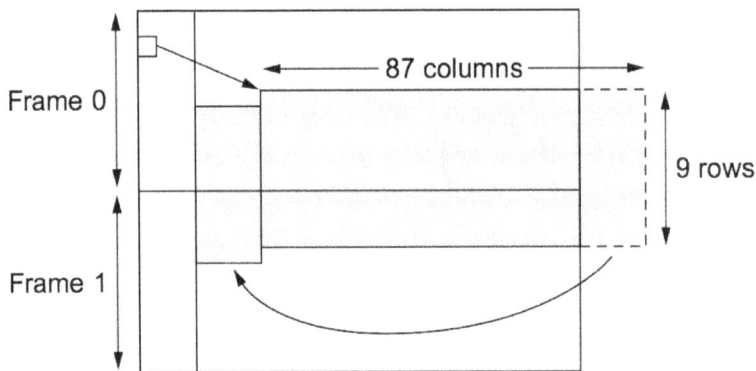

Figure 31. SONET frames out of phase.

The previous explanation of SONET is too simplistic as it implies that the payload of each frame is fully enclosed within the frame. (There is no reason why it wouldn't be.) Indeed, the STS-1 frame should be regarded merely as a temporary structure, serving as a placeholder for the frame, inside which the real payload may traverse between frame boundaries. The depicted scenario can be observed in Figure 31. In this image, we observe the STS-1 payload suspended between two STS-1 frames. Additionally, the payload has been relocated a certain amount of bytes to the right, resulting in it wrapping around. One of the fields in the frame above indicates the starting place of the payload. The significance of this capacity lies in its potential to streamline the process of synchronizing the clocks utilized across carriers' networks, a matter that consumes a substantial amount of carriers' time and concern.

2.4 Error Detection

As discussed in Chapter 1, bit errors are sometimes introduced into frames. This happens, for example, because of electrical interference or thermal noise. Although errors are rare, especially on optical links, some mechanism is needed to detect these errors so that corrective action can be taken. Otherwise, the end user is left wondering why the C program that successfully compiled just a moment ago now suddenly has a syntax error in it, when all that happened in the interim is that it was copied across a network file system.

There is a long history of techniques for dealing with bit errors in computer systems, dating back to at least the 1940s. Hamming and Reed-Solomon codes are two notable examples that were developed for use in punch card readers, when storing data on magnetic disks, and in early core memories. This section describes some of the error detection techniques most commonly used in networking.

Detecting errors is only one part of the problem. The other part is correcting errors once detected. Two basic approaches can be taken when the recipient of a message detects an error. One is to notify the sender that the message was corrupted so that the sender can retransmit a copy of the message. If bit errors are rare, then in all probability the retransmitted copy will be error free. Alternatively, some types of error detection algorithms allow the recipient to reconstruct the correct message even after it has been corrupted; such algorithms rely on error-correcting codes, discussed below.

One of the most common techniques for detecting transmission errors is a technique known as the cyclic redundancy check (CRC). It is used in nearly all the link-level protocols discussed in this chapter. This section outlines the basic CRC algorithm, but before discussing that approach, we first describe the simpler checksum scheme used by several Internet protocols.

The basic idea behind any error detection scheme is to add redundant information to a frame that can be used to determine if errors have been introduced. In the extreme, we could imagine transmitting two complete copies of the data. If the two copies are identical at the receiver, then it is probably the case that both are correct. If they differ, then an error was introduced into one (or both) of them, and they must be discarded. This is a rather poor error detection scheme for two reasons. First, it sends n redundant bits for an n-bit message. Second, many errors will go undetected—any error that happens to corrupt the same bit positions in the first and second copies of the message. In general, the goal of error detecting codes is to provide a high probability of detecting errors combined with a relatively low number of redundant bits.

Fortunately, we can do a lot better than this simple scheme. In general, we can provide quite strong error detection capability while sending only k redundant bits for an n-bit message, where k is much smaller than n. On an Ethernet, for example, a frame carrying up to 12,000 bits (1500 bytes) of data requires only a 32-bit CRC code, or as it is commonly expressed, uses CRC-32. Such a code will catch the overwhelming majority of errors, as we will see below.

We say that the extra bits we send are redundant because they add no new information to the message. Instead, they are derived directly from the original message using some well-defined algorithm. Both the sender and the receiver know exactly what that algorithm is. The sender applies the algorithm to the message to generate the redundant bits. It then transmits both the message and those few extra bits. When the receiver applies the same algorithm to the received message, it should (in the absence of errors) come up with the same result as the sender. It compares the result with the one sent to it by the sender. If they match, it can conclude (with high likelihood) that no errors were introduced in the message during transmission. If they do not match, it can be sure that either the message or the redundant bits were corrupted, and it must take appropriate action—that is, discarding the message or correcting it if that is possible.

One point to consider regarding the terminology for these additional components. Typically, they are known as error-detecting codes. Under certain circumstances, where the technique used to generate the code relies on addition, it may be referred to as a checksum. The Internet checksum is aptly titled. It is an error checking mechanism that use a summation method. Regrettably, the term "checksum" is frequently employed inaccurately to encompass any type of error-detecting code, including CRCs. To avoid confusion, we recommend using the term "checksum" just for codes that include addition, and using "error-detecting code" to refer to the broader category of codes discussed in this section.

2.4.1 Internet Checksum Algorithm

Our first approach to error detection is exemplified by the Internet checksum. Although it is not used at the link level, it nevertheless provides the same sort of functionality as CRCs, so we discuss it here.

The idea behind the Internet checksum is very simple—you add up all the words that are transmitted and then transmit the result of that sum. The result is the checksum. The receiver performs the same calculation on the received data and compares the result with the received checksum. If any transmitted data, including the checksum itself, is corrupted, then the results will not match, so the receiver knows that an error occurred.

You can imagine many different variations on the basic idea of a checksum. The exact scheme used by the Internet protocols works as follows. Consider the data being checksummed as a sequence of 16-bit integers. Add them together using 16-bit ones' complement arithmetic (explained below) and then take the ones' complement of the result. That 16-bit number is the checksum.

In ones' complement arithmetic, a negative integer (-x) is represented as the complement of x; that is, each bit of x is inverted. When adding numbers in ones' complement arithmetic, a carryout from the most significant bit needs to be added to the result. Consider, for example, the addition of -5 and -3 in ones' complement arithmetic on 4-bit integers: +5 is 0101, so -5 is 1010; +3 is 0011, so -3 is 1100. If we add 1010 and 1100, ignoring the carry, we get 0110. In ones' complement arithmetic, the fact that this operation caused a carry from the most significant bit causes us to increment the result, giving 0111, which is the ones' complement representation of -8 (obtained by inverting the bits in 1000), as we would expect.

The following routine gives a straightforward implementation of the Internet's checksum algorithm. The count argument gives the length of buf measured in 16-bit units. The routine assumes that buf has already been padded with 0s to a 16-bit boundary.

u_short

```
cksum(u_short *buf, int count)
{
  register u_long sum = 0;

  while (count--)
  {
    sum += *buf++;
    if (sum & 0xFFFF0000)
    {
      /* carry occurred, so wrap around */
      sum &= 0xFFFF;
      sum++;
    }
  }
  return ~(sum & 0xFFFF);
}
```

This code ensures that the calculation uses ones' complement arithmetic rather than the twos' complement that is used in most machines. Note the if statement inside the while loop. If there is a carry into the top 16 bits of sum, then we increment sum just as in the previous example.

Compared to our repetition code, this algorithm scores well for using a small number of redundant bits—only 16 for a message of any length—but it does not score extremely well for strength of error detection. For example, a pair of single-bit errors, one of which increments a word and one of which decrements another word by the same amount, will go undetected. The reason for using an algorithm like this in spite of its relatively weak protection against errors (compared to a CRC, for example) is simple: This algorithm is much easier to implement in software. Experience has suggested that a checksum of this form was adequate, but one reason it is adequate is that this checksum is the last line of defense in an end-to-end protocol. The majority of errors are picked up by stronger error detection algorithms, such as CRCs, at the link level.

2.4.2 Cyclic Redundancy Check

The primary objective in creating error detection algorithms is to optimize the likelihood of error detection while minimizing the use of redundant bits. Cyclic redundancy checks employ sophisticated mathematical techniques to accomplish this objective. For instance, a 32-bit CRC provides robust defense against typical bit mistakes in communications that have a length of hundreds of bytes. The theoretical basis of the cyclic redundancy check is derived from the mathematical discipline of finite fields. Although it may initially seem intimidating, the fundamental concepts may be readily comprehended. To start, think of an (n+1)-bit message as being represented by an n degree polynomial, that is, a polynomial whose highest-order term is x^n. The message is represented by a polynomial by using the value of each bit in the message as the coefficient for each term in the polynomial, starting with the most significant bit to represent the highest-order term. For example, an 8-bit message consisting of the bits 10011010 corresponds to the polynomial

$$(x) = (1 \times x7) + (0 \times x6) + (0 \times x5) + (1 \times x4) + (1 \times x3) + (0 \times x2) + (1 \times x1) + (0 \times x0)$$

$$(x) = x7 + x4 + x3 + x1$$

We can thus think of a sender and a receiver as exchanging polynomials with each other.

For the purposes of calculating a CRC, a sender and receiver have to agree on a divisor polynomial, (x). (x) is a polynomial of degree k. For example, suppose $(x) = x3+x2+1$. In this case, k = 3. The answer to the question "Where did (x) come from?" is, in most practical cases, "You look it up in a book." In fact, the choice of (x) has a significant impact on what types of errors can be reliably detected, as we discuss below. There are a handful of divisor polynomials that are very good choices for various environments, and the exact choice is normally made as part of the protocol design. For example, the Ethernet standard uses a well-known polynomial of degree 32.

When a sender wishes to transmit a message $M(x)$ that is n+1 bits long, what is actually sent is the (n+1)-bit message plus k bits. We call the complete transmitted message, including the redundant bits, $P(x)$. What we are going to do is contrive to make the polynomial representing (x) exactly divisible by $C(x)$; we explain how this is achieved below. If (x) is transmitted over a link and there are no errors introduced during transmission, then the receiver should be able to divide $P(x)$ by $C(x)$ exactly, leaving a remainder of zero. On the other hand, if some error is introduced into (x) during transmission, then in all likelihood the received polynomial will no longer be exactly divisible by $C(x)$, and thus the receiver will obtain a nonzero remainder implying that an error has occurred.

It will help to understand the following if you know a little about polynomial arithmetic; it is just slightly different from normal integer arithmetic. We are dealing with a special class of polynomial arithmetic here, where coefficients may be only one or zero, and operations on the coefficients are performed using modulo

2 arithmetic. This is referred to as "polynomial arithmetic modulo 2." Since this is a networking book, not a mathematics text, let's focus on the key properties of this type of arithmetic for our purposes (which we ask you to accept on faith):

- ⊙ Any polynomial (x) can be divided by a divisor polynomial $C(x)$ if $B(x)$ is of higher degree than $C(x)$.

- ⊙ Any polynomial (x) can be divided once by a divisor polynomial $C(x)$ if $B(x)$ is of the same degree as $C(x)$.

- ⊙ The remainder obtained when (x) is divided by $C(x)$ is obtained by performing the exclusive OR (XOR) operation on each pair of matching coefficients.

For example, the polynomial $x3 + 1$ can be divided by $x3 + x2 + 1$ (because they are both of degree 3) and the remainder would be $0 \times x3 + 1 \times x2 + 0 \times x1 + 0 \times x0 = x2$ (obtained by XORing the coefficients of each term). In terms of messages, we could say that 1001 can be divided by 1101 and leaves a remainder of 0100. You should be able to see that the remainder is just the bitwise exclusive OR of the two messages..

Now that we know the basic rules for dividing polynomials, we are able to do long division, which is necessary to deal with longer messages. An example appears below.

Recall that we wanted to create a polynomial for transmission that is derived from the original message M(x), is k bits longer than M(x), and is exactly divisible by C(x). We can do this in the following way:

- ⊙ Multiply(x) by xk; that is, add k zeros at the end of the message. Call this zero-extended message (x).

- ⊙ Divide (x) by $C(x)$ and find the remainder.

- ⊙ Subtract the remainder from (x).

It should be obvious that what is left at this point is a message that is exactly divisible by (x). We may also note that the resulting message consists of(x) followed by the remainder obtained in step 2, because when we subtracted the remainder (which can be no more than k bits long), we were just XORing it with the k zeros added in step 1. This part will become clearer with an example.

Consider the message $x7 + x4 + x3 + x1$, or 10011010. We begin by multiplying by $x3$, since our divisor polynomial is of degree 3. This gives 10011010000. We divide this by (x), which corresponds to 1101 in this case. Figure 32 shows the polynomial long-division operation. Given the rules of polynomial arithmetic described above, the long-division operation proceeds much as it would if we were dividing integers. Thus, in the first step of our example, we see that the divisor 1101 divides once into the first four bits of the message (1001), since they are of the same degree, and leaves a remainder of 100 (1101 XOR 1001). The next step is to bring down a digit from the message polynomial until we get another polynomial with the same degree as (x), in this case 1001. We calculate the remainder again (100) and continue until the calculation is complete. Note that the "result" of the long division, which appears at the top of he calculation, is not really of much interest—it is the remainder at the end that matters.

You can see from the very bottom of Figure 32 that the remainder of the example calculation is 101. So we know that 10011010000 minus 101 would be exactly divisible by C(x), and this is what we send. The minus operation in polynomial arithmetic is the logical XOR operation, so we actually send 10011010101. As noted above, this turns out to be just the original message with the remainder from the long division calculation appended to it. The recipient divides the received polynomial by C(x) and, if the result is 0, concludes that there were no errors. If the result is nonzero, it may be necessary to discard the corrupted message; with some codes, it may be possible to correct a small error (e.g., if the error affected only one bit). A code that enables error correction is called an error-correcting code (ECC).

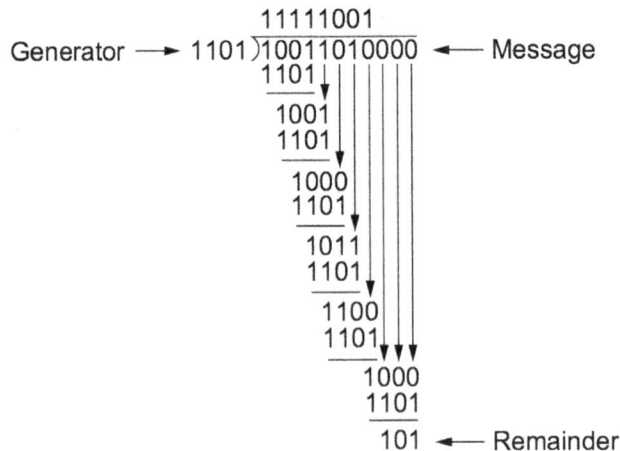

Figure 32. CRC calculation using polynomial long division.

Now we will consider the question of where the polynomial (x) comes from. Intuitively, the idea is to select this polynomial so that it is very unlikely to divide evenly into a message that has errors introduced into it. If the transmitted message is (x), we may think of the introduction of errors as the addition of another polynomial $E(x)$, so the recipient sees $P(x) + E(x)$. The only way that an error could slip by undetected would be if the received message could be evenly divided by (x), and since we know that $P(x)$ can be evenly divided by $C(x)$, this could only happen if $E(x)$ can be divided evenly by $C(x)$. The trick is to pick (x) so that this is very unlikely for common types of errors.

One common type of error is a single-bit error, which can be expressed as $(x) = xi$ when it affects bit position i. If we select (x) such that thefirst and the last term (that is, the xk and $x0$ terms) are nonzero, then we already have a two-term polynomial that cannot divide evenly into the one term $E(x)$. Such a (x) can, therefore, detect all single-bit errors. In general, it is possible to prove that the following types of errors can be detected by a (x) with the stated properties:

- All single-bit errors, as long as the Xk and X0 terms have nonzero coefficients
- All double-bit errors, as long as C(x) has a factor with at least three terms
- Any odd number of errors, as long as C(x) contains the factor (x+1)

We have mentioned that it is possible to use codes that not only detect the presence of errors but also enable errors to be corrected. Since the details of such codes require yet more complex mathematics than that required to understand CRCs, we will not dwell on them here. However, it is worth considering the merits of correction versus detection.

At first glance, it would seem that correction is always better, since with detection we are forced to throw away the message and, in general, ask for another copy to be transmitted. This uses up bandwidth and may introduce latency while waiting for the retransmission. However, there is a downside to correction, as it generally requires a greater number of redundant bits to send an error-correcting code that is as strong (that is, able to cope with the same range of errors) as a code that only detects errors. Thus, while error detection requires more bits to be sent when errors occur, error correction requires more bits to be sent all the time. As a result, error correction tends to be most useful when (1) errors are quite probable, as they may be, for example, in a wireless environment, or (2) the cost of retransmission is too high, for example, because of the latency involved retransmitting a packet over a satellite link.

The use of error-correcting codes in networking is sometimes referred to as forward error correction (FEC) because the correction of errors is handled "in advance" by sending extra information, rather than waiting for errors to happen and dealing with them later by retransmission. FEC is commonly used in wireless networks such as 802.11.

- Any "burst" error (i.e., sequence of consecutive errored bits) for which the length of the burst is less than k bits (Most burst errors of length greater than k bits can also be detected.)

Six versions of $C(x)$ are widely used in link-level protocols. For example, Ethernet uses CRC-32, which is defined as follows:

- CRC-32 = X32 + X26 + X23 + X22 + X16 + X12 + X11 + X10 + X8 + X7 + X5 + X4 +

X2 + X + 1

Finally, we note that the CRC algorithm, while seemingly complex, is easily implemented in hardware using a k-bit shift register and XOR gates. The number of bits in the shift register equals the degree of the generator polynomial (k). Figure 74 shows the hardware that would be used for the generator $x3 + x2 + 1$ from our previous example. The message is shifted in from the left, beginning with the most significant bit and ending with the string of k zeros that is attached to the message, just as in the long division example. When all the bits have been shifted in and appropriately XORed, the register contains the remainder—that is, the CRC (most significant bit on the right). The position of the XOR gates is determined as follows: If the bits in the shift register are labeled 0 through $k - 1$, left to right, then put an XOR gate in front of bit n if there is a term xn in the generator polynomial. Thus, we see an XOR gate in front of positions 0 and 2 for the generator $x3 + x2 + x0$.

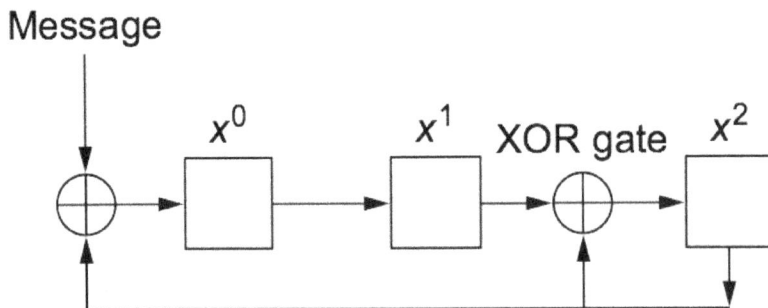

Figure 33. CRC calculation using shift register.

2.5 Reliable Transmission

As mentioned earlier, frames can become corrupted during transmission, and an error code such as CRC is used to identify and detect these mistakes. Although many error codes have the capability to rectify faults, the practicality of handling the wide variety of bit and burst errors that can occur over a network link is hindered by the excessive overhead. Despite the implementation of error-correcting codes, such as on wireless lines, certain faults may still be too severe to be rectified. Consequently, it is necessary to discard certain frames that are corrupt. In order to ensure reliable delivery of frames, a link-level protocol must have a mechanism to recover from discarded or lost frames. It's worth noting that reliability is a function that may be provided at the link level, but many modern link technologies omit this function. Furthermore, reliable delivery is frequently provided at higher levels, including both transport and sometimes, the application layer. Exactly where it should be provided is a matter of some debate and depends on many factors. We describe the basics of reliable delivery here, since the principles are common across layers, but you should be aware that we're not just talking about a link-layer function.

Reliable delivery is usually accomplished using a combination of two fundamental mechanisms—acknowledgments and timeouts. An acknowledgment (ACK for short) is a small control frame that a protocol sends back to its peer saying that it has received an earlier frame. By control frame we mean a header without any data, although a protocol can piggyback an ACK on a data frame it just happens to be sending in the opposite direction. The receipt of an acknowledgment indicates to the sender of the original frame that its frame was successfully delivered. If the sender does not receive an acknowledgment after a reasonable amount of time, then it retransmits the original frame. This action of waiting a reasonable amount of time is called a timeout.

The general strategy of using acknowledgments and timeouts to implement reliable delivery is sometimes called automatic repeat request (abbreviated ARQ). This section describes three different ARQ algorithms using generic language; that is, we do not give detailed information about a particular protocol's header fields.

2.5.1 Stop-and-Wait

The most basic ARQ technique is the stop-and-wait algorithm. The concept of stop-and-wait is simple: The sender engages in a process of transmitting one frame and then awaits an acknowledgment before proceeding to transmit the next frame. If the sender does not receive an acknowledgment within a specific timeframe, it will timeout and resend the original frame.

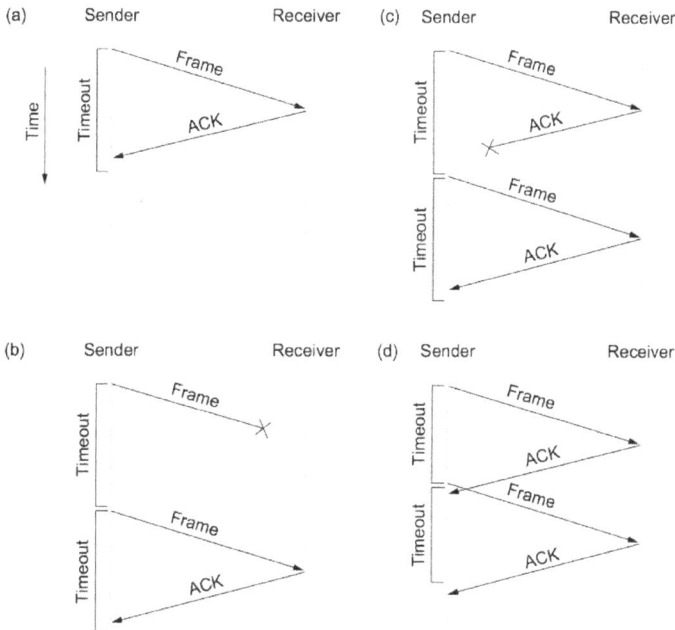

Figure 34. Timeline showing four different scenarios for the stop-and-wait algorithm. (a) The ACK is received before the timer expires; (b) the original frame is lost; (c) the ACK is lost; (d) the timeout fires too soon.

Figure 34 illustrates timelines for four different scenarios that result from this basic algorithm. The sending side is represented on the left, the receiving side is depicted on the right, and time flows from top to bottom. Figure 34(a) shows the situation in which the ACK is received before the timer expires; (b) and (c) show the situation in which the original frame and the ACK, respectively, are lost; and (d) shows the situation in which the timeout fires too soon. Recall that by "lost" we mean that the frame was corrupted while in transit, that this corruption was detected by an error code on the receiver, and that the frame was subsequently discarded.

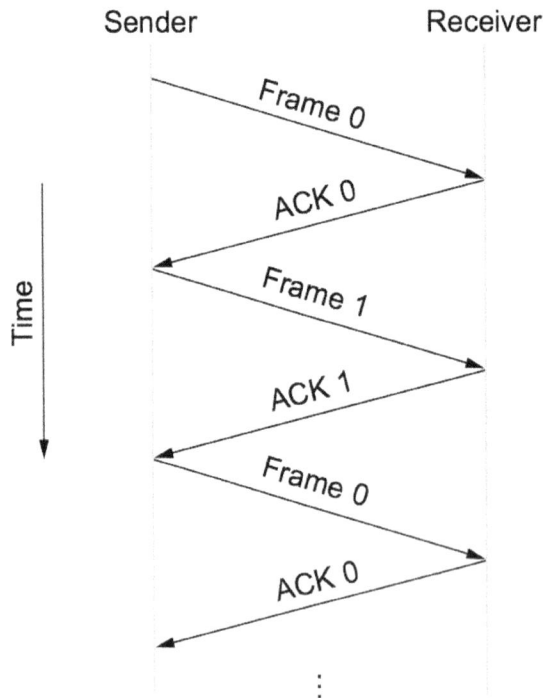

Figure 35. Timeline for stop-and-wait with 1-bit sequence number.

The packet timelines shown in this section are examples of a frequently used tool in teaching, explaining, and designing protocols. They are useful because they capture visually the behavior over time of a distributed system—something that can be quite hard to analyze. When designing a protocol, you often have to be prepared for the unexpected—a system crashes, a message gets lost, or something that you expected to happen quickly turns out to take a long time. These sorts of diagrams can often help us understand what might go wrong in such cases and thus help a protocol designer be prepared for every eventuality.

There is one important subtlety in the stop-and-wait algorithm. Suppose the sender sends a frame and the receiver acknowledges it, but the acknowledgment is either lost or delayed in arriving. This situation is illustrated in timelines (c) and (d) of Figure 34. In both cases, the sender times out and retransmits the original frame, but the receiver will think that it is the next frame, since it correctly received and acknowledged the first frame. This has the potential to cause duplicate copies of a frame to be delivered. To address this problem, the header for a stop-and-wait protocol usually includes a 1-bit sequence number—that is, the sequence number can take on the values 0 and 1—and the sequence numbers used for each frame alternate, as illustrated in Figure 35. Thus, when the sender retransmits frame 0, the receiver can determine that it is seeing a second copy of frame 0 rather than the first copy of frame 1 and therefore can ignore it (the receiver still acknowledges it, in case the first ACK was lost).

The main shortcoming of the stop-and-wait algorithm is that it allows the sender to have only one outstanding frame on the link at a time, and this may be far below the link's capacity. Consider, for example, a 1.5-Mbps link with a 45-ms round-trip time. This link has a delay × bandwidth product of 67.5 Kb, or approximately 8 KB. Since the sender can send only one frame per RTT, and assuming a frame size of 1 KB, this implies a maximum sending rate of

$$\text{Bits-Per-Frame} / \text{Time-Per-Frame} = 1024 \times 8 / 0.045 = 182 \text{ kbps}$$

or about one-eighth of the link's capacity. To use the link fully, then, we'd like the sender to be able to transmit up to eight frames before having to wait for an acknowledgment.

Key Takeaway

The significance of the delay × bandwidth product is that it represents the amount of data that could be in transit. We would like to be able to send this much data without waiting for the first acknowledgment. The principle at work here is often referred to as keeping the pipe full. The algorithms presented in the following two subsections do exactly this.

2.5.2 Sliding Window

Consider again the scenario in which the link has a delay × bandwidth product of 8 KB and frames are 1 KB in size. We would like the sender to be ready to transmit the ninth frame at pretty much the same moment that the ACK for the first frame arrives. The algorithm that allows us to do this is called sliding window, and an illustrative timeline is given in Figure 36.

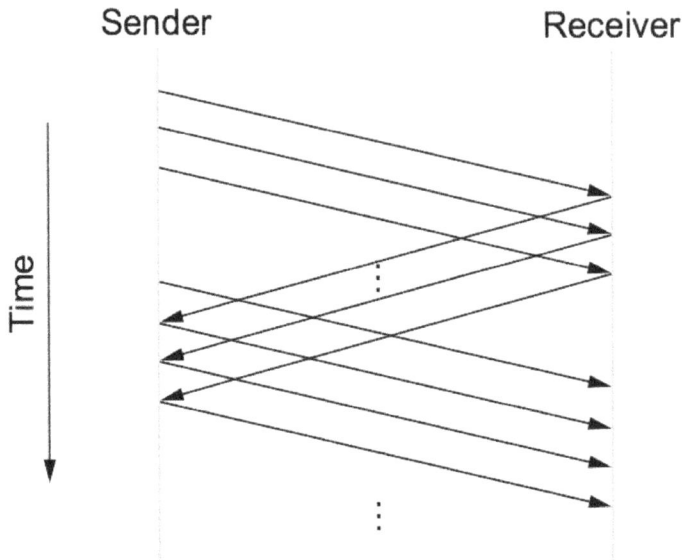

Figure 36. Timeline for the sliding window algorithm.

THE SLIDING WINDOW ALGORITHM

The sliding window algorithm works as follows. First, the sender assigns a sequence number, denoted SeqNum, to each frame. For now, let's ignore the fact that SeqNum is implemented by a finite-size header field and instead assume that it can grow infinitely large. The sender maintains three variables: The send window size, denoted SWS, gives the upper bound on the number of outstanding (unacknowledged) frames that the sender can transmit; LAR denotes the sequence number of the last acknowledgment received; and LFS denotes the sequence number of the last frame sent. The sender also maintains the following invariant:

$$LFS - LAR <= SWS$$

This situation is illustrated in Figure 37.

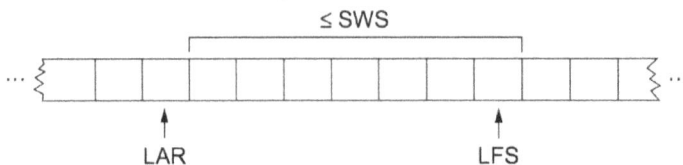

Figure 37. Sliding window on sender.

When an acknowledgment arrives, the sender moves LAR to the right, thereby allowing the sender to transmit another frame. Also, the sender associates a timer with each frame it transmits, and it retransmits the frame should the timer expire before an ACK is received. Notice that the sender has to be willing to buffer up to SWS frames since it must be prepared to retransmit them until they are acknowledged.

The receiver maintains the following three variables: The receive window size, denoted RWS, gives the upper bound on the number of out-of-order frames that the receiver is willing to accept; LAF denotes the sequence number of the largest acceptable frame; and LFR denotes the sequence number of the last frame received. The receiver also maintains the following invariant:

$$LAF - LFR <= RWS$$

This situation is illustrated in Figure 38.

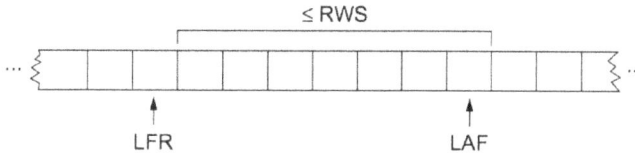

Figure 38. Sliding window on receiver.

When a frame with sequence number SeqNum arrives, the receiver takes the following action. If SeqNum <= LFR or SeqNum > LAF, then the frame is outside the receiver's window and it is discarded. If LFR < SeqNum <= LAF, then the frame is within the receiver's window and it is accepted. Now the receiver needs to decide whether or not to send an ACK. Let SeqNumToAck denote the largest sequence number not yet acknowledged, such that all frames with sequence numbers less than or equal to SeqNumToAck have been received. The receiver acknowledges the receipt of SeqNumToAck, even if higher numbered packets have been received. This acknowledgment is said to be cumulative. It then sets LFR = SeqNumToAck and adjusts LAF = LFR + RWS.

For example, suppose LFR = 5 (i.e., the last ACK the receiver sent was for sequence number 5), and RWS = 4. This implies that LAF = 9. Should frames 7 and 8 arrive, they will be buffered because they are within the receiver's window. However, no ACK needs to be sent since frame 6 has yet to arrive. Frames 7 and 8 are said to have arrived out of order. (Technically, the receiver could resend an ACK for frame 5 when frames 7 and 8 arrive.) Should frame 6 then arrive—perhaps it is late because it was lost the first time and had to be retransmitted, or perhaps it was simply delayed—the receiver acknowledges frame 8, bumps LFR to 8, and sets LAF to 12.2 If frame 6 was in fact lost, then a timeout will have occurred at the sender, causing it to retransmit frame 6.

We observe that when a timeout occurs, the amount of data in transit decreases, since the sender is unable to advance its window until frame 6 is acknowledged. This means that when packet losses occur, this scheme is no longer keeping the pipe full. The longer it takes to notice that a packet loss has occurred, the more severe this problem becomes.

Notice that, in this example, the receiver could have sent a negative acknowledgment (NAK) for frame 6 as soon as frame 7 arrived. However, this is unnecessary since the sender's timeout mechanism is sufficient to catch this situation, and sending NAKs adds additional complexity to the receiver. Also, as we mentioned, it would have been legitimate to send additional acknowledgments of frame 5 when frames 7 and 8 arrived; in some cases, a sender can use duplicate ACKs as a clue that a frame was lost. Both approaches help to improve performance by allowing early detection of packet losses.

Yet another variation on this scheme would be to use selective acknowledgments. That is, the receiver could acknowledge exactly those frames it has received rather than just the highest numbered frame received in order. So, in the above example, the receiver could acknowledge the receipt of frames 7 and 8. Giving more information to the sender makes it potentially easier for the sender to keep the pipe full but adds complexity to the implementation.

The sending window size is selected according to how many frames we want to have outstanding on the link at a given time; SWS is easy to compute for a given delay × bandwidth product. On the other hand, the receiver can set RWS to whatever it wants. Two common settings are RWS = 1, which implies that the receiver will not buffer any frames that arrive out of order, and RWS = SWS, which implies that the receiver can buffer any of the frames the sender transmits. It makes no sense to set RWS > SWS since it's impossible for more than SWS frames to arrive out of order.

FINITE SEQUENCE NUMBERS AND SLIDING WINDOW

We now return to the one simplification we introduced into the algorithm—our assumption that sequence numbers can grow infinitely large. In practice, of course, a frame's sequence number is specified in a header field of some finite size. For example, a 3-bit field means that there are eight possible sequence numbers, 0..7. This makes it necessary to reuse sequence numbers or, stated another way, sequence numbers wrap around. This introduces the problem of being able to distinguish between different incarnations of the same sequence numbers, which implies that the number of possible sequence numbers must be larger than the number of outstanding frames allowed. For example, stop-and-wait allowed one outstanding frame at a time and had two distinct sequence numbers.

Suppose we have one more number in our space of sequence numbers than we have potentially outstanding frames; that is, SWS <= MaxSeqNum - 1, where MaxSeqNum is the number of available sequence numbers. Is this sufficient? The answer depends on RWS. If RWS = 1, then MaxSeqNum >= SWS + 1 is sufficient. If RWS is equal to SWS, then having a MaxSeqNum just one greater than the sending window size is not good enough. To see this, consider the situation in which we have the eight sequence numbers 0 through 7, and SWS = RWS = 7. Suppose the sender transmits frames 0..6, they are successfully received, but the ACKs are lost. The receiver is now expecting frames 7, 0..5, but the sender times out and sends frames 0..6. Unfortunately, the receiver is expecting the second incarnation of frames 0..5 but gets the first incarnation of these frames. This is exactly the situation we wanted to avoid.

It turns out that the sending window size can be no more than half as big as the number of available sequence numbers when RWS = SWS, or stated more precisely,

$$SWS < (MaxSeqNum + 1)/ 2$$

Intuitively, what this is saying is that the sliding window protocol alternates between the two halves of the sequence number space, just as stop-and-wait alternates between sequence numbers 0 and 1. The only difference is that it continually slides between the two halves rather than discretely alternating between them.

Note that this rule is specific to the situation where RWS = SWS. We leave it as an exercise to determine the more general rule that works for arbitrary values of RWS and SWS. Also note that the relationship between the window size and the sequence number space depends on an assumption that is so obvious that it is easy to overlook, namely that frames are not reordered in transit. This cannot happen on a direct point-to-point link since there is no way for one frame to overtake another during transmission. However, we will see the sliding window algorithm used in a different environments, and we will need to devise another rule.

IMPLEMENTATION OF SLIDING WINDOW

The following routines illustrate how we might implement the sending and receiving sides of the sliding window algorithm. The routines are taken from a working protocol named, appropriately enough, Sliding Window Protocol (SWP). So as not to concern ourselves with the adjacent protocols in the protocol graph, we denote the protocol sitting above SWP as the high-level protocol (HLP) and the protocol sitting below SWP as the link-level protocol (LLP).

We start by defining a pair of data structures. First, the frame header is very simple: It contains a sequence number (SeqNum) and an acknowledgment number (AckNum). It also contains a Flags field that indicates whether the frame is an ACK or carries data.

```
typedef uint8_t SwpSeqno;
typedef struct {
    SwpSeqno  SeqNum;  /* sequence number of this frame */
    SwpSeqno  AckNum;  /* ack of received frame */
```

```
uint8_t    Flags;  /* up to 8 bits worth of flags */
} SwpHdr;
```

Next, the state of the sliding window algorithm has the following structure. For the sending side of the protocol, this state includes variables LAR and LFS, as described earlier in this section, as well as a queue that holds frames that have been transmitted but not yet acknowledged (sendQ). The sending state also includes a counting semaphore called sendWindowNotFull. We will see how this is used below, but generally a semaphore is a synchronization primitive that supports semWait and semSignal operations. Every invocation of semSignal increments the semaphore by 1, and every invocation of semWait decrements s by 1, with the calling process blocked (suspended) should decrementing the semaphore cause its value to become less than 0. A process that is blocked during its call to semWait will be allowed to resume as soon as enough semSignal operations have been performed to raise the value of the semaphore above 0.

For the receiving side of the protocol, the state includes the variable NFE. This is the next frame expected, the frame with a sequence number one more than the last frame received (LFR), described earlier in this section. There is also a queue that holds frames that have been received out of order (recvQ). Finally, although not shown, the sender and receiver sliding window sizes are defined by constants SWS and RWS, respectively.

```
typedef struct {
  /* sender side state: */
  SwpSeqno   LAR;      /* seqno of last ACK received */
  SwpSeqno   LFS;      /* last frame sent */
  Semaphore   sendWindowNotFull;
  SwpHdr    hdr;      /* pre-initialized header */
  struct sendQ_slot {
    Event  timeout;   /* event associated with send-timeout */
    Msg    msg;
  } sendQ[SWS];

  /* receiver side state: */
  SwpSeqno   NFE;     /* seqno of next frame expected */
  struct recvQ_slot {
    int    received; /* is msg valid? */
```

```
   Msg    msg;
} recvQ[RWS];
} SwpState;
```

The sending side of SWP is implemented by procedure sendSWP. This routine is rather simple. First, semWait causes this process to block on a semaphore until it is OK to send another frame. Once allowed to proceed, sendSWP sets the sequence number in the frame's header, saves a copy of the frame in the transmit queue (sendQ), schedules a timeout event to handle the case in which the frame is not acknowledged, and sends the frame to the next-lower-level protocol, which we denote as LINK.

One detail worth noting is the call to store_swp_hdr just before the call to msgAddHdr. This routine translates the C structure that holds the SWP header (state->hdr) into a byte string that can be safely attached to the front of the message (hbuf). This routine (not shown) must translate each integer field in the header into network byte order and remove any padding that the compiler has added to the C structure. The issue of byte order is a non-trivial issue, but for now it is enough to assume that this routine places the most significant bit of a multiword integer in the byte with the highest address.

Another piece of complexity in this routine is the use of semWait and the sendWindowNotFull semaphore. sendWindowNotFull is initialized to the size of the sender's sliding window, SWS (this initialization is not shown). Each time the sender transmits a frame, the semWait operation decrements this count and blocks the sender should the count go to 0. Each time an ACK is received, the semSignal operation invoked in deliverSWP (see below) increments this count, thus unblocking any waiting sender.

```
static int
sendSWP(SwpState *state, Msg *frame)
{
    struct sendQ_slot *slot;
    hbuf[HLEN];

    /* wait for send window to open */
    semWait(&state->sendWindowNotFull);
    state->hdr.SeqNum = ++state->LFS;
    slot = &state->sendQ[state->hdr.SeqNum % SWS];
```

```
store_swp_hdr(state->hdr, hbuf);
msgAddHdr(frame, hbuf, HLEN);
msgSaveCopy(&slot->msg, frame);
slot->timeout = evSchedule(swpTimeout, slot, SWP_SEND_TIMEOUT);
return send(LINK, frame);
}
```

Before continuing to the receive side of SWP, we need to reconcile a seeming inconsistency. On the one hand, we have been saying that a high-level protocol invokes the services of a low-level protocol by calling the send operation, so we would expect that a protocol that wants to send a message via SWP would call send(SWP, packet). On the other hand, the procedure that implements SWP's send operation is called sendSWP, and its first argument is a state variable (SwpState). What gives? The answer is that the operating system provides glue code that translates the generic call to send into a protocol-specific call to sendSWP. This glue code maps the first argument to send (the magic protocol variable SWP) into both a function pointer to sendSWP and a pointer to the protocol state that SWP needs to do its job. The reason we have the high-level protocol indirectly invoke the protocol-specific function through the generic function call is that we want to limit how much information the high-level protocol has coded in it about the low-level protocol. This makes it easier to change the protocol graph configuration at some time in the future.

Now we move on to SWP's protocol-specific implementation of the deliver operation, which is given in procedure deliverSWP. This routine actually handles two different kinds of incoming messages: ACKs for frames sent earlier from this node and data frames arriving at this node. In a sense, the ACK half of this routine is the counterpart to the sender side of the algorithm given in sendSWP. A decision as to whether the incoming message is an ACK or a data frame is made by checking the Flags field in the header. Note that this particular implementation does not support piggybacking ACKs on data frames.

When the incoming frame is an ACK, deliverSWP simply finds the slot in the transmit queue (sendQ) that corresponds to the ACK, cancels the timeout event, and frees the frame saved in that slot. This work is actually done in a loop since the ACK may be cumulative. The only other thing to notice about this case is the call to subroutine swpInWindow. This subroutine, which is given below, ensures that the sequence number for the frame being acknowledged is within the range of ACKs that the sender currently expects to receive.

When the incoming frame contains data, deliverSWP first calls msgStripHdr and load_swp_hdr to extract the header from the frame. Routine load_swp_hdr is the counterpart to store_swp_hdr discussed earlier; it translates a byte string into the C data structure that holds the SWP header. deliverSWP then calls swpInWindow to make sure the sequence number of the frame is within the range of sequence numbers that it expects. If it is, the routine loops over the set of consecutive frames it has received and passes them up to the higher-level protocol by invoking the deliverHLP routine. It also sends a cumulative ACK back to the sender, but does so by looping over the receive queue (it does not use the SeqNumToAck variable used in the prose description given earlier in this section).

```
static int
deliverSWP(SwpState state, Msg *frame)
{
  SwpHdr  hdr;
  char    *hbuf;

  hbuf = msgStripHdr(frame, HLEN);
  load_swp_hdr(&hdr, hbuf)
  if (hdr->Flags & FLAG_ACK_VALID)
  {
    /* received an acknowledgment—do SENDER side */
    if (swpInWindow(hdr.AckNum, state->LAR + 1, state->LFS))
    {
      do
      {
        struct sendQ_slot *slot;

        slot = &state->sendQ[++state->LAR % SWS];
        evCancel(slot->timeout);
        msgDestroy(&slot->msg);
        semSignal(&state->sendWindowNotFull);
      } while (state->LAR != hdr.AckNum);
    }
  }
```

```
if (hdr.Flags & FLAG_HAS_DATA)
{
    struct recvQ_slot *slot;

    /* received data packet—do RECEIVER side */
    slot = &state->recvQ[hdr.SeqNum % RWS];
    if (!swpInWindow(hdr.SeqNum, state->NFE, state->NFE + RWS - 1))
    {
        /* drop the message */
        return SUCCESS;
    }
    msgSaveCopy(&slot->msg, frame);
    slot->received = TRUE;
    if (hdr.SeqNum == state->NFE)
    {
        Msg m;

        while (slot->received)
        {
            deliver(HLP, &slot->msg);
            msgDestroy(&slot->msg);
            slot->received = FALSE;
            slot = &state->recvQ[++state->NFE % RWS];
        }
        /* send ACK: */
        prepare_ack(&m, state->NFE - 1);
        send(LINK, &m);
        msgDestroy(&m);
    }
}
return SUCCESS;
```

}

Finally,swpInWindow is a simple subroutine that checks to see if a given sequence number falls between some minimum and maximum sequence number.

static bool

swpInWindow(SwpSeqno seqno, SwpSeqno min, SwpSeqno max)

{

  SwpSeqno pos, maxpos;

  pos   = seqno - min;   /* pos *should* be in range [0..MAX) */

  maxpos = max - min + 1;   /* maxpos is in range [0..MAX] */

  return pos < maxpos;

}

FRAME ORDER AND FLOW CONTROL

The sliding window protocol is well recognized as one of the most prominent algorithms in the field of computer networking. One aspect of the algorithm that can cause confusion is its ability to fulfill three distinct functions. The primary objective we have been focusing on in this part is to consistently transmit frames over an unstable connection. (The technique can be utilized to consistently transmit messages over an unreliable network.) This is the fundamental operation of the algorithm.

Another function that the sliding window technique can fulfill is maintaining the sequential transmission of frames. At the receiver, the task is straightforward. Each frame is assigned a sequence number, and the receiver simply ensures that it does not transmit a frame to the next protocol level until all frames with a lower sequence number have already been transmitted. The receiver buffers, meaning it does not transmit out-of-order frames. The sliding window technique discussed in this section maintains the order of frames, although it is possible to conceive of a variation where the receiver forwards frames to the next protocol without waiting for the delivery of all preceding frames. One important topic to consider is whether the sliding window protocol is necessary for maintaining frame order at the link level, or if this task should be handled by a higher-level protocol. The third role that the sliding window algorithm sometimes plays is to support flow control—a feedback mechanism by which the receiver is able to throttle the sender. Such a mechanism is used to keep the sender from over-running the receiver—that is, from transmitting more data than the receiver is able to process. This is usually accomplished by augmenting the sliding window protocol so that the receiver not only acknowledges frames it has received but also informs the sender of how many frames it has room to receive. The number of frames that the receiver is capable of receiving corresponds to how much free buffer space it has. As in the case of ordered delivery, we need to make sure that flow control is necessary at the link level before incorporating it into the sliding window protocol.

Key Takeaway

One important concept to take away from this discussion is the system design principle we call separation of concerns. That is, you must be careful to distinguish between different functions that are sometimes rolled together in one mechanism, and you must make sure that each function is necessary and being supported in the most effective way. In this particular case, reliable delivery, ordered delivery, and flow control are sometimes combined in a single sliding window protocol, and we should ask ourselves if this is the right thing to do at the link level.

2.5.3 Concurrent Logical Channels

The data connection protocol utilized in the original ARPANET offers a compelling alternative to the sliding window protocol. It effectively maintains a continuous flow of data while employing the straightforward stop-and-wait method. An key implication of this method is that the frames transmitted over a certain link are not maintained in any specific sequence. The protocol does not provide any information or specifications on flow control.

The concept behind the ARPANET protocol, known as concurrent logical channels, involves combining several logical channels onto a single point-to-point link and implementing the stop-and-wait algorithm on each of these channels. There is no correlation between the frames sent on the logical channels. However, since there might be many outstanding frames on each logical channel, the sender can ensure that the connection remains fully utilized.More precisely, the sender keeps 3 bits of state for each channel: a boolean, saying whether the channel is currently busy; the 1-bit sequence number to use the next time a frame is sent on this logical channel; and the next sequence number to expect on a frame that arrives on this channel. When the node has a frame to send, it uses the lowest idle channel, and otherwise it behaves just like stop-and-wait.

In practice, the ARPANET supported 8 logical channels over each ground link and 16 over each satellite link. In the ground-link case, the header for each frame included a 3-bit channel number and a 1-bit sequence number, for a total of 4 bits. This is exactly the number of bits the sliding window protocol requires to support up to 8 outstanding frames on the link when RWS = SWS.

2.6 Multi-Access Networks

Developed in the mid-1970s by researchers at the Xerox Palo Alto Research Center (PARC), the Ethernet eventually became the dominant local area networking technology, emerging from a pack of competing technologies. Today, it competes mainly with 802.11 wireless networks but remains extremely popular in campus networks and data centers. The more general name for the technology behind the Ethernet is Carrier Sense, Multiple Access with Collision Detect (CSMA/CD).

As indicated by the CSMA name, the Ethernet is a multiple-access network, meaning that a set of nodes sends and receives frames over a shared link. You can, therefore, think of an Ethernet as being like a bus that has multiple stations plugged into it. The "carrier sense" in CSMA/CD means that all the nodes can distinguish between an idle and a busy link, and "collision detect" means that a node listens as it transmits and can therefore detect when a frame it is transmitting has interfered (collided) with a frame transmitted by another node.

The Ethernet has its roots in an early packet radio network, called Aloha, developed at the University of Hawaii to support computer communication across the Hawaiian Islands. Like the Aloha network, the fundamental problem faced by the Ethernet is how to mediate access to a shared medium fairly and efficiently (in Aloha, the medium was the atmosphere, while in the Ethernet the medium was originally a coax cable). The core idea in both Aloha and the Ethernet is an algorithm that controls when each node can transmit.

Modern Ethernet links are now largely point to point; that is, they connect one host to an Ethernet switch, or they interconnect switches. As a consequence, the "multiple access" algorithm is not used much in today's wired Ethernets, but a variant is now used in wireless networks, such as 802.11 networks (also known as Wi-Fi). Due to the enormous influence of Ethernet, we chose to describe its classic algorithm here, and then explain how it has been adapted to Wi-Fi in the next section. We will also discuss Ethernet switches elsewhere. For now, we'll focus on how a single Ethernet link works.

Digital Equipment Corporation and Intel Corporation joined Xerox to define a 10-Mbps Ethernet standard in 1978. This standard then formed the basis for IEEE standard 802.3, which additionally defines a much wider collection of physical media over which an Ethernet can operate, including 100-Mbps, 1-Gbps, 10-Gbps, 40-Gbps, and 100-Gbps versions.

2.6.1 Physical Properties

Ethernet segments were originally implemented using coaxial cable of length up to 500 m. (Modern Ethernets use twisted copper pairs, usually a particular type known as "Category 5," or optical fibers, and in some cases can be quite a lot longer than 500 m.) This cable was similar to the type used for cable TV. Hosts connected to an Ethernet segment by tapping into it. A transceiver, a small device directly attached to the tap, detected when the line was idle and drove the signal when the host was transmitting. It also received incoming signals. The transceiver, in turn, connected to an Ethernet adaptor, which was plugged into the host. This configuration is shown in Figure 39.

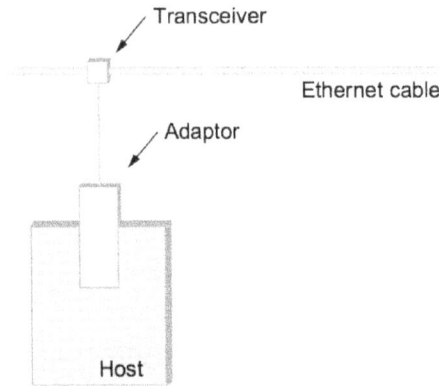

Figure 39. Ethernet transceiver and adaptor.

Multiple Ethernet segments can be joined together by repeaters (or a multiport variant of a repeater, called a hub). A repeater is a device that forwards digital signals, much like an amplifier forwards analog signals; repeaters do not understand bits or frames. No more than four repeaters could be positioned between any pair of hosts, meaning that a classical Ethernet had a total reach of only 2500 m. For example, using just two repeaters between any pair of hosts supports a configuration similar to the one illustrated in Figure 40; that is, a segment running down the spine of a building with a segment on each floor.

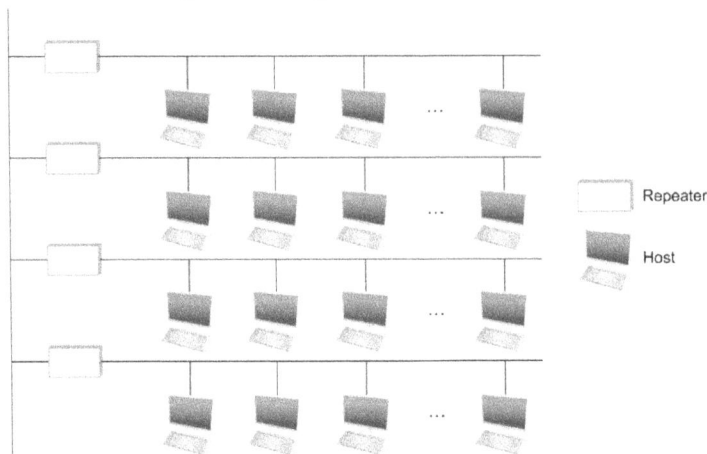

Figure 40. Ethernet repeater, interconnecting segments to form a larger collision domain.

Any signal placed on the Ethernet by a host is broadcast over the entire network; that is, the signal is propagated in both directions, and repeaters and hubs forward the signal on all outgoing segments. Terminators attached to the end of each segment absorb the signal and keep it from bouncing back and interfering with trailing signals. The original Ethernet specifications used the Manchester encoding scheme described in an earlier section, while 4B/5B encoding (or the similar 8B/10B) scheme is used today on higher speed Ethernets.

It is important to understand that whether a given Ethernet spans a single segment, a linear sequence of segments connected by repeaters, or multiple segments connected in a star configuration, data transmitted by any one host on that Ethernet reaches all the other hosts. This is the good news. The bad news is that all these hosts are competing for access to the same link, and, as a consequence, they are said to be in the same collision domain. The multi-access part of the Ethernet is all about dealing with the competition for the link that arises in a collision domain.

2.6.2 Access Protocol

Now, let's focus on the algorithm that manages access to a shared Ethernet link. This algorithm is usually referred to as the media access control (MAC) of Ethernet. Usually, it is executed in hardware on the network adapter. We will not provide a detailed description of the hardware itself, but rather concentrate on the specific algorithm that it executes. Initially, we will elucidate the structure and addresses of the Ethernet's frame.

Frame Format

Each Ethernet frame is defined by the format given in Figure 41. The 64-bit preamble allows the receiver to synchronize with the signal; it is a sequence of alternating 0s and 1s. Both the source and destination hosts are identified with a 48-bit address. The packet type field serves as the demultiplexing key; it identifies to which of possibly many higher-level protocols this frame should be delivered. Each frame contains up to 1500 bytes of data. Minimally, a frame must contain at least 46 bytes of data, even if this means the host has to pad the frame before transmitting it. The reason for this minimum frame size is that the frame must be long enough to detect a collision; we discuss this more below. Finally, each frame includes a 32-bit CRC. Like the HDLC protocol described in an earlier section, the Ethernet is a bit-oriented framing protocol. Note that from the host's perspective, an Ethernet frame has a 14-byte header: two 6-byte addresses and a 2-byte type field. The sending adaptor attaches the preamble and CRC before transmitting, and the receiving adaptor removes them.

64	48	48	16		32
Preamble	Dest addr	Src addr	Type	Body	CRC

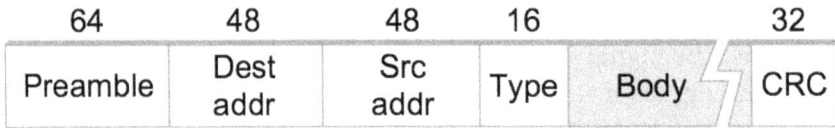

Figure 41. Ethernet frame format.

Addresses

Each host on an Ethernet—in fact, every Ethernet host in the world—has a unique Ethernet address. Technically, the address belongs to the adaptor, not the host; it is usually burned into ROM. Ethernet addresses are typically printed in a form humans can read as a sequence of six numbers separated by colons. Each number corresponds to 1 byte of the 6-byte address and is given by a pair of hexadecimal digits, one for each of the 4-bit nibbles in the byte; leading 0s are dropped. For example, 8:0:2b:e4:b1:2 is the human-readable representation of Ethernet address

00001000 00000000 00101011 11100100 10110001 00000010

To ensure that every adaptor gets a unique address, each manufacturer of Ethernet devices is allocated a different prefix that must be prepended to the address on every adaptor they build. For example, Advanced Micro Devices has been assigned the 24-bit prefix 080020 (or 8:0:20). A given manufacturer then makes sure the address suffixes it produces are unique.

Each frame transmitted on an Ethernet is received by every adaptor connected to that Ethernet. Each adaptor recognizes those frames addressed to its address and passes only those frames on to the host. (An adaptor can also be programmed to run in promiscuous mode, in which case it delivers all received frames to the host, but this is not the normal mode.) In addition to these unicast addresses, an Ethernet address consisting of all 1s is treated as a broadcast address; all adaptors pass frames addressed to the broadcast address up to the host. Similarly, an address that has the first bit set to 1 but is not the broadcast address is called a multicast address. A given host can program its adaptor to accept some set of multicast addresses. Multicast addresses are used to send messages to some subset of the hosts on an Ethernet (e.g., all file servers). To summarize, an Ethernet adaptor receives all frames and accepts

- Frames addressed to its own address
- Frames addressed to the broadcast address
- Frames addressed to a multicast address, if it has been instructed to listen to that address
- All frames, if it has been placed in promiscuous mode

It passes to the host only the frames that it accepts.

TRANSMITTER ALGORITHM

The receiver side of the Ethernet protocol is straightforward, but the sender's side is where the complex operations are carried out. The transmitter algorithm is precisely defined in the following manner.

When the adapter possesses a frame to transmit and the communication line is not in use, it promptly sends the frame without engaging in any negotiation with the other adapters. The maximum limit of 1500 bytes in the message indicates that the adaptor can only utilize the line for a predetermined duration.

When an adaptor has a frame to send and the line is busy, it waits for the line to go idle and then transmits immediately. (To be more precise, all adaptors wait 9.6 μs after the end of one frame before beginning to transmit the next frame. This is true for both the sender of the first frame as well as those nodes listening for the line to become idle.) The Ethernet is said to be a 1-persistent protocol because an adaptor with a frame to send transmits with probability 1 whenever a busy line goes idle. In general, a p-persistent algorithm transmits with probability $0 \le p \le 1$ after a line becomes idle and defers with probability $q = 1 - p$. The reasoning behind choosing a $p<1$ is that there might be multiple adaptors waiting for the busy line to become idle, and we don't want all of them to begin transmitting at the same time. If each adaptor transmits immediately with a probability of, say, 33%, then up to three adaptors can be waiting to transmit and the odds are that only one will begin transmitting when the line becomes idle. Despite this reasoning, an Ethernet adaptor always transmits immediately after noticing that the network has become idle and has been very effective in doing so.

To complete the story about p-persistent protocols for the case when $p<1$, you might wonder how long a sender that loses the coin flip (i.e., decides to defer) has to wait before it can transmit. The answer for the Aloha network, which originally developed this style of protocol, was to divide time into discrete slots, with each slot corresponding to the length of time it takes to transmit a full frame. Whenever a node has a frame to send and it senses an empty (idle) slot, it transmits with probability p and defers until the next slot with probability $q = 1 - p$. If that next slot is also empty, the node again decides to transmit or defer, with probabilities p and q, respectively. If that next slot is not empty—that is, some other station has decided to transmit—then the node simply waits for the next idle slot and the algorithm repeats.

Returning to our discussion of the Ethernet, because there is no centralized control it is possible for two (or more) adaptors to begin transmitting at the same time, either because both found the line to be idle or because both had been waiting for a busy line to become idle. When this happens, the two (or more) frames are said to collide on the network. Each sender, because the Ethernet supports collision detection, is able to determine that a collision is in progress. At the moment an adaptor detects that its frame is colliding with another, it first makes sure to transmit a 32-bit jamming sequence and then stops the transmission. Thus, a transmitter will minimally send 96 bits in the case of a collision: 64-bit preamble plus 32-bit jamming sequence.

One way that an adaptor will send only 96 bits—which is sometimes called a runt frame—is if the two hosts are close to each other. Had the two hosts been farther apart, they would have had to transmit longer, and thus send more bits, before detecting the collision. In fact, the worst-case scenario happens when the two hosts are at opposite ends of the Ethernet. To know for sure that the frame it just sent did not collide with another frame, the transmitter may need to send as many as 512 bits. Not coincidentally, every Ethernet frame must be at least 512 bits (64 bytes) long: 14 bytes of header plus 46 bytes of data plus 4 bytes of CRC.

Why 512 bits? The answer is related to another question you might ask about an Ethernet: Why is its length limited to only 2500 m? Why not 10 or 1000 km? The answer to both questions has to do with the fact that the farther apart two nodes are, the longer it takes for a frame sent by one to reach the other, and the network is vulnerable to a collision during this time.

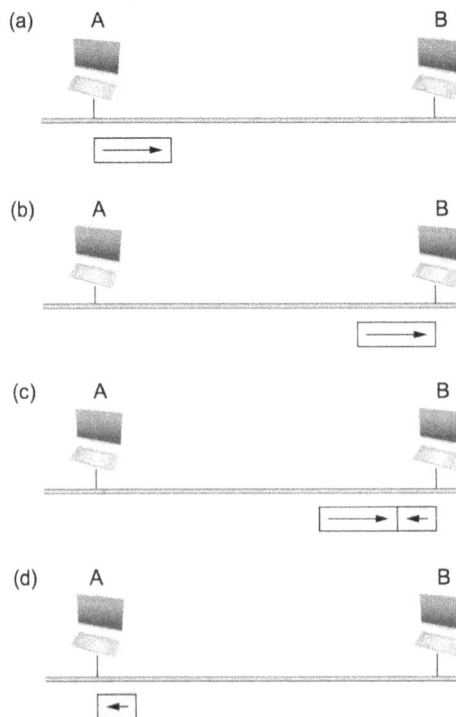

Figure 42. Worst-case scenario: (a) A sends a frame at time t; (b) A's frame arrives at B at time t+d; (c) B begins transmitting at time t+d and collides with A's frame; (d) B's runt (32-bit) frame arrives at A at time t+2×d.

Figure 42 illustrates the worst-case scenario, where hosts A and B are at opposite ends of the network. Suppose host A begins transmitting a frame at time t, as shown in (a). It takes it one link latency (let's denote the latency as d) for the frame to reach host B. Thus, the first bit of A's frame arrives at B at time t+d, as shown in (b). Suppose an instant before host A's frame arrives (i.e., B still sees an idle line), host B begins to transmit its own frame. B's frame will immediately collide with A's frame, and this collision will be detected by host B (c). Host B will send the 32-bit jamming sequence, as described above. (B's frame will be a runt.) Unfortunately, host A will not know that the collision occurred until B's frame reaches it, which will happen one link latency later, at time t+2×d, as shown in (d). Host A must continue to transmit until this time in order to detect the collision. In other words, host A must transmit for 2×d to be sure that it detects all possible collisions. Considering that a maximally configured Ethernet is 2500 m long, and that there may be up to four repeaters between any two hosts, the round-trip delay has been determined to be 51.2 μs, which on a 10-Mbps Ethernet corresponds to 512 bits. The other way to look at this situation is that we need to limit the Ethernet's maximum latency to a fairly small value (e.g., 51.2 μs) for the access algorithm to work; hence, an Ethernet's maximum length must be something on the order of 2500 m.

Once an adaptor has detected a collision and stopped its transmission, it waits a certain amount of time and tries again. Each time it tries to transmit but fails, the adaptor doubles the amount of time it waits before trying again. This strategy of doubling the delay interval between each retransmission attempt is a general technique known as exponential backoff. More precisely, the adaptor first delays either 0 or 51.2 μs, selected at random. If this effort fails, it then waits 0, 51.2, 102.4, or 153.6 μs (selected randomly) before trying again; this is $k \times 51.2$ for $k=0..3$. After the third collision, it waits $k \times 51.2$ for $k = 0..2^3 - 1$, again selected at random. In general, the algorithm randomly selects a k between 0 and $2^n - 1$ and waits $k \times 51.2$ μs, where n is the number of collisions experienced so far. The adaptor gives up after a given number of tries and reports a transmit error to the host. Adaptors typically retry up to 16 times, although the backoff algorithm caps n in the above formula at 10.

2.6.3 Longevity of Ethernet

Ethernet has been the dominant local area network technology for over 30 years. Today it is typically deployed point-to-point rather than tapping into a coax cable, it often runs at speeds of 1 or 10 Gbps rather than 10 Mbps, and it allows jumbo packets with up to 9000 bytes of data rather than 1500 bytes. But, it remains backwards compatible with the original standard. This makes it worth saying a few words about why Ethernets have been so successful, so that we can understand the properties we should emulate with any technology that tries to replace it.

First, an Ethernet is extremely easy to administer and maintain: There is no routing or configuration tables to be kept up-to-date, and it is easy to add a new host to the network. It is hard to imagine a simpler network to administer. Second, it is inexpensive: cable/fiber is relatively cheap, and the only other cost is the network adaptor on each host. Ethernet became deeply entrenched for these reasons, and any switch-based approach that aspired to displace it required additional investment in infrastructure (the switches), on top of the cost of each adaptor. The switch-based variant of Ethernet did eventually succeed in replacing multi-access Ethernet, but this is primarily because it could be deployed incrementally—with some hosts connected by point-to-point links to switches while others remained tapped into coax and connected to repeaters or hubs—all the while retaining the simplicity of network administration.

2.7 Wireless Networks

Wireless technologies exhibit distinct characteristics compared to traditional connections, however they also include numerous shared attributes. Similar to wired connections, the problem of bit errors is a significant concern, often exacerbated by the unpredictable noise conditions commonly found in wireless connections. Both framing and reliability must be considered and resolved. Wireless communications face significant power constraints, particularly due to their usage in small mobile devices such as phones and sensors, which have limited power resources, such as small batteries. In addition, it is not possible to transmit radio signals at excessively high power levels without considering the potential interference with other devices and the rules that limit the amount of power a device can emit at a specific frequency.

Wireless media provide inherent multi-access capabilities, making it challenging to specifically target a single receiver with radio transmissions or prevent the reception of radio signals from powerful transmitters in the vicinity. Therefore, ensuring media access control is a crucial concern for wireless connections. Furthermore, because to the inherent difficulty in regulating the recipients of your transmitted signal through the airwaves, the matter of potential eavesdropping must also be taken into consideration.

There is a baffling assortment of different wireless technologies, each of which makes different tradeoffs in various dimensions. One simple way to categorize the different technologies is by the data rates they provide and how far apart communicating nodes can be. Other important differences include which part of the electromagnetic spectrum they use (including whether it requires a license) and how much power they consume. In this section, we discuss two prominent wireless technologies: Wi-Fi (more formally known as 802.11), and Bluetooth. The next section discusses cellular networks in the context of ISP access services. Table 4 gives an overview of these technologies and how they compare to each other.

Table 4. Overview of Leading Wireless Technologies.

	Bluetooth (802.15.1)	Wi-Fi (802.11)	4G Cellular
Typical link length	10 m	100 m	Tens of kilometers
Typical data rate	2 Mbps (shared)	150-450 Mbps	1-5 Mbps
Typical use	Link a peripheral to a computer	Link a computer to a wired base	Link mobile phone to a wired tower
Wired technology analogy	USB	Ethernet	PON

Bandwidth can refer to either the width of a frequency band in hertz or the data rate of a network. Due to the frequent mention of both notions in wireless network talks, we will define bandwidth as the width of a frequency band, and data rate as the number of bits that may be transmitted per second via the link, as shown in Table 4.

2.7.1 Basic Issues

Due to the shared medium of wireless communications, the primary objective is to efficiently distribute the medium without causing excessive interference. The majority of this sharing is achieved by dividing it based on frequency and space dimensions. An individual organization, such as a business, may be granted the exclusive allocation of a specific frequency within a specific geographic area. It is possible to restrict the range of an electromagnetic signal since these signals diminish, or attenuate, as they move away from their source. In order to decrease the coverage area of your signal, simply lower the power output of your transmitter.

Government bodies, such as the Federal Communications Commission (FCC) in the United States, often set these allocations. Distinct frequency ranges are assigned to specific purposes. Certain bands are exclusively allocated for government utilization. Additional frequency bands are allocated for specific purposes, including AM radio, FM radio, television, satellite communication, and cellular phones. Particular frequencies within these bands are subsequently granted licenses to individual organizations for utilization within specific geographical regions. Ultimately, a number of frequency bands are designated specifically for license-exempt usage, meaning that a license is not required in certain channels.

Devices that utilize frequencies that do not require a license are still bound by specific limitations to ensure the smooth operation of unrestricted sharing. One of the most significant factors is the restriction on the amount of electricity that may be sent. By restricting the extent of a signal, it reduces the probability of it causing interference with another signal. As an illustration, a cordless phone, which is a frequently used unlicensed device, typically has a range of approximately 100 feet.

Spread spectrum is a commonly recurring concept in the context of sharing spectrum among multiple devices and applications. The concept of spread spectrum involves expanding the signal across a broader range of frequencies in order to reduce the effects of interference caused by other devices. (Spread spectrum was first developed for military applications, hence these "other devices" frequently aimed to disrupt the signal intentionally.) Frequency hopping is a spread spectrum technique that entails delivering the signal across a random sequence of frequencies. This means that the signal is initially transmitted at one frequency, then at a second frequency, then at a third frequency, and so on. The sequence of frequencies is not genuinely random, but rather generated algorithmically by a pseudorandom number generator. The receiver employs the identical technique as the sender and initializes it with the same seed, so enabling it to synchronize its frequency hopping with the transmitter in order to accurately receive the frame. This system minimizes interference by ensuring that it is highly improbable for two signals to utilize the same frequency for an extended period, except for occasional isolated instances.A second spread spectrum technique, called direct sequence, adds redundancy for greater tolerance of interference. Each bit of data is represented by multiple bits in the transmitted signal so that, if some of the transmitted bits are damaged by interference, there is usually enough redundancy to recover the original bit. For each bit the sender wants to transmit, it actually sends the exclusive-OR of that bit and n random bits. As with frequency hopping, the sequence of random bits is generated by a pseudorandom number generator known to both the sender and the receiver. The transmitted values, known as an n-bit chipping code, spread the signal across a frequency band that is n times wider than the frame would have otherwise required. Figure 43 gives an example of a 4-bit chipping sequence.

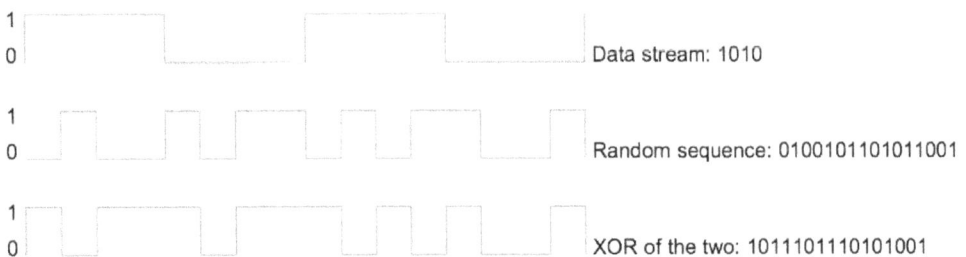

Data stream: 1010

Random sequence: 0100101101011001

XOR of the two: 1011101110101001

Figure 43. Example 4-bit chipping sequence.

Different parts of the electromagnetic spectrum have different properties, making some better suited to communication, and some less so. For example, some can penetrate buildings and some cannot. Governments regulate only the prime communication portion: the radio and microwave ranges. As demand for prime spectrum increases, there is great interest in the spectrum that is becoming available as analog television is phased out in favor of digital.

In many wireless networks today we observe that there are two different classes of endpoints. One endpoint, sometimes described as the base station, usually has no mobility but has a wired (or at least high-bandwidth) connection to the Internet or other networks, as shown in Figure 44. The node at the other end of the link—shown here as a client node—is often mobile and relies on its link to the base station for all of its communication with other nodes.

Observe that in Figure 44 we have used a wavy pair of lines to represent the wireless "link" abstraction provided between two devices (e.g., between a base station and one of its client nodes). One of the interesting aspects of wireless communication is that it naturally supports point-to-multipoint communication, because radio waves sent by one device can be simultaneously received by many devices. However, it is often useful to create a point-to-point link abstraction for higher layer protocols, and we will see examples of how this works later in this section.

Note that in Figure 44 communication between non-base (client) nodes is routed via the base station. This is in spite of the fact that radio waves emitted by one client node may well be received by other client nodes—the common base station model does not permit direct communication between the client nodes.

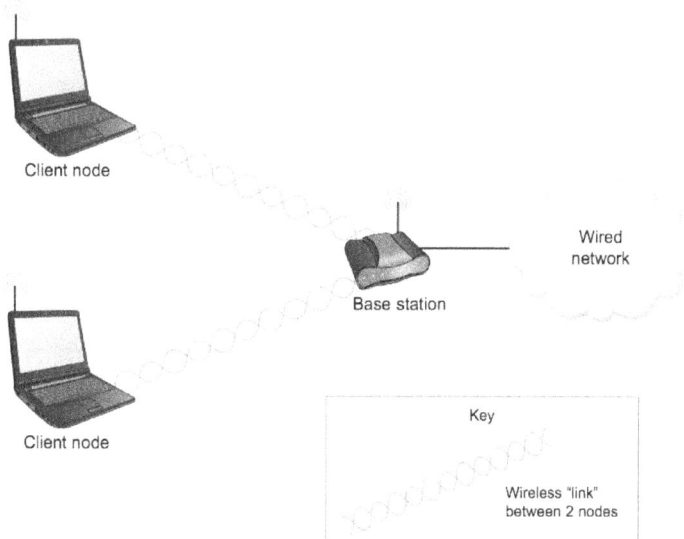

Figure 44. A wireless network using a base station.

This topology implies three qualitatively different levels of mobility. The first level is no mobility, such as when a receiver must be in a fixed location to receive a directional transmission from the base station. The second level is mobility within the range of a base, as is the case with Bluetooth. The third level is mobility between bases, as is the case with cell phones and Wi-Fi.

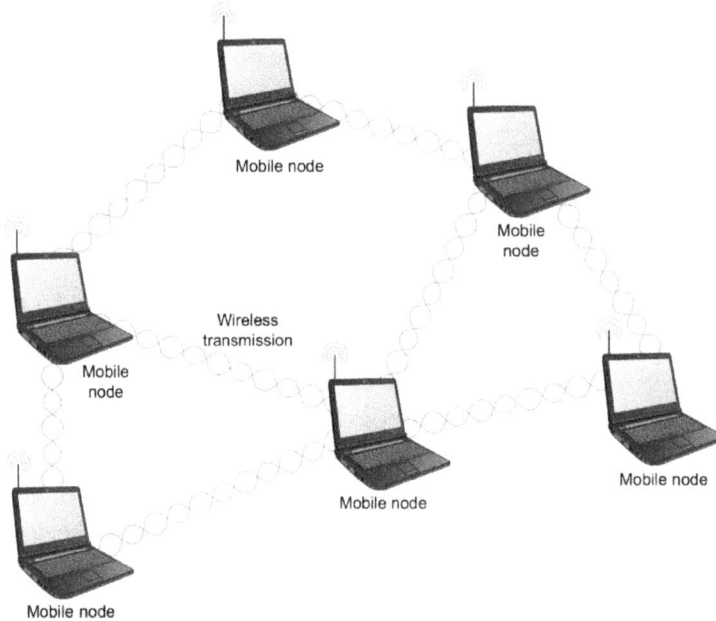

Figure 45. A wireless ad hoc or mesh network.

An alternative topology that is seeing increasing interest is the mesh or ad hoc network. In a wireless mesh, nodes are peers; that is, there is no special base station node. Messages may be forwarded via a chain of peer nodes as long as each node is within range of the preceding node. This is illustrated in Figure 45. This allows the wireless portion of a network to extend beyond the limited range of a single radio. From the point of view of competition between technologies, this allows a shorter-range technology to extend its range and potentially compete with a longer-range technology. Meshes also offer fault tolerance by providing multiple routes for a message to get from point A to point B. A mesh network can be extended incrementally, with incremental costs. On the other hand, a mesh network requires non-base nodes to have a certain level of sophistication in their hardware and software, potentially increasing per-unit costs and power consumption, a critical consideration for battery-powered devices. Wireless mesh networks are of considerable research interest, but they are still in their relative infancy compared to networks with base stations. Wireless sensor networks, another hot emerging technology, often form wireless meshes.

Now that we have covered some of the common wireless issues, let's take a look at the details of two common wireless technologies.

2.7.2 Wi-Fi (802.11)

Most readers will have used a wireless network based on the IEEE 802.11 standards, often referred to as Wi-Fi. Wi-Fi is technically a trademark, owned by a trade group called the Wi-Fi Alliance, which certifies product compliance with 802.11. Like Ethernet, 802.11 is designed for use in a limited geographical area (homes, office buildings, campuses), and its primary challenge is to mediate access to a shared communication medium—in this case, signals propagating through space.

PHYSICAL PROPERTIES

802.11 defines a number of different physical layers that operate in various frequency bands and provide a range of different data rates.

The original 802.11 standard defined two radio-based physical layers standards, one using frequency hopping (over 79 1-MHz-wide frequency bandwidths) and the other using direct sequence spread spectrum (with an 11-bit chipping sequence). Both provided data rates in the 2 Mbps range. Subsequently, the physical layer standard 802.11b was added, and using a variant of direct sequence, supported up to 11 Mbps. These three standards all operated in the license-exempt 2.4-GHz frequency band of the electromagnetic spectrum. Then came 802.11a, which delivered up to 54 Mbps using a variant of frequency division multiplexing called orthogonal frequency division multiplexing (OFDM). 802.11a runs in the license-exempt 5-GHz band. 802.11g followed, and also using OFDM, delivered up to 54 Mbps. 802.11g is backward compatible with 802.11b (and returns to the 2.4-GHz band).

At the time of writing, many devices support 802.11n or 802.11ac, which typically achieve per-device data rates of 150 Mbps to 450 Mbps, respectively. This improvement is partly due to the use of multiple antennas and allowing greater wireless channel bandwidths. The use of multiple antennas is often called MIMO for multiple-input, multiple-output. The latest emerging standard, 802.11ax, promises another substantial improvement in throughput, in part by adopting many of the coding and modulation techniques used in the 4G/5G cellular network, which we describe in the next section. It is common for commercial products to support more than one flavor of 802.11; many base stations support all five variants (a,b, g, n, and ac). This not only ensures compatibility with any device that supports any one of the standards but also makes it possible for two such products to choose the highest bandwidth option for a particular environment.

It is worth noting that while all the 802.11 standards define a maximum bit rate that can be supported, they mostly support lower bit rates as well (e.g., 802.11a allows for bit rates of 6, 9, 12, 18, 24, 36, 48, and 54 Mbps). At lower bit rates, it is easier to decode transmitted signals in the presence of noise. Different modulation schemes are used to achieve the various bit rates. In addition, the amount of redundant information in the form of error-correcting codes is varied. More redundant information means higher resilience to bit errors at the cost of lowering the effective data rate (since more of the transmitted bits are redundant).

The systems aim to select an appropriate bit rate by considering the noisy environment they are in. The algorithms used for bit rate selection can be highly intricate. Curiously, the 802.11 specifications do not explicitly define a specific method, instead allowing the suppliers to determine the algorithms. The fundamental method for selecting a bit rate involves estimating the bit error rate, which can be achieved by directly measuring the signal-to-noise ratio (SNR) at the physical layer or by estimating the SNR through the measurement of successful packet transmission and acknowledgment frequency. Some methods involve the sender occasionally testing a higher data transmission speed by transmitting one or more packets at that speed to determine if it is successful.

COLLISION AVOIDANCE

At first glance, it might seem that a wireless protocol would follow the same algorithm as the Ethernet—wait until the link becomes idle before transmitting and back off should a collision occur—and, to a first approximation, this is what 802.11 does. The additional complication for wireless is that, while a node on an Ethernet receives every other node's transmissions and can transmit and receive at the same time, neither of these conditions holds for wireless nodes. This makes detection of collisions rather more complex. The reason why wireless nodes cannot usually transmit and receive at the same time (on the same frequency) is that the power generated by the transmitter is much higher than any received is likely to be and so swamps the receiving circuitry. The reason why a node may not receive transmissions from another node is because that node may be too far away or blocked by an obstacle. This situation is a bit more complex than it first appears, as the following discussion will illustrate.

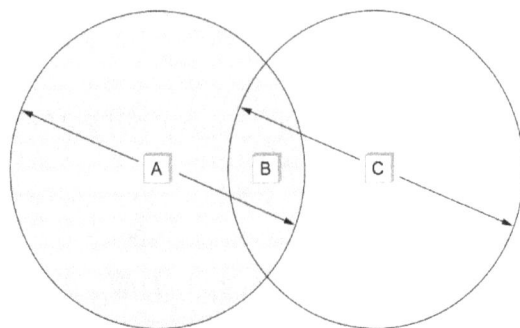

Figure 46. The hidden node problem. Although A and C are hidden from each other, their signals can collide at B. (B's reach is not shown.)

Consider the situation depicted in Figure 46, where A and C are both within range of B but not each other. Suppose both A and C want to communicate with B and so they each send it a frame. A and C are unaware of each other since their signals do not carry that far. These two frames collide with each other at B, but unlike an Ethernet, neither A nor C is aware of this collision. A and C are said to be hidden nodes with respect to each other.

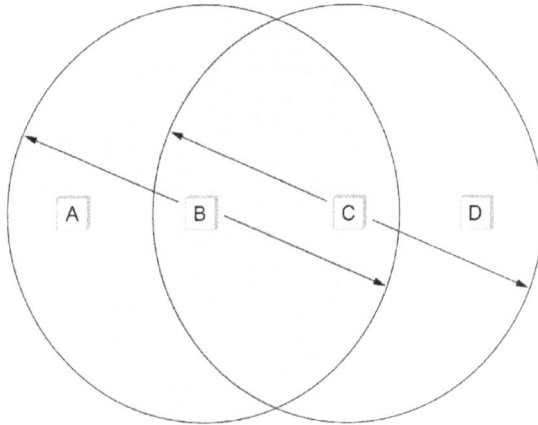

Figure 47. The exposed node problem. Although B and C are exposed to each other's signals, there is no interference if B transmits to A while C transmits to D. (A and D's reaches are not shown.)

A related problem, called the exposed node problem, occurs under the circumstances illustrated in Figure 47, where each of the four nodes is able to send and receive signals that reach just the nodes to its immediate left and right. For example, B can exchange frames with A and C but it cannot reach D, while C can reach B and D but not A. Suppose B is sending to A. Node C is aware of this communication because it hears B's transmission. It would be a mistake, however, for C to conclude that it cannot transmit to anyone just because it can hear B's transmission. For example, suppose C wants to transmit to node D. This is not a problem since C's transmission to D will not interfere with A's ability to receive from B. (It would interfere with A sending to B, but B is transmitting in our example.)

802.11 addresses these problems by using CSMA/CA, where the CA stands for collision avoidance, in contrast to the collision detection of CSMA/CD used on Ethernets. There are a few pieces to make this work.

The Carrier Sense part seems simple enough: Before sending a packet, the transmitter checks if it can hear any other transmissions; if not, it sends. However, because of the hidden node problem, just waiting for the absence of signals from other transmitters does not guarantee that a collision will not occur from the perspective of the receiver. For this reason, one part of CSMA/CA is an explicit ACK from the receiver to the sender. If the packet was successfully decoded and passed its CRC at the receiver, the receiver sends an ACK back to the sender.

Note that if a collision does occur, it will render the entire packet useless. For this reason, 802.11 adds an optional mechanism called RTS-CTS (Ready to Send-Clear to Send). This goes some way toward addressing the hidden node problem. The sender sends an RTS—a short packet—to the intended receiver, and if that packet is received successfully the receiver responds with another short packet, the CTS. Even though the RTS may not have been heard by a hidden node, the CTS probably will be. This effectively tells the nodes within range of the receiver that they should not send anything for a while—the amount of time of the intended transmission is included in the RTS and CTS packets. After that time plus a small interval has passed, the carrier can be assumed to be available again, and another node is free to try to send.

Of course, two nodes might detect an idle link and try to transmit an RTS frame at the same time, causing their RTS frames to collide with each other. The senders realize the collision has happened when they do not receive the CTS frame after a period of time, in which case they each wait a random amount of time before trying again. The amount of time a given node delays is defined by an exponential backoff algorithm very much like that used on the Ethernet.

After a successful RTS-CTS exchange, the sender sends its data packet and, if all goes well, receives an ACK for that packet. In the absence of a timely ACK, the sender will try again to request usage of the channel again, using the same process described above. By this time, of course, other nodes may again be trying to get access to the channel as well.

DISTRIBUTION SYSTEM

As described so far, 802.11 would be suitable for a network with a mesh (ad hoc) topology, and development of an 802.11s standard for mesh networks is nearing completion. At the current time, however, nearly all 802.11 networks use a base-station-oriented topology.

Instead of all nodes being created equal, some nodes are allowed to roam (e.g., your laptop) and some are connected to a wired network infrastructure. 802.11 calls these base stations access points (APs), and they are connected to each other by a so-called distribution system. Figure 48 illustrates a distribution system that connects three access points, each of which services the nodes in some region. Each access point operates on some channel in the appropriate frequency range, and each AP will typically be on a different channel than its neighbors.

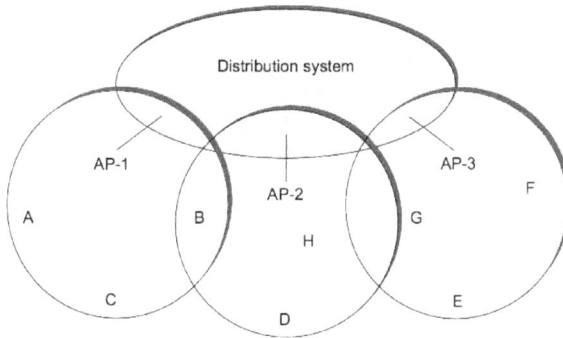

Figure 48. Access points connected to a distribution system.

The details of the distribution system are not important to this discussion—it could be an Ethernet, for example. The only important point is that the distribution network operates at the link layer, the same protocol layer as the wireless links. In other words, it does not depend on any higher-level protocols (such as the network layer).

Although two nodes can communicate directly with each other if they are within reach of each other, the idea behind this configuration is that each node associates itself with one access point. For node A to communicate with node E, for example, A first sends a frame to its access point (AP-1), which forwards the frame across the distribution system to AP-3, which finally transmits the frame to E. How AP-1 knew to forward the message to AP-3 is beyond the scope of 802.11; it may have used a bridging protocol. What 802.11 does specify is how nodes select their access points and, more interestingly, how this algorithm works in light of nodes moving from one cell to another.

The technique for selecting an AP is called scanning and involves the following four steps:

- ⊙ The node sends a Probe frame.
- ⊙ All APs within reach reply with a Probe Response frame.
- ⊙ The node selects one of the access points and sends that AP an Association Request frame.
- ⊙ The AP replies with an Association Response frame.

A node engages this protocol whenever it joins the network, as well as when it becomes unhappy with its current AP. This might happen, for example, because the signal from its current AP has weakened due to the node moving away from it. Whenever a node acquires a new AP, the new AP notifies the old AP of the change (this happens in step 4) via the distribution system.

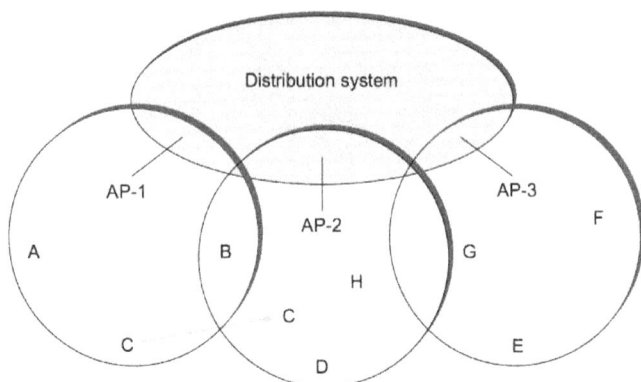

Figure 49. Node mobility.

Consider the situation shown in Figure 49, where node C moves from the cell serviced by AP-1 to the cell serviced by AP-2. As it moves, it sends Probe frames, which eventually result in Probe Response frames from AP-2. At some point, C prefers AP-2 over AP-1, and so it associates itself with that access point.

The mechanism just described is called active scanning since the node is actively searching for an access point. APs also periodically send a Beacon frame that advertises the capabilities of the access point; these include the transmission rates supported by the AP. This is called passive scanning, and a node can change to this AP based on the Beacon frame simply by sending an Association Request frame back to the access point.

FRAME FORMAT

Most of the 802.11 frame format, which is depicted in Figure 50, is exactly what we would expect. The frame contains the source and destination node addresses, each of which is 48 bits long; up to 2312 bytes of data; and a 32-bit CRC. The Control field contains three subfields of interest (not shown): a 6-bit Type field that indicates whether the frame carries data, is an RTS or CTS frame, or is being used by the scanning algorithm, and a pair of 1-bit fields—called ToDS and FromDS—that are described below.

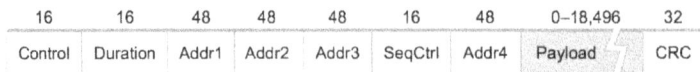

16	16	48	48	48	16	48	0–18,496	32
Control	Duration	Addr1	Addr2	Addr3	SeqCtrl	Addr4	Payload	CRC

Figure 50. 802.11 frame format.

The peculiar thing about the 802.11 frame format is that it contains four, rather than two, addresses. How these addresses are interpreted depends on the settings of the ToDS and FromDS bits in the frame's Control field. This is to account for the possibility that the frame had to be forwarded across the distribution system, which would mean that the original sender is not necessarily the same as the most recent transmitting node. Similar reasoning applies to the destination address. In the simplest case, when one node is sending directly to another, both the DS bits are 0, Addr1 identifies the target node, and Addr2 identifies the source node. In the most complex case, both DS bits are set to 1, indicating that the message went from a wireless node onto the distribution system, and then from the distribution system to another wireless node. With both bits set, Addr1 identifies the ultimate destination, Addr2 identifies the immediate sender (the one that forwarded the frame from the distribution system to the ultimate destination), Addr3 identifies the intermediate destination (the one that accepted the frame from a wireless node and forwarded it across the distribution system), and Addr4 identifies the original source. In terms of the example given in Figure 48, Addr1 corresponds to E, Addr2 identifies AP-3, Addr3 corresponds to AP-1, and Addr4 identifies A.

SECURITY OF WIRELESS LINKS

One of the inherent drawbacks of wireless connectivity, in contrast to wired or fiber connections, is the lack of certainty regarding the destination of your data. You can likely determine whether the intended recipient received it, but it is impossible to ascertain how many additional recipients may have intercepted your transmission. If you have concerns regarding the privacy of your data, wireless networks provide a significant obstacle.

Even if you are not prioritizing data privacy or have already addressed it through alternative means, you may still be worried about the possibility of an unauthorized user introducing data into your network. At the very least, such a user could potentially utilize resources that you would rather use for yourself, such as the limited bandwidth between your residence and your internet service provider.For these reasons, wireless networks typically come with some sort of mechanism to control access to both the link itself and the transmitted data. These mechanisms are often categorized as wireless security. The widely adopted WPA2 is described in Chapter 8.

2.7.3 Bluetooth (802.15.1)

Bluetooth technology serves the purpose of facilitating close-range communication between mobile phones, PDAs, laptop computers, and other personal or peripheral devices. For instance, Bluetooth technology enables the connection of a mobile phone to a headset or a notebook computer to a keyboard. In essence, Bluetooth serves as a more expedient substitute for physically linking two devices via a cable. In these types of applications, there is no need to provide a significant amount of range or bandwidth. Consequently, Bluetooth radios have the capability to utilize low power transmission due to the significant impact of transmission power on the bandwidth and range of wireless connections. Bluetooth-enabled devices, like the commonly used phone headset, are typically battery powered. Therefore, it is crucial that these devices have low power consumption.

Bluetooth functions inside the unlicensed frequency range of 2.45 GHz. Bluetooth connections typically have bandwidths ranging from 1 to 3 Mbps and a range of approximately 10 meters. Due to this rationale, and the fact that the connecting devices usually pertain to a single individual or group, Bluetooth is occasionally classified as a Personal Area Network (PAN).

The Bluetooth Special Interest Group is the industry organization responsible for defining the specifications of Bluetooth. The specification encompasses a comprehensive set of protocols that extend beyond the link layer and establish application protocols, referred to as profiles, for various applications. For instance, there exists a profile specifically designed for the purpose of syncing a Personal Digital Assistant (PDA) with a personal computer. Another profile enables a portable computer to connect to a wired Local Area Network (LAN) using the 802.11 standard, even though this was not the original intention of Bluetooth. The IEEE 802.15.1 standard is derived from Bluetooth, although it does not include the application protocols.

A piconet, which is the fundamental configuration of a Bluetooth network, comprises of a master device and a maximum of seven slave devices, as illustrated in Figure 51. Communication within the network occurs exclusively between the master and a slave, with no direct communication between the slaves themselves. Due of the less complex nature of slaves' responsibilities, their Bluetooth hardware and software can be designed to be less intricate and most cost effective.

Since Bluetooth operates in an license-exempt band, it is required to use a spread spectrum technique to deal with possible interference in the band. It uses frequency-hopping with 79 channels (frequencies), using each for 625 µs at a time. This provides a natural time slot for Bluetooth to use for synchronous time division multiplexing. A frame takes up 1, 3, or 5 consecutive time slots. Only the master can start to transmit in odd-numbered slots. A slave can start to transmit in an even-numbered slot—but only in response to a request from the master during the previous slot, thereby preventing any contention between the slave devices.

A slave device can be parked; that is, it is set to an inactive, low-power state. A parked device cannot communicate on the piconet; it can only be reactivated by the master. A piconet can have up to 255 parked devices in addition to its active slave devices.

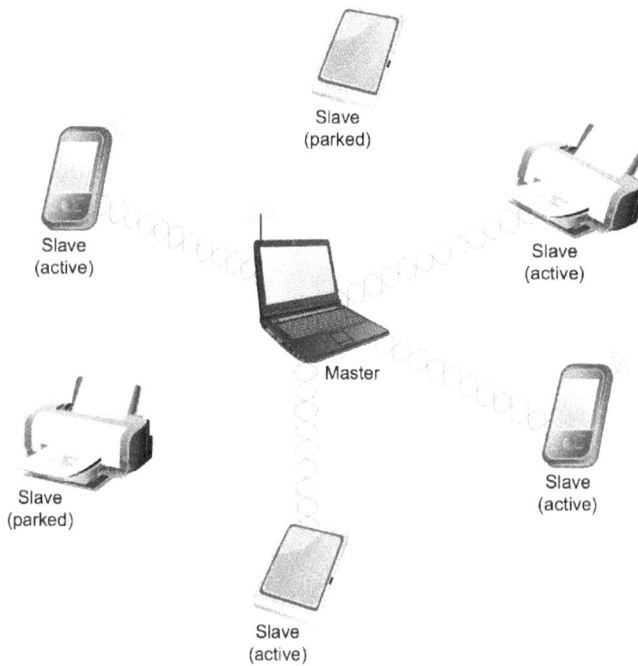

Figure 51. A Bluetooth piconet.

In the realm of very low-power, short-range communication there are a few other technologies besides Bluetooth. One of these is ZigBee, devised by the ZigBee alliance and standardized as IEEE 802.15.4. It is designed for situations where the bandwidth requirements are low and power consumption must be very low to give very long battery life. It is also intended to be simpler and cheaper than Bluetooth, making it feasible to incorporate in cheaper devices such as sensors. Sensors are gaining significance as a networked device category due to technological advancements that enable the deployment of numerous inexpensive and compact devices to monitor variables such as temperature, humidity, and energy usage in buildings.

2.8 Access Networks

Aside from the conventional Ethernet and Wi-Fi connections often utilized for Internet access in residential, professional, educational, and public environments, the majority of individuals connect to the Internet through an access or broadband service that is purchased from an Internet Service Provider (ISP). This section outlines two specific technologies: Passive Optical Networks (PON), sometimes known as fiber-to-the-home, and Cellular Networks that facilitate connectivity for our mobile devices. Both Ethernet and Wi-Fi networks are considered multi-access networks. However, their methods of regulating access differ significantly.

To set a little more context, ISPs (e.g., Telco or Cable companies) often operate a national backbone, and connected to the periphery of that backbone are hundreds or thousands of edge sites, each of which serves a city or neighborhood. These edge sites are commonly called Central Offices in the Telco world and Head Ends in the cable world, but despite their names implying "centralized" and "root of the hierarchy" these sites are at the very edge of the ISP's network; the ISP-side of the last-mile that directly connects to customers. PON and Cellular access networks are anchored in these facilities.3

2.8.1 Passive Optical Network

PON, or Passive Optical Network, is the prevailing technology for providing fiber-based broadband connectivity to residential and commercial premises. PON utilizes a point-to-multipoint architecture, where the network is organized in a tree-like form. It originates from a single point in the ISP's network and extends outward to connect with a maximum of 1024 residences. PON is named for its passive splitters, which efficiently transmit optical signals in both the downstream and upstream directions without the need for active frame storage and forwarding. Thus, they serve as the optical equivalent of repeaters employed in traditional Ethernet networks. Framing occurs at the source at the premises of the Internet Service Provider (ISP), using an Optical Line Terminal (OLT) device, and at the endpoints in individual houses, using an Optical Network Unit (ONU) device.

Figure 52 shows an example PON, simplified to depict just one ONU and one OLT. In practice, a Central Office would include multiple OLTs connecting to thousands of customer homes. For completeness, Figure 52 also includes two other details about how the PON is connected to the ISP's backbone (and hence, to the rest of the Internet). The Agg Switch aggregates traffic from a set of OLTs, and the BNG (Broadband Network Gateway) is a piece of Telco equipment that, among many other things, meters Internet traffic for the sake of billing. As its name implies, the BNG is effectively the gateway between the access network (everything to the left of the BNG) and the Internet (everything to the right of the BNG).

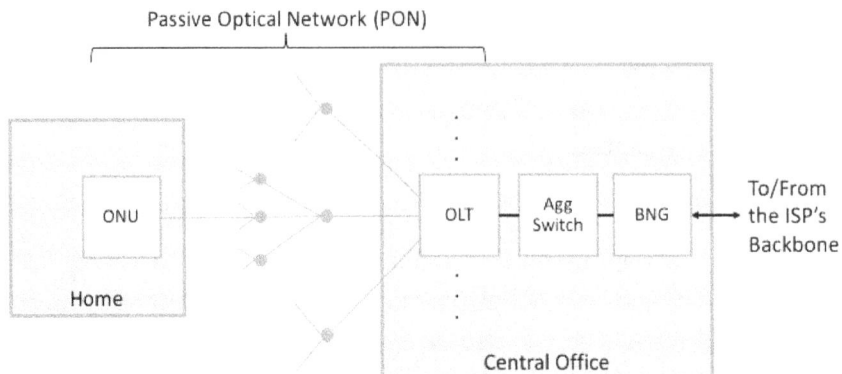

Figure 52. An example PON that connects OLTs in the Central Office to ONUs in homes and businesses.

Because the splitters are passive, PON has to implement some form of multi-access protocol. The approach it adopts can be summarized as follows. First, upstream and downstream traffic are transmitted on two different optical wavelengths, so they are completely independent of each other. Downstream traffic starts at the OLT and the signal is propagated down every link in the PON. As a consequence, every frame reaches every ONU. This device then looks at a unique identifier in the individual frames sent over the wavelength, and either keeps the frame (if the identifier is for it) or drops it (if not). Encryption is used to keep ONUs from eavesdropping on their neighbors' traffic.

Upstream traffic is then time-division multiplexed on the upstream wavelength, with each ONU periodically getting a turn to transmit. Because the ONUs are distributed over a fairly wide area (measured in kilometers) and at different distances from the OLT, it is not practical for them to transmit based on synchronized clocks, as in SONET. Instead, the OLT transmits grants to the individual ONUs, giving them a time interval during which they can transmit. In other words, the single OLT is responsible for centrally implementing the round-robin sharing of the shared PON. This includes the possibility that the OLT can grant each ONU a different share of time, effectively implementing different levels of service.

PON is similar to Ethernet in the sense that it defines a sharing algorithm that has evolved over time to accommodate higher and higher bandwidths. G-PON (Gigabit-PON) is the most widely deployed today, supporting a bandwidth of 2.25-Gbps. XGS-PON (10 Gigabit-PON) is just now starting to be deployed.

2.8.2 Cellular Network

While cellular telephone technology had its roots in analog voice communication, data services based on cellular standards are now the norm. Like Wi-Fi, cellular networks transmit data at certain bandwidths in the radio spectrum. Unlike Wi-Fi, which permits anyone to use a channel at either 2.4 or 5 GHz (all you have to do is set up a base station, as many of us do in our homes), exclusive use of various frequency bands have been auctioned off and licensed to service providers, who in turn sell mobile access service to their subscribers.

The frequency bands that are used for cellular networks vary around the world, and are complicated by the fact that ISPs often simultaneously support both old/legacy technologies and new/next-generation technologies, each of which occupies a different frequency band. The high-level summary is that traditional cellular technologies range from 700-MHz to 2400-MHz, with new mid-spectrum allocations now happening at 6-GHz and millimeter-wave (mmWave) allocations opening above 24-GHz.

CITIZENS BROADBAND RADIO SERVICE (CBRS)

In addition to the licensed bands, there is also an unlicensed band at 3.5-GHz set aside in North America, called Citizens Broadband Radio Service (CBRS), that anyone with a cellular radio can use. Similar unlicensed bands are being set up in other countries, as well. This opens the door for setting up private cellular networks, for example, within a University campus, an enterprise, or a manufacturing plant.

To be more precise, the CBRS band allows three tiers of users to share the spectrum: first right of use goes to the original owners of this spectrum, naval radars and satellite ground stations; followed by priority users who receive this right over 10MHz bands for three years via regional auctions; and finally the rest of the population, who can access and utilize a portion of this band as long as they first check with a central database of registered users.

Like 802.11, cellular technology relies on the use of base stations that are connected to a wired network. In the case of the cellular network, the base stations are often called Broadband Base Units (BBU), the mobile devices that connect to them are usually referred to as User Equipment (UE), and the set of BBUs are anchored at an Evolved Packet Core (EPC) hosted in a Central Office. The wireless network served by the EPC is often called a Radio Access Network (RAN).

BBUs officially go by another name—Evolved NodeB, often abbreviated eNodeB or eNB—where NodeB is what the radio unit was called in an early incarnation of cellular networks (and has since evolved). Given that the cellular world continues to evolve at a rapid pace and eNB's are soon to be upgraded to gNB's, we have decided to use the more generic and less cryptic BBU.

Figure 53 depicts one possible configuration of the end-to-end scenario, with a few additional bits of detail. The EPC has multiple subcomponents, including an MME (Mobility Management Entity), an HSS (Home Subscriber Server), and an S/PGW (Session/Packet Gateway) pair; the first tracks and manages the movement of UEs throughout the RAN, the second is a database that contains subscriber-related information, and the Gateway pair processes and forwards packets between the RAN and the Internet (it forms the EPC's user plane). We say "one possible configuration" because the cellular standards allow wide variability in how many S/PGWs a given MME is responsible for, making it possible for a single MME to manage mobility across a wide geographic area that is served by multiple Central Offices. Finally, while not explicitly spelled out in Figure 53, it is sometimes the case that the ISP's PON network is used to connect the remote BBUs back to the Central Office.

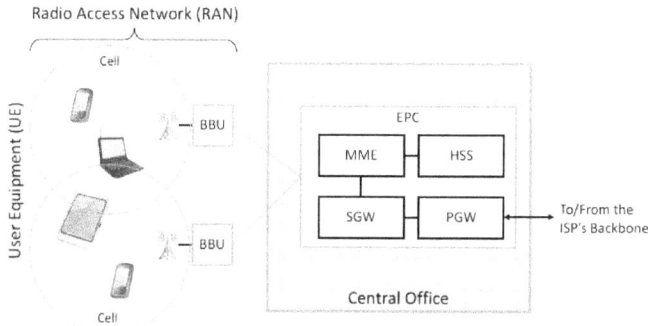

Figure 53. A Radio Access Network (RAN) connecting a set of cellular devices (UEs) to an Evolved Packet Core (EPC) hosted in a Central Office.

The geographic area served by a BBU's antenna is called a cell. A BBU could serve a single cell or use multiple directional antennas to serve multiple cells. Cells don't have crisp boundaries, and they overlap. Where they overlap, an UE could potentially communicate with multiple BBUs. At any time, however, the UE is in communication with, and under the control of, just one BBU. As the device begins to leave a cell, it moves into an area of overlap with one or more other cells. The current BBU senses the weakening signal from the phone and gives control of the device to whichever base station is receiving the strongest signal from it. If the device is involved in a call or other network session at the time, the session must be transferred to the new base station in what is called a handoff. The decision making process for handoffs is under the purview of the MME, which has historically been a proprietary aspect of the cellular equipment vendors (although open source MME implementations are now starting to be available).

There have been multiple generations of protocols implementing the cellular network, colloquially known as 1G, 2G, 3G, and so on. The first two generations supported only voice, with 3G defining the transition to broadband access, supporting data rates measured in hundreds of kilobits per second. Today, the industry is at 4G (supporting data rates typically measured in the few megabits per second) and is in the process of transitioning to 5G (with the promise of a tenfold increase in data rates).

As of 3G, the generational designation actually corresponds to a standard defined by the 3GPP (3rd Generation Partnership Project). Even though its name has "3G" in it, the 3GPP continues to define the standard for 4G and 5G, each of which corresponds to a release of the standard. Release 15, which is now published, is considered the demarcation point between 4G and 5G. By another name, this sequence of releases and generations is called LTE, which stands for Long-Term Evolution. The main takeaway is that while standards are published as a sequence of discrete releases, the industry as a whole has been on a fairly well-defined evolutionary path known as LTE. This section uses LTE terminology, but highlights the changes coming with 5G when appropriate.

The main innovation of LTE's air interface is how it allocates the available radio spectrum to UEs. Unlike Wi-Fi, which is contention-based, LTE uses a reservation-based strategy. This difference is rooted in each system's fundamental assumption about utilization: Wi-Fi assumes a lightly loaded network (and hence optimistically transmits when the wireless link is idle and backs off if contention is detected), while cellular networks assume (and strive for) high utilization (and hence explicitly assign different users to different "shares" of the available radio spectrum).

The state-of-the-art media access mechanism for LTE is called Orthogonal Frequency-Division Multiple Access (OFDMA). The idea is to multiplex data over a set of 12 orthogonal subcarrier frequencies, each of which is modulated independently. The "Multiple Access" in OFDMA implies that data can simultaneously be sent on behalf of multiple users, each on a different subcarrier frequency and for a different duration of time. The subbands are narrow (e.g., 15kHz), but the coding of user data into OFDMA symbols is designed to minimize the risk of data loss due to interference between adjacent bands.

The use of OFDMA naturally leads to conceptualizing the radio spectrum as a two-dimensional resource, as shown in Figure 54. The minimal schedulable unit, called a Resource Element (RE), corresponds to a 15kHz-wide band around one subcarrier frequency and the time it takes to transmit one OFDMA symbol. The number of bits that can be encoded in each symbol depends on the modulation rate, so for example using Quadrature Amplitude Modulation (QAM), 16-QAM yields 4 bits per symbol and 64-QAM yields 6 bits per symbol.

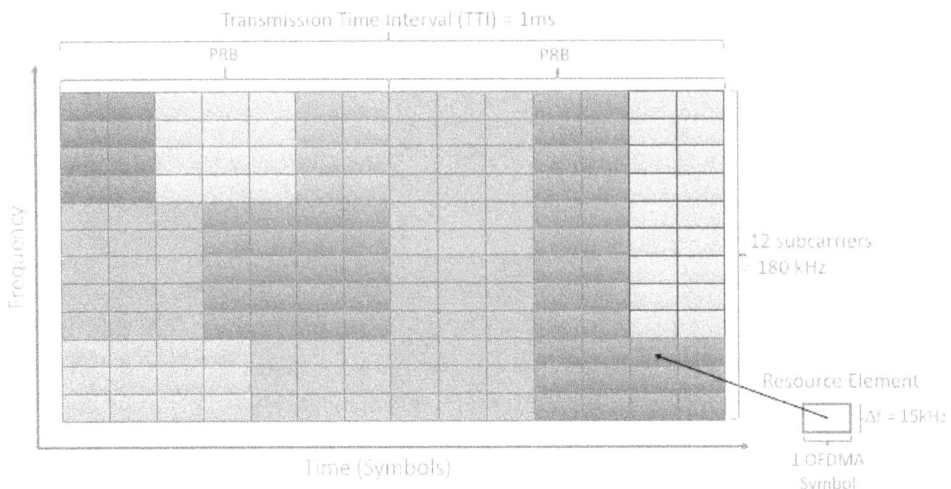

Figure 54. The available radio spectrum abstractly represented by a 2-D grid of schedulable Resource Elements.

A scheduler makes allocation decisions at the granularity of blocks of 7x12=84 resource elements, called a Physical Resource Block (PRB). Figure 54 shows two back-to-back PRBs, where UEs are depicted by different colored blocks. Of course time continues to flow along one axis, and depending on the size of the licensed frequency band, there may be many more subcarrier slots (and hence PRBs) available along the other axis, so the scheduler is essentially scheduling a sequence of PRBs for transmission.

The 1ms Transmission Time Interval (TTI) shown in Figure 54 corresponds to the time frame in which the BBU receives feedback from UEs about the quality of the signal they are experiencing. This feedback, called a Channel Quality Indicator (CQI), essentially reports the observed signal-to-noise ratio, which impacts the UE's ability to recover the data bits. The base station then uses this information to adapt how it allocates the available radio spectrum to the UEs it is serving.

Up to this point, the description of how we schedule the radio spectrum is specific to 4G. The transition from 4G to 5G introduces additional degrees-of-freedom in how the radio spectrum is scheduled, making it possible to adapt the cellular network to a more diverse set of devices and applications domains.

Fundamentally, 5G defines a family of waveforms—unlike 4G, which specified only one waveform—each optimized for a different band in the radio spectrum.4 The bands with carrier frequencies below 1GHz are designed to deliver mobile broadband and massive IoT services with a primary focus on range. Carrier frequencies between 1GHz-6GHz are designed to offer wider bandwidths, focusing on mobile broadband and mission-critical applications. Carrier frequencies above 24GHz (mmWaves) are designed to provide super wide bandwidths over short, line-of-sight coverage.

These different waveforms affect the scheduling and subcarrier intervals (i.e., the "size" of the Resource Elements just described).

◉ For sub-1GHz bands, 5G allows maximum 50MHz bandwidths. In this case, there are two waveforms: one with subcarrier spacing of 15kHz and another of 30kHz. (We used 15kHz in the example shown in Figure 54. The corresponding scheduling intervals are 0.5ms and 0.25ms, respectively. (We used 0.5ms in the example shown in Figure 54.)

◉ For 1GHz-6GHz bands, maximum bandwidths go up to 100MHz. Correspondingly, there are three waveforms with subcarrier spacings of 15kHz, 30kHz and 60kHz, corresponding to scheduling intervals of 0.5ms, 0.25ms and 0.125ms, respectively.

◉ For millimeter bands, bandwidths may go up to 400MHz. There are two waveforms, with subcarrier spacings of 60kHz and 120kHz. Both have scheduling intervals of 0.125ms.

This range of options is important because it adds another degree of freedom to the scheduler. In addition to allocating resource blocks to users, it has the ability to dynamically adjust the size of the resource blocks by changing the wave form being used in the band it is responsible for scheduling.

Whether 4G or 5G, the scheduling algorithm is a challenging optimization problem, with the objective of simultaneously (a) maximizing utilization of the available frequency band, and (b) ensuring that every UE receives the level of service it requires. This algorithm is not specified by 3GPP, but rather, is the proprietary intellectual property of the BBU vendors.

PERSPECTIVE: RACE TO THE EDGE

As we start to explore how softwarization is transforming the network, we should recognize that it is the access network that connects homes, businesses, and mobile users to the Internet that is undergoing the most radical change. The fiber-to-the-home and cellular networks described in Section 2.8 are currently constructed from complex hardware appliances (e.g., OLTs, BNGs, BBUs, EPCs). Not only have these devices historically been closed and proprietary, but the vendors that sell them have typically bundled a broad and diverse collection of functionality in each. As a consequence, they have become expensive to build, complicated to operate, and slow to change.

In response, network operators are actively transitioning from these purpose-built appliances to open software running on commodity servers, switches, and access devices. This initiative is often called CORD, which is an acronym for Central Office Re-architected as a Datacenter, and as the name suggests, the idea is to build the Telco Central Office (or the Cable Head End, resulting in the acronym HERD) using exactly the same technologies as in the large datacenters that make up the cloud.

The motivation for operators to do this is in part to benefit from the cost savings that come from replacing purpose-built appliances with commodity hardware, but it is mostly driven by the need to accelerate the pace of innovation. Their goal is to enable new classes of edge services—e.g., Public Safety, Autonomous Vehicles, Automated Factories, Internet-of-Things (IoT), Immersive User Interfaces—that benefit from low latency connectivity to end users, and more importantly, to the increasing number of devices those users surround themselves with. This results in a multi-tier cloud similar to the one shown in Figure 55.

This is all part of the growing trend to move functionality out of the datacenter and closer to the network edge, a trend that puts cloud providers and network operators on a collision course. Cloud providers, in pursuit of low-latency/high-bandwidth applications, are moving out of the datacenter and towards the edge at the same time network operators are adopting the best practices and technologies of the cloud to the edge that already exists and implements the access network. It's impossible to say how this will all play out over time; both industries have their particular advantages.

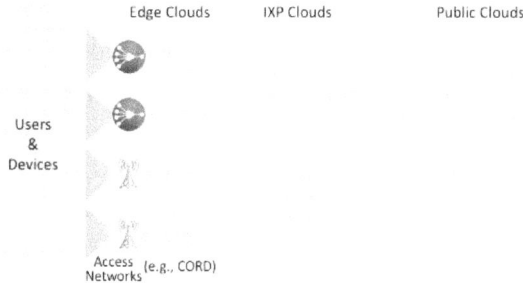

Figure 55. Emerging multi-tier cloud includes datacenter-based public clouds, IXP-hosted distributed clouds, and access-based edge clouds, such as CORD. While there are on the order of 150 IXP-hosted clouds worldwide, we can expect there to be thousands or even tens of thousands of edge clouds.

On the one hand, cloud providers believe that by saturating metro areas with edge clusters and abstracting away the access network, they can build an edge presence with low enough latency and high enough bandwidth to serve the next generation of edge applications. In this scenario, the access network remains a dumb bit-pipe, allowing cloud providers to excel at what they do best: run scalable cloud services on commodity hardware.

On the other hand, network operators believe that by building the next generation access network using cloud technology, they will be able to co-locate edge applications in the access network. This scenario comes with built-in advantages: an existing and widely distributed physical footprint, existing operational support, and native support for both mobility and guaranteed service.

While acknowledging both of these possibilities, there is a third outcome that is not only worth considering, but also worth working towards: the democratization of the network edge. The idea is to make the access-edge cloud accessible to anyone, and not strictly the domain of incumbent cloud providers or network operators. There are three reasons to be optimistic about this possibility:

- ⊙ Hardware and software for the access network is becoming commoditized and open. This is a key enabler that we were just talking about. If it helps Telcos and CableCos be agile, then it can provide the same value to anyone.

- ⊙ There is demand. Enterprises in the automotive, factory, and warehouse space increasingly want to deploy private 5G networks for a variety of physical automation use cases (e.g., a garage where a remote valet parks your car or a factory floor making use of automation robots).

- Spectrum is becoming available. 5G is opening up for use in an unlicensed or lightly licensed model in the US and Germany as two prime examples, with other countries soon to follow. This means 5G should have around 100-200 MHz of spectrum available for private use.

Traditionally, the access network has been controlled by telecommunications companies, cable companies, and vendors who provide them with specialized equipment. However, the transformation of the access network into software-based and virtualized systems now allows various entities, such as smart cities, underserved rural areas, apartment complexes, and manufacturing plants, to create their own access-edge cloud and connect it to the public Internet. We anticipate that this task will become as effortless as the current process of installing a WiFi router. By doing this, not only does it introduce the access-edge to more daring surroundings, but it also has the capacity to allow developers who naturally seek for chances for innovation to enter the access network.

Broader Perspective

To continue reading about the cloudification of the Internet, see Perspective: Virtual Networks All the Way Down.

To learn more about the transformation taking place in access networks, we recommend: CORD: Central Office Re-architected as a Datacenter, IEEE Communications, October 2016 and Democratizing the Network Edge SIGCOMM CCR, April 2019.

CHAPTER-3
INTERNETWORKING

PROBLEM: NOT ALL NETWORKS ARE DIRECTLY CONNECTED

As we have seen, there are many technologies that can be used to build last-mile links or to connect a modest number of nodes together, but how do we build networks of global scale? A single Ethernet can interconnect no more than 1024 hosts; a point-to-point link connects only two. Wireless networks are limited by the range of their radios. To build a global network, we need a way to interconnect these different types of links and multi-access networks. The concept of interconnecting different types of networks to build a large, global network is the core idea of the Internet and is often referred to as internetworking.

We can divide the internetworking problem up into a few subproblems. First of all, we need a way to interconnect links. Devices that interconnect links of the same type are often called switches, or sometimes Layer 2 (L2) switches. These devices are the first topic of this chapter. A particularly important class of L2 switches in use today are those used to interconnect Ethernet segments. These switches are also sometimes called bridges.

The core job of a switch is to take packets that arrive on an input and forward (or switch) them to the right output so that they will reach their appropriate destination. There are a variety of ways that the switch can determine the "right" output for a packet, which can be broadly categorized as connectionless and connection-oriented approaches. These two approaches have both found important application areas over the years.

Given the enormous diversity of network types, we also need a way to interconnect disparate networks and links (i.e., deal with heterogeneity). Devices that perform this task, once called gateways, are now mostly known as routers, or alternatively, Layer 3 (L3) switches. The protocol that was invented to deal with interconnection of disparate network types, the Internet Protocol (IP), is the topic of our second section.

Once we interconnect a whole lot of links and networks with switches and routers, there are likely to be many different possible ways to get from one point to another. Finding a suitable path or route through a network is one of the fundamental problems of networking. Such paths should be efficient (e.g., no longer than necessary), loop free, and able to respond to the fact that networks are not static—nodes may fail or reboot, links may break, and new nodes or links may be added. Our third section looks at some of the algorithms and protocols that have been developed to address these issues.

After comprehending the challenges associated with switching and routing, it becomes necessary to get devices that can execute these tasks. This chapter finishes by providing a detailed analysis of the various methods used to implement switches and routers. Although packet switches and routers share similarities with general-purpose computers, specialized architectures are often employed in specific scenarios. This is especially true in the upper echelons, where there appears to be a constant demand for additional switching capacity capable of managing the continuously growing traffic load in the central part of the Internet.

3.1 Switching Basics

Essentially, a switch is a device that enables the connection of multiple links to create a more extensive network. A switch is a device with many inputs and outputs that moves packets from an input to one or more outputs. Therefore, a switch incorporates the star topology (refer to Figure 56) into the available network configurations. The star topology possesses numerous appealing characteristics:

⊙ Even though a switch has a fixed number of inputs and outputs, which limits the number of hosts that can be connected to a single switch, large networks can be built by interconnecting a number of switches.

⊙ We can connect switches to each other and to hosts using point-to-point links, which typically means that we can build networks of large geographic scope.

⊙ Adding a new host to the network by connecting it to a switch does not necessarily reduce the performance of the network for other hosts already connected.

The assertion stated in the last chapter cannot be applied to the shared-media networks mentioned. Two hosts on the same 10-Mbps Ethernet segment cannot transmit constantly at 10 Mbps due to the fact that they share the same transmission medium. Each host on a switched network is connected to the switch through its own dedicated link. This means that multiple hosts can potentially transfer data at the maximum link speed, as long as the switch has sufficient overall capacity. Ensuring a high level of combined data transfer capacity is a primary objective when designing a switch. We will revisit this subject at a later point. Switched networks are often seen as more scalable than shared-media networks due to their capacity to support numerous hosts at full speed, allowing for significant growth in the number of nodes.

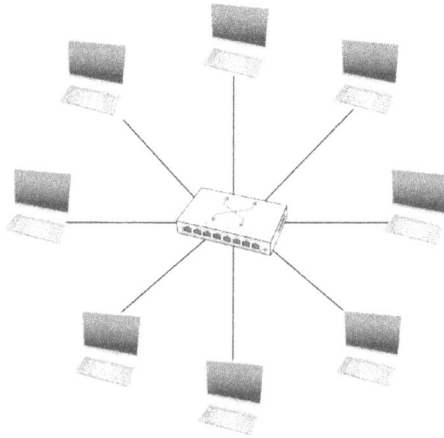

Figure 56. A switch provides a star topology.

DENSE WAVELENGTH DIVISION MULTIPLEXING

Our focus on packet-switched networks obscures the fact that, especially in wide-area networks, the underlying physical transport is all-optical: there are no packets. At this layer, commercially available DWDM (Dense Wavelength Division Multiplexing) equipment is able to transmit a large numbers of optical wavelengths (colors) down a single fiber. For example, one might send data on 100 or more different wavelengths, and each wavelength might carry as much as 100 Gbps of data.

Connecting these fibers is an optical device called a ROADM (Reconfigurable Optical Add/Drop Multiplexers). A collection of ROADMs (nodes) and fibers (links) form an optical transport network, where each ROADM is able to forward individual wavelengths along a multi-hop path, creating a logical end-to-end circuit. From the perspective of a packet-switched network that might be constructed on top of this optical transport, one wavelength, even if it crosses multiple ROADMs, appears to be a single point-to-point link between two switches, over which one might elect to run SONET or 100-Gbps Ethernet as the framing protocol. The reconfigurability feature of ROADMs means that it is possible to change these underlying end-to-end wavelengths, effectively creating a new topology at the packet-switching layer.

A switch is connected to a set of links and, for each of these links, runs the appropriate data link protocol to communicate with the node at the other end of the link. A switch's primary job is to receive incoming packets on one of its links and to transmit them on some other link. This function is sometimes referred to as either switching or forwarding, and in terms of the Open Systems Interconnection (OSI) architecture, it is considered a function of the network layer. (This is a case where OSI layering isn't a perfect reflection of the real world, as we'll see later.)

The question, then, is how does the switch decide which output link to place each packet on? The general answer is that it looks at the header of the packet for an identifier that it uses to make the decision. The details of how it uses this identifier vary, but there are two common approaches. The first is the datagram or connectionless approach. The second is the virtual circuit or connection-oriented approach. A third approach, source routing, is less common than these other two, but it does have some useful applications.

One thing that is common to all networks is that we need to have a way to identify the end nodes. Such identifiers are usually called addresses. We have already seen examples of addresses, such as the 48-bit address used for Ethernet. The only requirement for Ethernet addresses is that no two nodes on a network have the same address. This is accomplished by making sure that all Ethernet cards are assigned a globally unique identifier. For the following discussion, we assume that each host has a globally unique address. Later on, we consider other useful properties that an address might have, but global uniqueness is adequate to get us started.

Another prerequisite we must consider is the existence of a method to discern the input and output ports of every switch. There are a minimum of two logical methods to identify ports: There are two methods for identifying ports. The first method involves assigning a number to each port. The second method involves using the name of the node (such as a switch or host) that the port connects to. Currently, we employ port numbering.

3.1.1 Datagrams

The idea behind datagrams is incredibly simple: You just include in every packet enough information to enable any switch to decide how to get it to its destination. That is, every packet contains the complete destination address. Consider the example network illustrated in Figure 57, in which the hosts have addresses A, B, C, and so on. To decide how to forward a packet, a switch consults a forwarding table (sometimes called a routing table), an example of which is depicted in Table 5. This particular table shows the forwarding information that switch 2 needs to forward datagrams in the example network. It is pretty easy to figure out such a table when you have a complete map of a simple network like that depicted here; we could imagine a network operator configuring the tables statically. It is a lot harder to create the forwarding tables in large, complex networks with dynamically changing topologies and multiple paths between destinations. That harder problem is known as routing and is the topic of a later section. We can think of routing as a process that takes place in the background so that, when a data packet turns up, we will have the right information in the forwarding table to be able to forward, or switch, the packet.

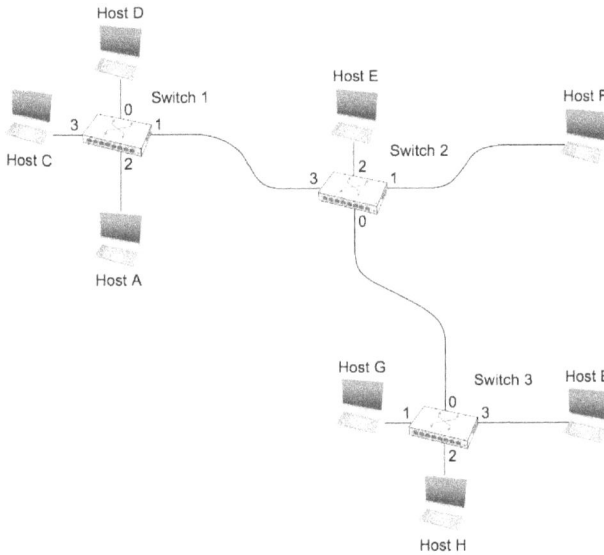

Figure 57. Datagram forwarding: an example network.

Table 5. Forwarding Table for Switch 2.

Destination	Port
A	3
B	0
C	3
D	3
E	2
F	1
G	0
H	0

Datagram networks have the following characteristics:

⊙ A host can send a packet anywhere at any time, since any packet that turns up at a switch can be immediately forwarded (assuming a correctly populated forwarding table). For this reason, datagram networks are often called connectionless; this contrasts with the connection-oriented networks described below, in which some connection state needs to be established before the first data packet is sent.

- ⊙ When a host sends a packet, it has no way of knowing if the network is capable of delivering it or if the destination host is even up and running.

- ⊙ Each packet is forwarded independently of previous packets that might have been sent to the same destination. Thus, two successive packets from host A to host B may follow completely different paths (perhaps because of a change in the forwarding table at some switch in the network).

- ⊙ A switch or link failure might not have any serious effect on communication if it is possible to find an alternate route around the failure and to update the forwarding table accordingly.

This final point is of particular significance to the history of datagram networks. An essential objective in designing the Internet is to ensure resilience in the face of failures, and historical evidence has demonstrated its remarkable effectiveness in achieving this objective. Given that datagram-based networks are the prevailing technology addressed in this book, we will defer the provision of illustrative examples to subsequent parts and proceed to analyze the two primary choices.

3.1.2 Virtual Circuit Switching

A second technique for packet switching uses the concept of a virtual circuit (VC). This approach, which is also referred to as a connection-oriented model, requires setting up a virtual connection from the source host to the destination host before any data is sent. To understand how this works, consider Figure 58, where host A again wants to send packets to host B. We can think of this as a two-stage process. The first stage is "connection setup." The second is data transfer. We consider each in turn.

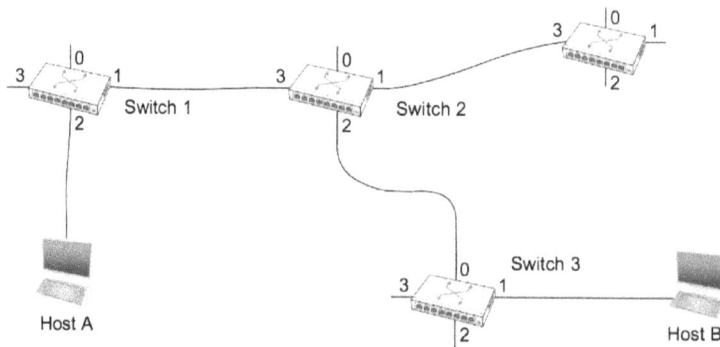

Figure 58. An example of a virtual circuit network.

In the connection setup phase, it is necessary to establish a "connection state" in each of the switches between the source and destination hosts. The connection state for a single connection consists of an entry in a "VC table" in each switch through which the connection passes. One entry in the VC table on a single switch contains:

- A virtual circuit identifier (VCI) that uniquely identifies the connection at this switch and which will be carried inside the header of the packets that belong to this connection

- An incoming interface on which packets for this VC arrive at the switch

- An outgoing interface in which packets for this VC leave the switch

- A potentially different VCI that will be used for outgoing packets

The semantics of one such entry is as follows: If a packet arrives on the designated incoming interface and that packet contains the designated VCI value in its header, then that packet should be sent out the specified outgoing interface with the specified outgoing VCI value having been first placed in its header.

Note that the combination of the VCI of packets as they are received at the switch and the interface on which they are received uniquely identifies the virtual connection. There may of course be many virtual connections established in the switch at one time. Also, we observe that the incoming and outgoing VCI values are generally not the same. Thus, the VCI is not a globally significant identifier for the connection; rather, it has significance only on a given link (i.e., it has link-local scope).

Whenever a new connection is created, we need to assign a new VCI for that connection on each link that the connection will traverse. We also need to ensure that the chosen VCI on a given link is not currently in use on that link by some existing connection.

There are two broad approaches to establishing connection state. One is to have a network administrator configure the state, in which case the virtual circuit is "permanent." Of course, it can also be deleted by the administrator, so a permanent virtual circuit (PVC) might best be thought of as a long-lived or administratively configured VC. Alternatively, a host can send messages into the network to cause the state to be established. This is referred to as signalling, and the resulting virtual circuits are said to be switched. The salient characteristic of a switched virtual circuit (SVC) is that a host may set up and delete such a VC dynamically without the involvement of a network administrator. Note that an SVC should more accurately be called a signalled VC, since it is the use of signalling (not switching) that distinguishes an SVC from a PVC.

Let's assume that a network administrator wants to manually create a new virtual connection from host A to host B. First, the administrator needs to identify a path through the network from A to B. In the example network of Figure 58, there is only one such path, but in general, this may not be the case. The administrator then picks a VCI value that is currently unused on each link for the connection. For the purposes of our example, let's suppose that the VCI value 5 is chosen for the link from host A to switch 1, and that 11 is chosen for the link from switch 1 to switch 2. In that case, switch 1 needs to have an entry in its VC table configured as shown in Table 6.

Table 6. Example Virtual Circuit Table Entry for Switch 1.

Incoming Interface	Incoming VCI	Outgoing Interface	Outgoing VCI
2	5	1	11

Similarly, suppose that the VCI of 7 is chosen to identify this connection on the link from switch 2 to switch 3 and that a VCI of 4 is chosen for the link from switch 3 to host B. In that case, switches 2 and 3 need to be configured with VC table entries as shown in Table 7 and Table 8, respectively. Note that the "outgoing" VCI value at one switch is the "incoming" VCI value at the next switch.

Table 7. Virtual Circuit Table Entry at Switch 2.

Incoming Interface	Incoming VCI	Outgoing Interface	Outgoing VCI
3	11	2	7

Table 8. Virtual Circuit Table Entry at Switch 3.

Incoming Interface	Incoming VCI	Outgoing Interface	Outgoing VCI
0	7	1	4

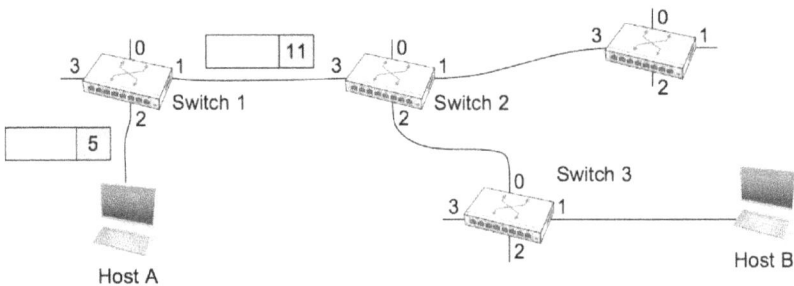

Figure 59. A packet is sent into a virtual circuit network.

Once the VC tables have been set up, the data transfer phase can proceed, as illustrated in Figure 59. For any packet that it wants to send to host B, A puts the VCI value of 5 in the header of the packet and sends it to switch 1. Switch 1 receives any such packet on interface 2, and it uses the combination of the interface and the VCI in the packet header to find the appropriate VC table entry. As shown in Table 6, the table entry in this case tells switch 1 to forward the packet out of interface 1 and to put the VCI value 11 in the header when the packet is sent. Thus, the packet will arrive at switch 2 on interface 3 bearing VCI 11. Switch 2 looks up interface 3 and VCI 11 in its VC table (as shown in Table 7) and sends the packet on to switch 3 after updating the VCI value in the packet header appropriately, as shown in

Figure 60. This process continues until it arrives at host B with the VCI value of 4 in the packet. To host B, this identifies the packet as having come from host A.

In real networks of reasonable size, the burden of configuring VC tables correctly in a large number of switches would quickly become excessive using the above procedures. Thus, either a network management tool or some sort of signalling (or both) is almost always used, even when setting up "permanent" VCs. In the case of PVCs, signalling is initiated by the network administrator, while SVCs are usually set up using signalling by one of the hosts. We consider now how the same VC just described could be set up by signalling from the host.

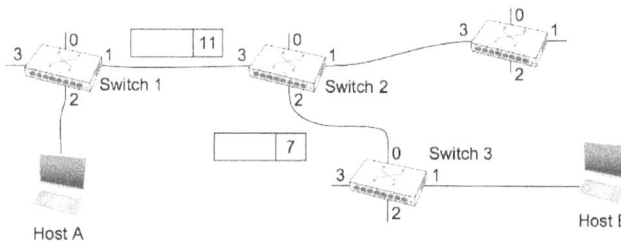

Figure 60. A packet makes its way through a virtual circuit network.

To start the signalling process, host A sends a setup message into the network— that is, to switch 1. The setup message contains, among other things, the complete destination address of host B. The setup message needs to get all the way to B to create the necessary connection state in every switch along the way. We can see that getting the setup message to B is a lot like getting a datagram to B, in that the switches have to know which output to send the setup message to so that it eventually reaches B. For now, let's just assume that the switches know enough about the network topology to figure out how to do that, so that the setup message flows on to switches 2 and 3 before finally reaching host B.

When switch 1 receives the connection request, in addition to sending it on to switch 2, it creates a new entry in its virtual circuit table for this new connection. This entry is exactly the same as shown previously in Table 6. The main difference is that now the task of assigning an unused VCI value on the interface is performed by the switch for that port. In this example, the switch picks the value 5. The virtual circuit table now has the following information: "When packets arrive on port 2 with identifier 5, send them out on port 1." Another issue is that, somehow, host A will need to learn that it should put the VCI value of 5 in packets that it wants to send to B; we will see how that happens below.

When switch 2 receives the setup message, it performs a similar process; in this example, it picks the value 11 as the incoming VCI value. Similarly, switch 3 picks 7 as the value for its incoming VCI. Each switch can pick any number it likes, as long as that number is not currently in use for some other connection on that port of that switch. As noted above, VCIs have link-local scope; that is, they have no global significance.

Finally, the setup message arrives as host B. Assuming that B is healthy and willing to accept a connection from host A, it too allocates an incoming VCI value, in this case 4. This VCI value can be used by B to identify all packets coming from host A.

Now, to complete the connection, everyone needs to be told what their downstream neighbor is using as the VCI for this connection. Host B sends an acknowledgment of the connection setup to switch 3 and includes in that message the VCI that it chose (4). Now switch 3 can complete the virtual circuit table entry for this connection, since it knows the outgoing value must be 4. Switch 3 sends the acknowledgment on to switch 2, specifying a VCI of 7. Switch 2 sends the message on to switch 1, specifying a VCI of 11. Finally, switch 1 passes the acknowledgment on to host A, telling it to use the VCI of 5 for this connection.

By now, everyone possesses all the essential knowledge required to facilitate the movement of data from host A to host B. Every switch contains a comprehensive virtual circuit table entry for the connection. Moreover, host A possesses a definite confirmation that all necessary arrangements are in order, extending to host B. Currently, the connection table entries have been successfully established in all three switches, mirroring the administratively configured example mentioned earlier. However, this entire procedure occurred automatically in response to the signaling message transmitted from A. The data transfer phase can now commence and is identical to that employed in the PVC scenario. When host A wishes to terminate the transmission of data to host B, it initiates the disconnection process by transmitting a teardown message to switch 1. The switch eliminates the corresponding entry from its table and transmits the message to the other switches along the path, which also delete the relevant table entries. If host A were to send a packet with a Virtual Circuit Identifier (VCI) of 5 to switch 1 at this moment, the packet would be discarded as if the link between them had never been established.

There are several things to note about virtual circuit switching:

- ⊙ Since host A has to wait for the connection request to reach the far side of the network and return before it can send its first data packet, there is at least one round-trip time (RTT) of delay before data is sent.

- ⊙ While the connection request contains the full address for host B (which might be quite large, being a global identifier on the network), each data packet contains only a small identifier, which is only unique on one link. Thus, the per-packet overhead caused by the header is reduced relative to the datagram model. More importantly, the lookup is fast because the virtual circuit number can be treated as an index into a table rather than as a key that has to be looked up.

⊙ If a switch or a link in a connection fails, the connection is broken and a new one will need to be established. Also, the old one needs to be torn down to free up table storage space in the switches.

⊙ The issue of how a switch decides which link to forward the connection request on has been glossed over. In essence, this is the same problem as building up the forwarding table for datagram forwarding, which requires some sort of routing algorithm. Routing is described in a later section, and the algorithms described there are generally applicable to routing setup requests as well as datagrams.

One of the nice aspects of virtual circuits is that by the time the host gets the go-ahead to send data, it knows quite a lot about the network—for example, that there really is a route to the receiver and that the receiver is willing and able to receive data. It is also possible to allocate resources to the virtual circuit at the time it is established. For example, X.25 (an early and now largely obsolete virtual-circuit-based networking technology) employed the following three-part strategy:

⊙ Buffers are allocated to each virtual circuit when the circuit is initialized.

⊙ The sliding window protocol is run between each pair of nodes along the virtual circuit, and this protocol is augmented with flow control to keep the sending node from over-running the buffers allocated at the receiving node.

⊙ The circuit is rejected by a given node if not enough buffers are available at that node when the connection request message is processed.

In doing these three things, each node is ensured of having the buffers it needs to queue the packets that arrive on that circuit. This basic strategy is usually called hop-by-hop flow control.

By comparison, a datagram network has no connection establishment phase, and each switch processes each packet independently, making it less obvious how a datagram network would allocate resources in a meaningful way. Instead, each arriving packet competes with all other packets for buffer space. If there are no free buffers, the incoming packet must be discarded. We observe, however, that even in a datagram-based network a source host often sends a sequence of packets to the same destination host. It is possible for each switch to distinguish among the set of packets it currently has queued, based on the source/destination pair, and thus for the switch to ensure that the packets belonging to each source/destination pair are receiving a fair share of the switch's buffers.

In the virtual circuit model, we could imagine providing each circuit with a different quality of service (QoS). In this setting, the term quality of service is usually taken to mean that the network gives the user some kind of performance-related guarantee, which in turn implies that switches set aside the resources they need to meet this guarantee. For example, the switches along a given virtual circuit might allocate a percentage of each outgoing link's bandwidth to that circuit. As another example, a sequence of switches might ensure that packets belonging to a particular circuit not be delayed (queued) for more than a certain amount of time.

There have been a number of successful examples of virtual circuit technologies over the years, notably X.25, Frame Relay, and Asynchronous Transfer Mode (ATM). With the success of the Internet's connectionless model, however, none of them enjoys great popularity today. One of the most common applications of virtual circuits for many years was the construction of virtual private networks (VPNs), a subject discussed in a later section. Even that application is now mostly supported using Internet-based technologies today.

ASYNCHRONOUS TRANSFER MODE (ATM)

Asynchronous Transfer Mode (ATM) is probably the most well-known virtual circuit-based networking technology, although it is now well past its peak in terms of deployment. ATM became an important technology in the 1980s and early 1990s for a variety of reasons, not the least of which is that it was embraced by the telephone industry, which at that point in time was less active in computer networks (other than as a supplier of links from which other people built networks). ATM also happened to be in the right place at the right time, as a high-speed switching technology that appeared on the scene just when shared media like Ethernet and token rings were starting to look a bit too slow for many users of computer networks. In some ways ATM was a competing technology with Ethernet switching, and it was seen by many as a competitor to IP as well.

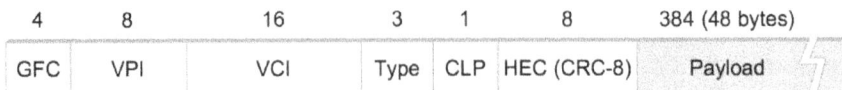

4	8	16	3	1	8	384 (48 bytes)
GFC	VPI	VCI	Type	CLP	HEC (CRC-8)	Payload

Figure 61. ATM cell format at the UNI.

The approach ATM takes has some interesting properties, which makes it worth examining a bit further. The picture of the ATM packet format—more commonly called an ATM cell—in Figure 61 will illustrate the main points. We'll skip the generic flow control (GFC) bits, which never saw much use, and start with the 24 bits that are labelled VPI (virtual path identifier—8 bits) and VCI (virtual circuit identifier—16 bits). If you consider these bits together as a single 24-bit field, they correspond to the virtual circuit identifier introduced above. The reason for breaking the field into two parts was to allow for a level of hierarchy: All the circuits with the same VPI could, in some cases, be treated as a group (a virtual path) and could all be switched together looking only at the VPI, simplifying the work of a switch that could ignore all the VCI bits and reducing the size of the VC table considerably.

Skipping to the last header byte we find an 8-bit cyclic redundancy check (CRC), known as the header error check (HEC). It uses CRC-8 and provides error detection and single-bit error correction capability on the cell header only. Protecting the cell header is particularly important because an error in the VCI will cause the cell to be misdelivered.

Probably the most significant thing to notice about the ATM cell, and the reason it is called a cell and not a packet, is that it comes in only one size: 53 bytes. What was the reason for this? One big reason was to facilitate the implementation of hardware switches. When ATM was being created in the mid- and late 1980s, 10-Mbps Ethernet was the cutting-edge technology in terms of speed. To go much faster, most people thought in terms of hardware. Also, in the telephone world, people think big when they think of switches—telephone switches often serve tens of thousands of customers. Fixed-length packets turn out to be a very helpful thing if you want to build fast, highly scalable switches. There are two main reasons for this:

- It is easier to build hardware to do simple jobs, and the job of processing packets is simpler when you already know how long each one will be.

- If all packets are the same length, then you can have lots of switching elements all doing much the same thing in parallel, each of them taking the same time to do its job.

This second reason, the enabling of parallelism, greatly improves the scalability of switch designs. It would be overstating the case to say that fast parallel hardware switches can only be built using fixed-length cells. However, it is certainly true that cells ease the task of building such hardware and that there was a lot of knowledge available about how to build cell switches in hardware at the time the ATM standards were being defined. As it turns out, this same principle is still applied in many switches and routers today, even if they deal in variable length packets—they cut those packets into some sort of cell in order to forward them from input port to output port, but this is all internal to the switch.

There is another good argument in favor of small ATM cells, having to do with end-to-end latency. ATM was designed to carry both voice phone calls (the dominant use case at the time) and data. Because voice is low-bandwidth but has strict delay requirements, the last thing you want is for a small voice packet queued behind a large data packet at a switch. If you force all packets to be small (i.e., cell-sized), then large data packets can still be supported by reassembling a set of cells into a packet, and you get the benefit of being able to interleave the forwarding of voice cells and data cells at every switch along the path from source to destination. This idea of using small cells to improve end-to-end latency is alive and well today in cellular access networks.

Having decided to use small, fixed-length packets, the next question was what is the right length to fix them at? If you make them too short, then the amount of header information that needs to be carried around relative to the amount of data that fits in one cell gets larger, so the percentage of link bandwidth that is actually used to carry data goes down. Even more seriously, if you build a device that processes cells at some maximum number of cells per second, then as cells get shorter the total data rate drops in direct proportion to cell size. An example of such a device might be a network adaptor that reassembles cells into larger units before handing them up to the host. The performance of such a device depends directly on cell size. On the other hand, if you make the cells too big, then there is a problem of wasted bandwidth caused by the need to pad transmitted data to fill a complete cell. If the cell payload size is 48 bytes and you want to send 1 byte, you'll need to send 47 bytes of padding. If this happens a lot, then the utilization of the link will be very low. The combination of relatively high header-to-payload ratio plus the frequency of sending partially filled cells did actually lead to some noticeable inefficiency in ATM networks that some detractors called the cell tax.

As it turns out, 48 bytes was picked for the ATM cell payload as a compromise. There were good arguments for both larger and smaller cells, and 48 made almost no one happy—a power of two would certainly have been better for computers to process.

3.1.3 Source Routing

A third approach to switching that uses neither virtual circuits nor conventional datagrams is known as source routing. The name derives from the fact that all the information about network topology that is required to switch a packet across the network is provided by the source host.

There are various ways to implement source routing. One would be to assign a number to each output of each switch and to place that number in the header of the packet. The switching function is then very simple: For each packet that arrives on an input, the switch would read the port number in the header and transmit the packet on that output. However, since there will in general be more than one switch in the path between the sending and the receiving host, the header for the packet needs to contain enough information to allow every switch in the path to determine which output the packet needs to be placed on. One way to do this would be to put an ordered list of switch ports in the header and to rotate the list so that the next switch in the path is always at the front of the list. Figure 62 illustrates this idea.

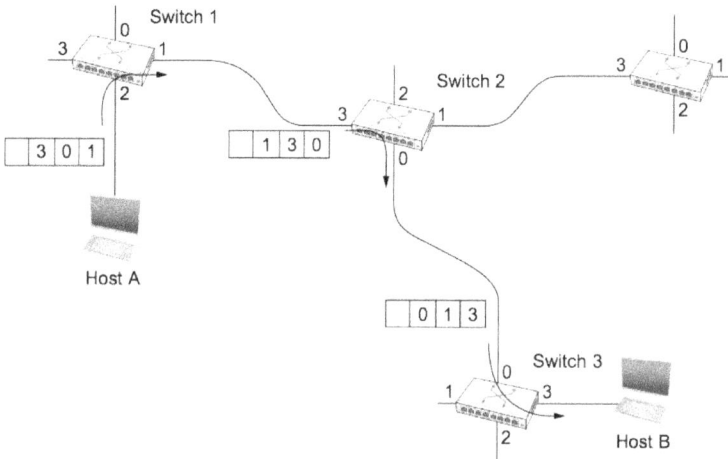

Figure 62. Source routing in a switched network (where the switch reads the rightmost number).

In this example, the packet needs to traverse three switches to get from host A to host B. At switch 1, it needs to exit on port 1, at the next switch it needs to exit at port 0, and at the third switch it needs to exit at port 3. Thus, the original header when the packet leaves host A contains the list of ports (3, 0, 1), where we assume that each switch reads the rightmost element of the list. To make sure that the next switch gets the appropriate information, each switch rotates the list after it has read its own entry. Thus, the packet header as it leaves switch 1 en route to switch 2 is now (1, 3, 0); switch 2 performs another rotation and sends out a packet with (0, 1, 3) in the header. Although not shown, switch 3 performs yet another rotation, restoring the header to what it was when host A sent it.

There are several things to note about this approach. First, it assumes that host A knows enough about the topology of the network to form a header that has all the right directions in it for every switch in the path. This is somewhat analogous to the problem of building the forwarding tables in a datagram network or figuring out where to send a setup packet in a virtual circuit network. In practice, however, it is the first switch at the ingress to the network (as opposed to the end host connected to that switch) that appends the source route.

Second, observe that we cannot predict how big the header needs to be, since it must be able to hold one word of information for every switch on the path. This implies that headers are probably of variable length with no upper bound, unless we can predict with absolute certainty the maximum number of switches through which a packet will ever need to pass.

Third, there are some variations on this approach. For example, rather than rotate the header, each switch could just strip the first element as it uses it. Rotation has an advantage over stripping, however: Host B gets a copy of the complete header, which may help it figure out how to get back to host A. Yet another alternative is to have the header carry a pointer to the current "next port" entry, so that each switch just updates the pointer rather than rotating the header; this may be more efficient to implement. We show these three approaches in Figure 63. In each case, the entry that this switch needs to read is A, and the entry that the next switch needs to read is B.

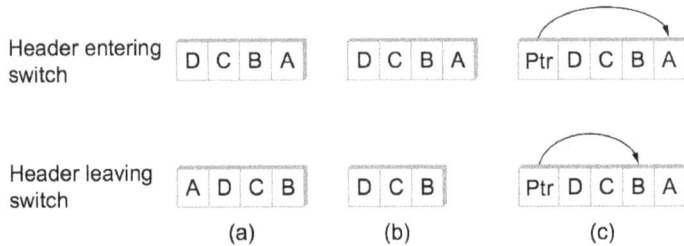

Header entering switch | D C B A | D C B A | Ptr D C B A

Header leaving switch | A D C B | D C B | Ptr D C B A

(a)   (b)   (c)

Figure 63. Three ways to handle headers for source routing: (a) rotation; (b) stripping; (c) pointer. The labels are read right to left.

Source routing can be used in both datagram networks and virtual circuit networks. For example, the Internet Protocol, which is a datagram protocol, includes a source route option that allows selected packets to be source routed, while the majority are switched as conventional datagrams. Source routing is also used in some virtual circuit networks as the means to get the initial setup request along the path from source to destination.

Source routes are sometimes categorized as strict or loose. In a strict source route, every node along the path must be specified, whereas a loose source route only specifies a set of nodes to be traversed, without saying exactly how to get from one node to the next. A loose source route can be thought of as a set of waypoints rather than a completely specified route. The loose option can be helpful to limit the amount of information that a source must obtain to create a source route. In any reasonably large network, it is likely to be hard for a host to get the complete path information it needs to construct correctly a strict source route to any destination. But both types of source routes do find application in certain scenarios, as we will see in later chapters.

3.2 Switched Ethernet

Having discussed some of the basic ideas behind switching, we now focus more closely on a specific switching technology: Switched Ethernet. The switches used to build such networks, which are often referred to as L2 switches, are widely used in campus and enterprise networks. Historically, they were more commonly referred to as bridges because they were used to "bridge" ethernet segments to build an extended LAN. But today most networks deploy Ethernet in a point-to-point configuration, with these links interconnected by L2 switches to form a switched Ethernet.

The following starts with the historical perspective (using bridges to connect a set of Ethernet segments), and then shifts to the perspective in wide-spread use today (using L2 switches to connect a set of point-to-point links). But whether we call the device a bridge or a switch—and the network you build an extended LAN or a switched Ethernet—the two behave in exactly the same way.

To begin, suppose you have a pair of Ethernets that you want to interconnect. One approach you might try is to put a repeater between them. This would not be a workable solution, however, if doing so exceeded the physical limitations of the Ethernet. (Recall that no more than two repeaters between any pair of hosts and no more than a total of 2500 m in length are allowed.) An alternative would be to put a node with a pair of Ethernet adaptors between the two Ethernets and have the node forward frames from one Ethernet to the other. This node would differ from a repeater, which operates on bits, not frames, and just blindly copies the bits received on one interface to another. Instead, this node would fully implement the Ethernet's collision detection and media access protocols on each interface. Hence, the length and number-of-host restrictions of the Ethernet, which are all about managing collisions, would not apply to the combined pair of Ethernets connected in this way. This device operates in promiscuous mode, accepting all frames transmitted on either of the Ethernets, and forwarding them to the other.

In their simplest variants, bridges simply accept LAN frames on their inputs and forward them out on all other outputs. This simple strategy was used by early bridges but has some pretty serious limitations as we'll see below. A number of refinements were added over the years to make bridges an effective mechanism for interconnecting a set of LANs. The rest of this section fills in the more interesting details.

3.2.1 Learning Bridges

The first optimization we can make to a bridge is to observe that it need not forward all frames that it receives. Consider the bridge in Figure 64. Whenever a frame from host A that is addressed to host B arrives on port 1, there is no need for the bridge to forward the frame out over port 2. The question, then, is how does a bridge come to learn on which port the various hosts reside?

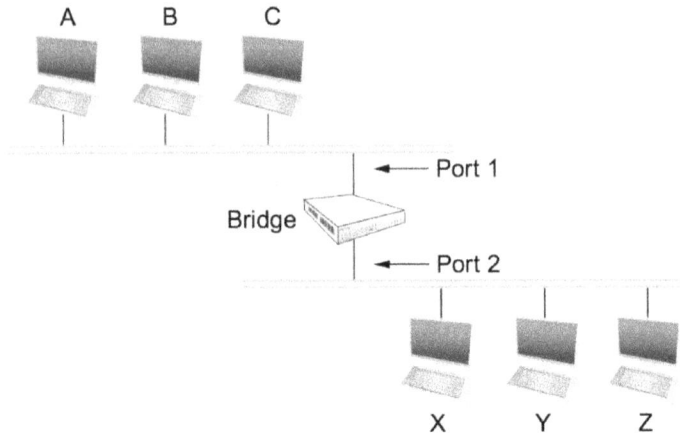

Figure 64. Illustration of a learning bridge.

One option would be to have a human download a table into the bridge similar to the one given in Table 9. Then, whenever the bridge receives a frame on port 1 that is addressed to host A, it would not forward the frame out on port 2; there would be no need because host A would have already directly received the frame on the LAN connected to port 1. Anytime a frame addressed to host A was received on port 2, the bridge would forward the frame out on port 1.

Table 9. Forwarding Table Maintained by a Bridge.

Host	Port
A	1
B	1
C	1
X	2
Y	2
Z	2

Having a human maintain this table is too burdensome, and there is a simple trick by which a bridge can learn this information for itself. The idea is for each bridge to inspect the source address in all the frames it receives. Thus, when host A sends a frame to a host on either side of the bridge, the bridge receives this frame and records the fact that a frame from host A was just received on port 1. In this way, the bridge can build a table just like Table 9.

Note that a bridge using such a table implements a version of the datagram (or connectionless) model of forwarding described earlier. Each packet carries a global address, and the bridge decides which output to send a packet on by looking up that address in a table.

Upon initial boot, the bridge's table is devoid of any entries, which are subsequently added as time progresses. In addition, each entry is assigned a timeout, and the bridge will discard the entry once the set time period has elapsed. This is done to safeguard against the scenario where a host, and consequently its LAN address, is relocated from one network to another. Therefore, this table may not be entirely comprehensive. If the bridge receives a frame that is addressed to a host not already listed in the table, it will proceed to forward the frame through all the other ports. Put simply, this table serves as an optimization that selectively removes some frames, but it is not necessary for ensuring accuracy.

3.2.2 Implementation

The code that implements the learning bridge algorithm is quite simple, and we sketch it here. Structure BridgeEntry defines a single entry in the bridge's forwarding table; these are stored in a Map structure (which supports mapCreate, mapBind, and mapResolve operations) to enable entries to be efficiently located when packets arrive from sources already in the table. The constant MAX_TTL specifies how long an entry is kept in the table before it is discarded.

```
#define BRIDGE_TAB_SIZE   1024  /* max size of bridging table */

#define MAX_TTL          120   /* time (in seconds) before an entry is flushed */


typedef struct {
    MacAddr    destination;   /* MAC address of a node */
    int        ifnumber;      /* interface to reach it */
    u_short    TTL;           /* time to live */
    Binding    binding;       /* binding in the Map */
} BridgeEntry;


int    numEntries = 0;
Map    bridgeMap = mapCreate(BRIDGE_TAB_SIZE, sizeof(BridgeEntry));
```

The routine that updates the forwarding table when a new packet arrives is given by updateTable. The arguments passed are the source media access control (MAC) address contained in the packet and the interface number on which it was received. Another routine, not shown here, is invoked at regular intervals, scans the entries in the forwarding table, and decrements the TTL (time to live) field of each entry, discarding any entries whose TTL has reached 0. Note that the TTL is reset to MAX_TTL every time a packet arrives to refresh an existing table entry and that the interface on which the destination can be reached is updated to reflect the most recently received packet.

```
void
updateTable (MacAddr src, int inif)
{
  BridgeEntry    *b;

  if (mapResolve(bridgeMap, &src, (void **)&b) == FALSE )
  {
    /* this address is not in the table, so try to add it */
    if (numEntries < BRIDGE_TAB_SIZE)
    {
      b = NEW(BridgeEntry);
      b->binding = mapBind( bridgeMap, &src, b);
      /* use source address of packet as dest. address in table */
      b->destination = src;
      numEntries++;
    }
    else
    {
      /* can't fit this address in the table now, so give up */
      return;
    }
  }
  /* reset TTL and use most recent input interface */
  b->TTL = MAX_TTL;
  b->ifnumber = inif;
}
```

Note that this implementation adopts a simple strategy in the case where the bridge table has become full to capacity—it simply fails to add the new address. Recall that completeness of the bridge table is not necessary for correct forwarding; it just optimizes performance. If there is some entry in the table that is not currently being used, it will eventually time out and be removed, creating space for a new entry. An alternative approach would be to invoke some sort of cache replacement algorithm on finding the table full; for example, we might locate and remove the entry with the smallest TTL to accommodate the new entry.

3.2.3 Spanning Tree Algorithm

The preceding strategy works just fine until the network has a loop in it, in which case it fails in a horrible way—frames potentially get forwarded forever. This is easy to see in the example depicted in Figure 65, where switches S1, S4, and S6 form a loop.

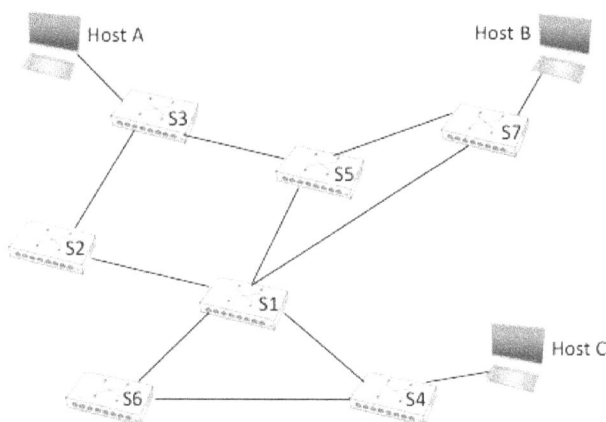

Figure 65. Switched Ethernet with loops.

Note that we are now making the shift from calling the each forwarding device a bridge (connecting segments that might reach multiple other devices) to instead calling them L2 switches (connecting point-to-point links that reach just one other device). To keep the example manageable, we include just three hosts. In practice, switches typically have 16, 24, or 48 ports, meaning they are able to connect to that many hosts (and other switches).

In our example switched network, suppose that a packet enters switch S4 from Host C and that the destination address is one not yet in any switch's forwarding table: S4 sends a copy of the packet out its two other ports: to switches S1 and S6. Switch S6 forwards the packet onto S1 (and meanwhile, S1 forwards the packet onto S6), both of which in turn forward their packets back to S4. Switch S4 still doesn't have this destination in its table, so it forwards the packet out its two other ports. There is nothing to stop this cycle from repeating endlessly, with packets looping in both directions among S1, S4, and S6.

Why would a switched Ethernet (or extended LAN) come to have a loop in it? One possibility is that the network is managed by more than one administrator, for example, because it spans multiple departments in an organization. In such a setting, it is possible that no single person knows the entire configuration of the network, meaning that a switch that closes a loop might be added without anyone knowing. A second, more likely scenario is that loops are built into the network on purpose—to provide redundancy in case of failure. After all, a network with no loops needs only one link failure to become split into two separate partitions.

Whatever the cause, switches must be able to correctly handle loops. This problem is addressed by having the switches run a distributed spanning tree algorithm. If you think of the network as being represented by a graph that possibly has loops (cycles), then a spanning tree is a subgraph of this graph that covers (spans) all the vertices but contains no cycles. That is, a spanning tree keeps all of the vertices of the original graph but throws out some of the edges. For example, Figure 66 shows a cyclic graph on the left and one of possibly many spanning trees on the right.

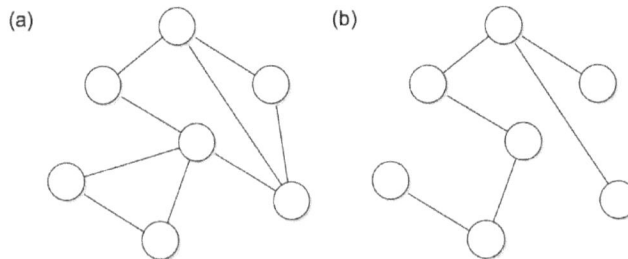

Figure 66. Example of (a) a cyclic graph; (b) a corresponding spanning tree.

The idea of a spanning tree is simple enough: It's a subset of the actual network topology that has no loops and that reaches all the devices in the network. The hard part is how all of the switches coordinate their decisions to arrive at a single view of the spanning tree. After all, one topology is typically able to be covered by multiple spanning trees. The answer lies in the spanning tree protocol, which we'll describe now.

The spanning tree algorithm, which was developed by Radia Perlman, then at the Digital Equipment Corporation, is a protocol used by a set of switches to agree upon a spanning tree for a particular network. (The IEEE 802.1 specification is based on this algorithm.) In practice, this means that each switch decides the ports over which it is and is not willing to forward frames. In a sense, it is by removing ports from the topology that the network is reduced to an acyclic tree. It is even possible that an entire switch will not participate in forwarding frames, which seems kind of strange at first glance. The algorithm is dynamic, however, meaning that the switches are always prepared to reconfigure themselves into a new spanning tree should some switch fail, and so those unused ports and switches provide the redundant capacity needed to recover from failures.

The main idea of the spanning tree is for the switches to select the ports over which they will forward frames. The algorithm selects ports as follows. Each switch has a unique identifier; for our purposes, we use the labels S1, S2, S3, and so on. The algorithm first elects the switch with the smallest ID as the root of the spanning tree; exactly how this election takes place is described below. The root switch always forwards frames out over all of its ports. Next, each switch computes the shortest path to the root and notes which of its ports is on this path. This port is also selected as the switch's preferred path to the root. Finally, to account for the possibility there could be another switch connected to its ports, the switch elects a single designated switch that will be responsible for forwarding frames toward the root. Each designated switch is the one that is closest to the root. If two or more switches are equally close to the root, then the switches' identifiers are used to break ties, and the smallest ID wins. Of course, each switch might be connected to more than one other switch, so it participates in the election of a designated switch for each such port. In effect, this means that each switch decides if it is the designated switch relative to each of its ports. The switch forwards frames over those ports for which it is the designated switch.

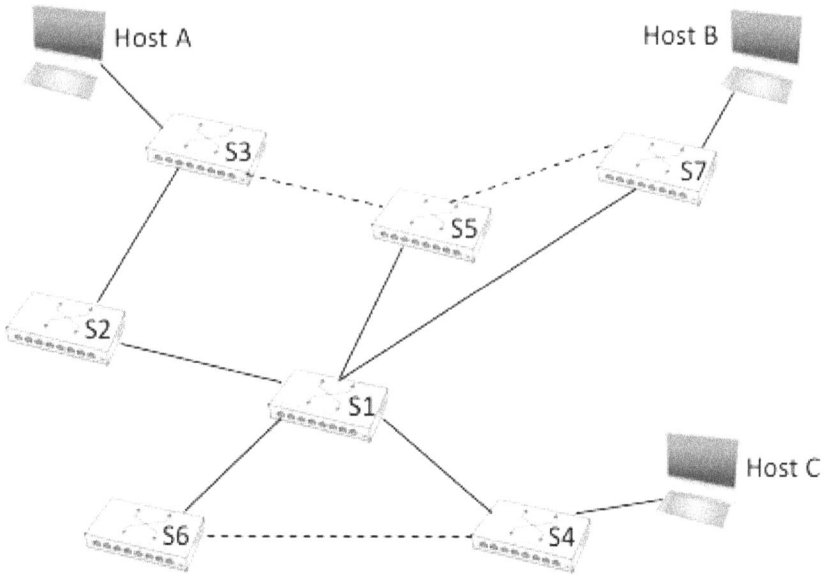

Figure 67. Spanning tree with some ports not selected.

Figure 67 shows the spanning tree that corresponds to the network shown in Figure 65. In this example, S1 is the root, since it has the smallest ID. Notice that S3 and S5 are connected to each other, but S5 is the designated switch since it is closer to the root. Similarly, S5 and S7 are connected to each other, but in this case S5 is the designated switch since it has the smaller ID; both are an equal distance from S1.

While it is possible for a human to look at the network given in Figure 65 and to compute the spanning tree given in the Figure 67 according to the rules given above, the switches do not have the luxury of being able to see the topology of the entire network, let alone peek inside other switches to see their ID. Instead, they have to exchange configuration messages with each other and then decide whether or not they are the root or a designated switch based on these messages.

Specifically, the configuration messages contain three pieces of information:

- The ID for the switch that is sending the message.

- The ID for what the sending switch believes to be the root switch.

- The distance, measured in hops, from the sending switch to the root switch.

Each switch records the current best configuration message it has seen on each of its ports ("best" is defined below), including both messages it has received from other switches and messages that it has itself transmitted.

Initially, each switch thinks it is the root, and so it sends a configuration message out on each of its ports identifying itself as the root and giving a distance to the root of 0. Upon receiving a configuration message over a particular port, the switch checks to see if that new message is better than the current best configuration message recorded for that port. The new configuration message is considered better than the currently recorded information if any of the following is true:

- It identifies a root with a smaller ID.

- It identifies a root with an equal ID but with a shorter distance.

- The root ID and distance are equal, but the sending switch has a smaller ID

If the new message is better than the currently recorded information, the switch discards the old information and saves the new information. However, it first adds 1 to the distance-to-root field since the switch is one hop farther away from the root than the switch that sent the message.

When a switch receives a configuration message indicating that it is not the root—that is, a message from a switch with a smaller ID—the switch stops generating configuration messages on its own and instead only forwards configuration messages from other switches, after first adding 1 to the distance field. Likewise, when a switch receives a configuration message that indicates it is not the designated switch for that port—that is, a message from a switch that is closer to the root or equally far from the root but with a smaller ID—the switch stops sending configuration messages over that port. Thus, when the system stabilizes, only the root switch is still generating configuration messages, and the other switches are forwarding these messages only over ports for which they are the designated switch. At this point, a spanning tree has been built, and all the switches are in agreement on which ports are in use for the spanning tree. Only those ports may be used for forwarding data packets.

Let's see how this works with an example. Consider what would happen in Figure 67 if the power had just been restored to a campus, so that all the switches boot at about the same time. All the switches would start off by claiming to be the root. We denote a configuration message from node X in which it claims to be distance d from root node Y as (Y,d,X). Focusing on the activity at S3, a sequence of events would unfold as follows:

- ◉ S3 receives (S2, 0, S2).
- ◉ Since 2 < 3, S3 accepts S2 as root.
- ◉ S3 adds one to the distance advertised by S2 (0) and thus sends (S2, 1, S3) toward S5.
- ◉ Meanwhile, S2 accepts S1 as root because it has the lower ID, and it sends (S1, 1, S2) toward S3.
- ◉ S5 accepts S1 as root and sends (S1, 1, S5) toward S3.
- ◉ S3 accepts S1 as root, and it notes that both S2 and S5 are closer to the root than it is, but S2 has the smaller id, so it remains on S3's path to the root.

This leaves S3 with active ports as shown in Figure 67. Note that Hosts A and B are not able to communicate over the shortest path (via S5) because frames have to "flow up the tree and back down," but that's the price you pay to avoid loops.

Even after the system has stabilized, the root switch continues to send configuration messages periodically, and the other switches continue to forward these messages as just described. Should a particular switch fail, the downstream switches will not receive these configuration messages, and after waiting a specified period of time they will once again claim to be the root, and the algorithm will kick in again to elect a new root and new designated switches.

One important thing to notice is that although the algorithm is able to reconfigure the spanning tree whenever a switch fails, it is not able to forward frames over alternative paths for the sake of routing around a congested switch.

3.2.4 Broadcast and Multicast

The previous discourse centers on the manner in which switches direct unicast frames from one port to another. Switches must have both broadcast and multicast functionalities in order to seamlessly extend a LAN across several networks, as this is their primary objective. Broadcasting is a straightforward process where a switch sends a frame with a destination broadcast address over every active port, save the one it received the frame on. Implementing multicast involves each host independently determining whether or not to accept the message. This is precisely the practical approach. It is important to note that not all hosts belong to a specific multicast group, which means there is room for improvement. More precisely, the spanning tree approach can be expanded to trim networks where multicast frames do not need to be sent. Let's examine a frame that is transmitted by a host A to group M, as shown in Figure 67. If host C is not a member of group M, switch S4 does not need to forward the frames via that network.

How would a given switch learn whether it should forward a multicast frame over a given port? It learns exactly the same way that a switch learns whether it should forward a unicast frame over a particular port—by observing the source addresses that it receives over that port. Of course, groups are not typically the source of frames, so we have to cheat a little. In particular, each host that is a member of group M must periodically send a frame with the address for group M in the source field of the frame header. This frame would have as its destination address the multicast address for the switches.

Although the multicast extension just described was once proposed, it was not widely adopted. Instead, multicast is implemented in exactly the same way as broadcast.

3.2.5 Virtual LANs (VLANs)

An inherent constraint of switches is their lack of scalability. Connecting more than a few switches, in practical terms, is not feasible, with "few" generally referring to a quantity in the range of tens. One explanation for this is that the spanning tree technique exhibits linear scalability, meaning that it does not have a mechanism for establishing a hierarchical structure within the collection of switches. Another explanation is because switches route all broadcast frames. While it is justifiable for all hosts in a confined context (such as a department) to have access to each other's broadcast messages, it is improbable that all hosts in a more extensive environment (such as a major firm or university) would like to be inconvenienced by one another's broadcast messages. In other words, the broadcast function is not able to handle large amounts of data, and as a result, networks based on Layer 2 do not have the ability to handle large-scale operations.

One approach to increasing the scalability is the virtual LAN (VLAN). VLANs allow a single extended LAN to be partitioned into several seemingly separate LANs. Each virtual LAN is assigned an identifier (sometimes called a color), and packets can only travel from one segment to another if both segments have the same identifier. This has the effect of limiting the number of segments in an extended LAN that will receive any given broadcast packet.

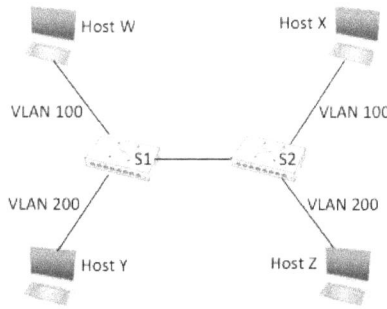

Figure 68. Two virtual LANs share a common backbone.

We can see how VLANs work with an example. Figure 68 shows four hosts and two switches. In the absence of VLANs, any broadcast packet from any host will reach all the other hosts. Now let's suppose that we define the segments connected to hosts W and X as being in one VLAN, which we'll call VLAN 100. We also define the segments that connect to hosts Y and Z as being in VLAN 200. To do this, we need to configure a VLAN ID on each port of switches S1 and S2. The link between S1 and S2 is considered to be in both VLANs.

When a packet sent by host X arrives at switch S2, the switch observes that it came in a port that was configured as being in VLAN 100. It inserts a VLAN header between the Ethernet header and its payload. The interesting part of the VLAN header is the VLAN ID; in this case, that ID is set to 100. The switch now applies its normal rules for forwarding to the packet, with the extra restriction that the packet may not be sent out an interface that is not part of VLAN 100. Thus, under no circumstances will the packet—even a broadcast packet—be sent out the interface to host Z, which is in VLAN 200. The packet, however, is forwarded on to switch S1, which follows the same rules and thus may forward the packet to host W but not to host Y.

An attractive feature of VLANs is that it is possible to change the logical topology without moving any wires or changing any addresses. For example, if we wanted to make the link that connects to host Z be part of VLAN 100 and thus enable X, W, and Z to be on the same virtual LAN, then we would just need to change one piece of configuration on switch S2.

Supporting VLANs requires a fairly simple extension to the original 802.1 header specification, inserting a 12-bit VLAN ID (VID) field between the SrcAddr and Type fields, as shown in Figure 69. (This VID is typically referred to as a VLAN Tag.) There are actually 32-bits inserted in the middle of the header, but the first 16-bits are used to preserve backwards compatibility with the original specification (they use Type = 0x8100 to indicate that this frame includes the VLAN extension); the other four bits hold control information used to prioritize frames. This means it is possible to map $2^{12} = 4096$ virtual networks onto a single physical LAN.

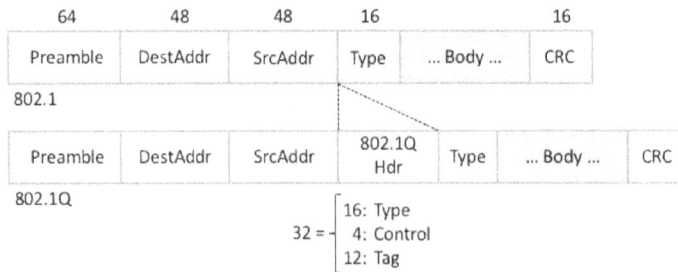

Figure 69. 802.1Q VLAN tag embedded within an Ethernet (802.1) header.

In conclusion, it is worth noting that networks constructed by interconnecting L2 switches have a notable drawback, which is the absence of support for heterogeneity. Switches have limitations in terms of the types of networks they can link. Switches rely on the frame header of the network and hence can only handle networks that have identical address formats. Switches can facilitate the connection between Ethernet and 802.11-based networks because to their same header structure. However, switches are not easily adaptable to other networks having distinct addressing forms, such as ATM, SONET, PON, or the cellular network. The following part elucidates the method to overcome this constraint and expand the size of switched networks to even greater magnitudes.

3.3 Internet (IP)

In the preceding section, we observed that it was feasible to construct LANs of considerable size by employing bridges and LAN switches. However, these methods had some limitations in terms of scalability and the capacity to handle heterogeneity. This section delves into many methods for surpassing the constraints of bridging networks, allowing us to construct extensive, diverse networks with reasonably effective routing. These kind of networks are called internetworks. In the next chapter, we will further explain the process of constructing a genuinely worldwide internetwork. However, for the time being, we will focus on understanding the fundamental principles. Firstly, let us analyze the definition of the term "internetwork" in a more meticulous manner.

3.3.1 What Is an Internetwork?

The word "internetwork," or often just "internet" with a lowercase "i," is used to describe a diverse group of networks that are interconnected to provide a host-to-host packet delivery service. For instance, a large firm may create a private internetwork by linking the local area networks (LANs) at their various sites using dedicated point-to-point links obtained through leasing from the telecommunications carrier. The Internet, denoted with a capital I, refers to the extensively utilized worldwide internetwork that currently connects a significant proportion of networks. Consistent with the fundamental approach of this book, our primary objective is for you to acquire knowledge about the principles of "lowercase i" internetworking. However, we support these concepts by providing real-world illustrations from the "big I" Internet. Another phrase that can cause confusion is the distinction between networks, subnetworks, and internetworks. We will defer the discussion of subnetworks (or subnets) until a later section. Currently, the term "network" refers to either a directly connected or a switched network as explained in the preceding section and chapter. This type of network utilizes a single technology, such as 802.11 or Ethernet. An internetwork refers to a network that is composed of multiple interconnected networks. Occasionally, in order to eliminate any confusion, we designate the networks that we are connecting as physical networks. An internet is a virtual network constructed from a group of tangible networks. Within this particular framework, a grouping of Ethernet segments that are linked together by bridges or switches would continue to be regarded as a unified network.

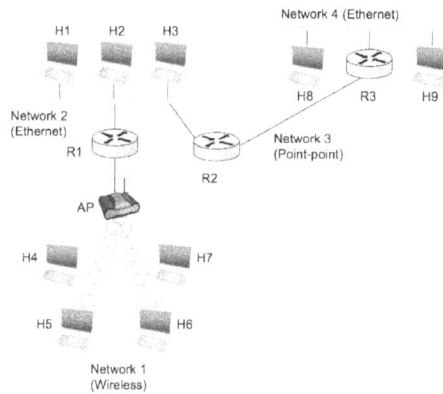

Figure 70. A simple internetwork. H denotes a host and R denotes a router.

Figure 70 shows an example internetwork. An internetwork is often referred to as a "network of networks" because it is made up of lots of smaller networks. In this figure, we see Ethernets, a wireless network, and a point-to-point link. Each of these is a single-technology network. The nodes that interconnect the networks are called routers. They are also sometimes called gateways, but since this term has several other connotations, we restrict our usage to router.

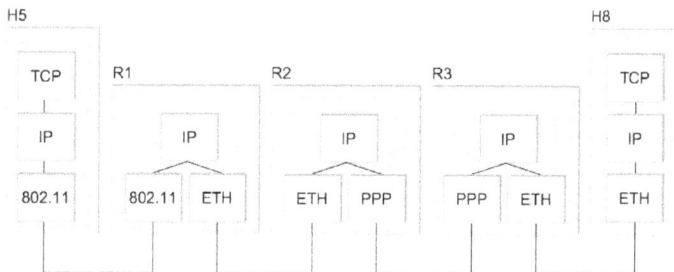

Figure 71. A simple internetwork, showing the protocol layers used to connect H5 to H8 in the above figure. ETH is the protocol that runs over the Ethernet.

The Internet Protocol is the key tool used today to build scalable, heterogeneous internetworks. It was originally known as the Kahn-Cerf protocol after its inventors. One way to think of IP is that it runs on all the nodes (both hosts and routers) in a collection of networks and defines the infrastructure that allows these nodes and networks to function as a single logical internetwork. For example, Figure 71 shows how hosts H5 and H8 are logically connected by the internet in Figure 70, including the protocol graph running on each node. Note that higher-level protocols, such as TCP and UDP, typically run on top of IP on the hosts.

The rest of this and the next chapter are about various aspects of IP. While it is certainly possible to build an internetwork that does not use IP—and in fact, in the early days of the Internet there were alternative solutions—IP is the most interesting case to study simply because of the size of the Internet. Said another way, it is only the IP Internet that has really faced the issue of scale. Thus, it provides the best case study of a scalable internetworking protocol.

L2 VS L3 NETWORKS

As seen in the previous section, an Ethernet can be treated as a point-to-point link interconnecting a pair of switches, with a mesh of interconnected switches forming a Switched Ethernet. This configuration is also known as an L2 Network.

But as we'll discover in this section, an Ethernet (even when arranged in a point-to-point configuration rather than a shared CSMA/CD network) can be treated as a network interconnecting a pair of routers, with a mesh of such routers forming an Internet. This configuration is also known as an L3 Network.

Confusingly, this is because a point-to-point Ethernet is both a link and a network (albeit a trivial two-node network in the second case), depending on whether it's connected to a pair of L2 switches running the spanning tree algorithm, or to a pair of L3 routers running IP (plus the routing protocols described later in this chapter). Why pick one configuration over the other? It partly depends on whether you want the network to be a single broadcast domain (if yes, pick L2), and whether you want the hosts connected to the network to be on different networks (if yes, select L3).

The good news is that when you fully understand the implications of this duality, you will have cleared a major hurdle in mastering modern packet-switched networks.

3.3.2 Service Model

When constructing an internetwork, it is advisable to begin by establishing its service model, which refers to the specific host-to-host services that you intend to offer. The first consideration when establishing a service model for an internetwork is ensuring that a host-to-host service is feasible on each of the underlying physical networks. For instance, it would be ineffective to determine that our internetwork service model would ensure the delivery of each packet in 1 ms or less if there were underlying network technologies that may randomly delay packets. The idea employed in formulating the IP service model was to ensure its simplicity, allowing any potential network technology inside an internetwork to adequately offer the required service. The IP service model consists of two components: an addressing scheme, which facilitates the identification of all hosts in the internetwork, and a datagram (connectionless) model for delivering data. This service paradigm is commonly referred to as "best effort" since while IP makes diligent attempts to send datagrams, it does not provide any assurances or promises. Let's temporarily delay our discussion on the addressing system and focus on examining the data delivery paradigm.

DATAGRAM DELIVERY

The IP datagram is a crucial component of the Internet Protocol. As mentioned previously, a datagram refers to a packet that is transmitted in a connectionless manner via a network. Each datagram contains sufficient information for the network to route the packet to its intended destination, eliminating the need for any pre-established method to instruct the network on how to handle the packet upon arrival. Simply transmit the data, and the network will do its utmost endeavor to deliver it to the intended recipient. The term "best-effort" indicates that if any issues arise, such as packet loss, corruption, misdelivery, or any other failure to reach the intended destination, the network does not take any further action. It simply makes its best attempt and considers that to be its sole responsibility. It exhibits no effort to rectify the failure. This is occasionally referred to as an untrustworthy service. The best-effort, connectionless service is the most basic service that can be requested from an internetwork, and this is its primary advantage. For instance, if you offer a best-effort service on a network that guarantees a dependable service, then you will have a best-effort service that consistently delivers the packets. Conversely, if you own a dependable service model operating on an unreliable network, you would need to incorporate more functionality into the routers to compensate for the shortcomings of the underlying network. One of the primary design objectives of IP was to maintain the routers in a straightforward and uncomplicated manner. The versatility of IP to traverse any network infrastructure is often highlighted as one of its main attributes. It is worth mentioning that several of the technologies that currently utilize IP were not in existence at the time IP was created. Thus yet, no networking technology has emerged that has been deemed too unconventional for IP. IP can be implemented on a network that utilizes carrier pigeons to carry messages. Best-effort delivery encompasses more than simply the possibility of packet loss. Occasionally, packets may be delivered in a non-sequential manner, and it is possible for the same packet to be delivered many times. It is necessary for the higher-level protocols or programs that operate above IP to be cognizant of all potential failure modes.

PACKET FORMAT

Clearly, a key part of the IP service model is the type of packets that can be carried. The IP datagram, like most packets, consists of a header followed by a number of bytes of data. The format of the header is shown in Figure 72. Note that we have adopted a different style of representing packets than the one we used in previous chapters. This is because packet formats at the internetworking layer and above, where we will be focusing our attention for the next few chapters, are almost invariably designed to align on 32-bit boundaries to simplify the task of processing them in software. Thus, the common way of representing them (used in Internet Requests for Comments, for example) is to draw them as a succession of 32-bit words. The top word is the one transmitted first, and the leftmost byte of each word is the one transmitted first. In this representation, you can easily recognize fields that are a multiple of 8 bits long. On the odd occasion when fields are not an even multiple of 8 bits, you can determine the field lengths by looking at the bit positions marked at the top of the packet.

Looking at each field in the IP header, we see that the "simple" model of best-effort datagram delivery still has some subtle features. The Version field specifies the version of IP. The still-assumed version of IP is 4, which is typically called IPv4. Observe that putting this field right at the start of the datagram makes it easy for everything else in the packet format to be redefined in subsequent versions; the header processing software starts off by looking at the version and then branches off to process the rest of the packet according to the appropriate format. The next field, HLen, specifies the length of the header in 32-bit words. When there are no options, which is most of the time, the header is 5 words (20 bytes) long. The 8-bit TOS (type of service) field has had a number of different definitions over the years, but its basic function is to allow packets to be treated differently based on application needs. For example, the TOS value might determine whether or not a packet should be placed in a special queue that receives low delay.

The next 16 bits of the header contain the Length of the datagram, including the header. Unlike the HLen field, the Length field counts bytes rather than words. Thus, the maximum size of an IP datagram is 65,535 bytes. The physical network over which IP is running, however, may not support such long packets. For this reason, IP supports a fragmentation and reassembly process. The second word of the header contains information about fragmentation, and the details of its use are presented in the following section entitled "Fragmentation and Reassembly."

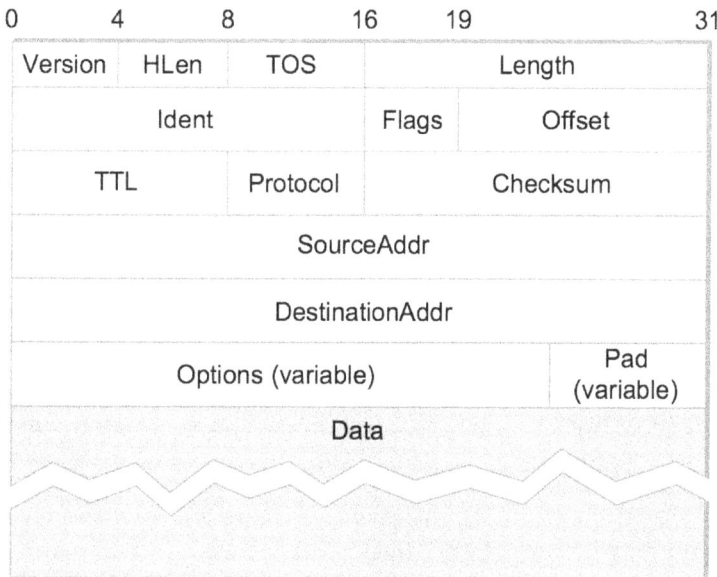

Figure 72. IPv4 packet header.

Moving on to the third word of the header, the next byte is the TTL (time to live) field. Its name reflects its historical meaning rather than the way it is commonly used today. The intent of the field is to catch packets that have been going around in routing loops and discard them, rather than let them consume resources indefinitely. Originally, TTL was set to a specific number of seconds that the packet would be allowed to live, and routers along the path would decrement this field until it reached 0. However, since it was rare for a packet to sit for as long as 1 second in a router, and routers did not all have access to a common clock, most routers just decremented the TTL by 1 as they forwarded the packet. Thus, it became more of a hop count than a timer, which is still a perfectly good way to catch packets that are stuck in routing loops. One subtlety is in the initial setting of this field by the sending host: Set it too high and packets could circulate rather a lot before getting dropped; set it too low and they may not reach their destination. The value 64 is the current default.

The Protocol field is simply a demultiplexing key that identifies the higher-level protocol to which this IP packet should be passed. There are values defined for the TCP (Transmission Control Protocol—6), UDP (User Datagram Protocol—17), and many other protocols that may sit above IP in the protocol graph.

The Checksum is calculated by considering the entire IP header as a sequence of 16-bit words, adding them up using ones' complement arithmetic, and taking the ones' complement of the result. Thus, if any bit in the header is corrupted in transit, the checksum will not contain the correct value upon receipt of the packet. Since a corrupted header may contain an error in the destination address—and, as a result, may have been misdelivered—it makes sense to discard any packet that fails the checksum. It should be noted that this type of checksum does not have the same strong error detection properties as a CRC, but it is much easier to calculate in software.

The last two required fields in the header are the SourceAddr and the DestinationAddr for the packet. The latter is the key to datagram delivery: Every packet contains a full address for its intended destination so that forwarding decisions can be made at each router. The source address is required to allow recipients to decide if they want to accept the packet and to enable them to reply. IP addresses are discussed in a later section—for now, the important thing to know is that IP defines its own global address space, independent of whatever physical networks it runs over. As we will see, this is one of the keys to supporting heterogeneity.

Finally, there may be a number of options at the end of the header. The presence or absence of options may be determined by examining the header length (HLen) field. While options are used fairly rarely, a complete IP implementation must handle them all.

FRAGMENTATION AND REASSEMBLY

One of the problems of providing a uniform host-to-host service model over a heterogeneous collection of networks is that each network technology tends to have its own idea of how large a packet can be. For example, classic Ethernet can accept packets up to 1500 bytes long, but modern-day variants can deliver larger (jumbo) packets that carry up to 9000 bytes of payload. This leaves two choices for the IP service model: Make sure that all IP datagrams are small enough to fit inside one packet on any network technology, or provide a means by which packets can be fragmented and reassembled when they are too big to go over a given network technology. The latter turns out to be a good choice, especially when you consider the fact that new network technologies are always turning up, and IP needs to run over all of them; this would make it hard to pick a suitably small bound on datagram size. This also means that a host will not send needlessly small packets, which wastes bandwidth and consumes processing resources by requiring more headers per byte of data sent.

The central idea here is that every network type has a maximum transmission unit (MTU), which is the largest IP datagram that it can carry in a frame.1 Note that this value is smaller than the largest packet size on that network because the IP datagram needs to fit in the payload of the link-layer frame.

When a host sends an IP datagram, therefore, it can choose any size that it wants. A reasonable choice is the MTU of the network to which the host is directly attached. Then, fragmentation will only be necessary if the path to the destination includes a network with a smaller MTU. Should the transport protocol that sits on top of IP give IP a packet larger than the local MTU, however, then the source host must fragment it.

Fragmentation typically occurs in a router when it receives a datagram that it wants to forward over a network that has an MTU that is smaller than the received datagram. To enable these fragments to be reassembled at the receiving host, they all carry the same identifier in the Ident field. This identifier is chosen by the sending host and is intended to be unique among all the datagrams that might arrive at the destination from this source over some reasonable time period. Since all fragments of the original datagram contain this identifier, the reassembling host will be able to recognize those fragments that go together. Should all the fragments not arrive at the receiving host, the host gives up on the reassembly process and discards the fragments that did arrive. IP does not attempt to recover from missing fragments.

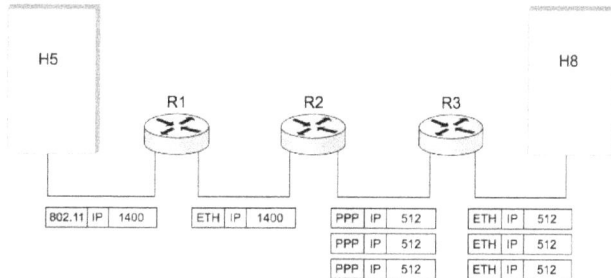

Figure 73. IP datagrams traversing the sequence of physical networks graphed in the earlier figure.

To see what this all means, consider what happens when host H5 sends a datagram to host H8 in the example internet shown in Figure 70. Assuming that the MTU is 1500 bytes for the two Ethernets and the 802.11 network, and 532 bytes for the point-to-point network, then a 1420-byte datagram (20-byte IP header plus 1400 bytes of data) sent from H5 makes it across the 802.11 network and the first Ethernet without fragmentation but must be fragmented into three datagrams at router R2. These three fragments are then forwarded by router R3 across the second Ethernet to the destination host. This situation is illustrated in Figure 73. This figure also serves to reinforce two important points:

⊙ Each fragment is itself a self-contained IP datagram that is transmitted over a sequence of physical networks, independent of the other fragments.

⊙ Each IP datagram is re-encapsulated for each physical network over which it travels.

(a)

Start of header	
Ident = x	0 Offset = 0
Rest of header	
1400 data bytes	

(b)

Start of header	
Ident = x	1 Offset = 0
Rest of header	
512 data bytes	

Start of header	
Ident = x	1 Offset = 64
Rest of header	
512 data bytes	

Start of header	
Ident = x	0 Offset = 128
Rest of header	
376 data bytes	

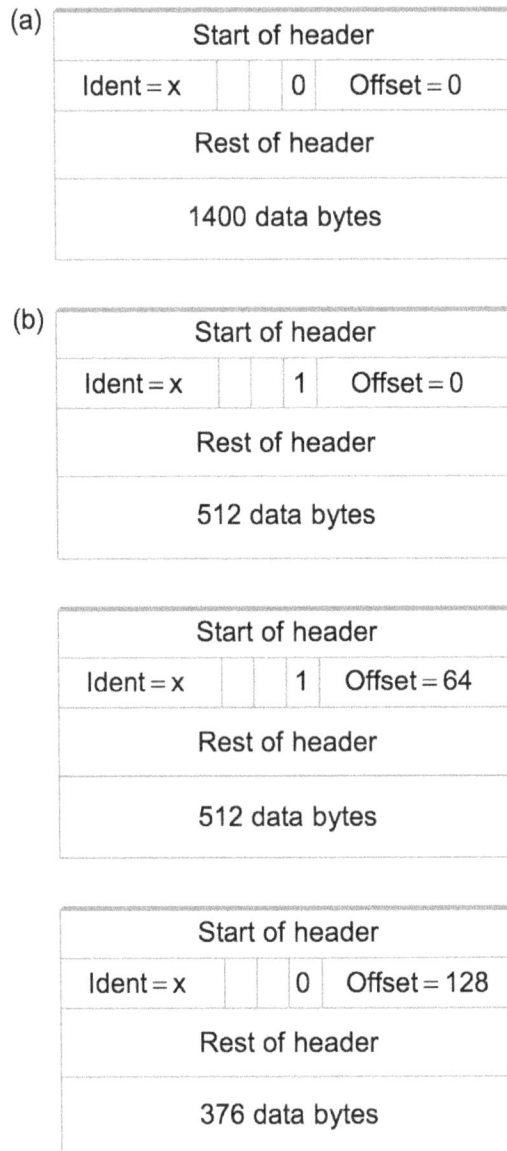

Figure 74. Header fields used in IP fragmentation:
(a) unfragmented packet; (b) fragmented packets.

The fragmentation process can be understood in detail by looking at the header fields of each datagram, as is done in Figure 74. The unfragmented packet, shown at the top, has 1400 bytes of data and a 20-byte IP header. When the packet arrives at router R2, which has an MTU of 532 bytes, it has to be fragmented. A 532-byte MTU leaves 512 bytes for data after the 20-byte IP header, so the first fragment contains 512 bytes of data. The router sets the M bit in the Flags field (see Figure 72), meaning that there are more fragments to follow, and it sets the Offset to 0, since this fragment contains the first part of the original datagram. The data carried in the second fragment starts with the 513th byte of the original data, so the Offset field in this header is set to 64, which is 512/8. Why the division by 8? Because the designers of IP decided that fragmentation should always happen on 8-byte boundaries, which means that the Offset field counts 8-byte chunks, not bytes. (We leave it as an exercise for you to figure out why this design decision was made.) The third fragment contains the last 376 bytes of data, and the offset is now $2 \times 512/8 = 128$. Since this is the last fragment, the M bit is not set.

Observe that the fragmentation process is done in such a way that it could be repeated if a fragment arrived at another network with an even smaller MTU. Fragmentation produces smaller, valid IP datagrams that can be readily reassembled into the original datagram upon receipt, independent of the order of their arrival. Reassembly is done at the receiving host and not at each router.

IP reassembly is far from a simple process. For example, if a single fragment is lost, the receiver will still attempt to reassemble the datagram, and it will eventually give up and have to garbage-collect the resources that were used to perform the failed reassembly. Getting a host to tie up resources needlessly can be the basis of a denial-of-service attack.

For this reason, among others, IP fragmentation is generally considered a good thing to avoid. Hosts are now strongly encouraged to perform "path MTU discovery," a process by which fragmentation is avoided by sending packets that are small enough to traverse the link with the smallest MTU in the path from sender to receiver.

3.3.3 Global Addresses

In the previous discourse on the IP service model, we highlighted that one of its provisions is an addressing system. In order to achieve the capability of transmitting data to any host on any network, it is essential to establish a method for identifying all the hosts. Therefore, it is necessary to establish a universal addressing scheme that ensures no two hosts share the same address. The first essential characteristic that an addressing scheme should possess is global uniqueness.

While Ethernet addresses are really globally unique, this characteristic alone is insufficient to serve as an effective addressing scheme in a big internetwork. Ethernet addresses are devoid of any hierarchical structure and offer minimal information for routing protocols. (Ethernet addresses actually possess a structure for assignment, with the initial 24 bits serving to identify the manufacturer. However, this structure does not offer any valuable information to routing protocols as it is unrelated to network topology.) IP addresses are hierarchical, meaning they consist of multiple pieces that represent a hierarchy inside the internetwork.

IP addresses are composed of two distinct components, commonly known as the network portion and the host portion. This is a highly rational configuration for an internetwork, consisting of numerous interconnected networks. The network portion of an IP address serves to identify the specific network to which a host is connected. In other words, all hosts that are connected to the same network will have identical network portions in their IP addresses. The host portion serves to uniquely identify each individual host within the given network. In the given internetwork diagram in Figure 70, the hosts on network 1 would have identical network portions in their addresses, while their host portions would differ. It should be noted that the routers depicted in Figure 70 are connected to two networks. Each network requires an address for each interface. For instance, router R1, positioned between the wireless network and an Ethernet, possesses an IP address on the interface to the wireless network with a network portion that matches all the hosts on that network. The interface to the Ethernet likewise possesses an IP address with a network portion identical to the hosts on that Ethernet. Considering that a router can be set up as a host with two network interfaces, it is more accurate to see IP addresses as being associated with interfaces rather than hosts. What is the appearance of these hierarchical addresses? In contrast to certain other types of hierarchical addresses, the sizes of the two sections are not uniform across all addresses. Initially, IP addresses were categorized into three distinct classes, as seen in Figure 75, with each class specifying varying sizes for the network and host components. (Additionally, there exist class D addresses which designate a multicast group, and class E addresses which are presently not in use.) Regardless of the situation, the address consists of 32 bits. The class of an IP address is determined by the most important bits. A class A address is indicated by a first bit of 0. A binary value of 10 in the first bit and 0 in the second bit indicates a class B address. A binary number with the first two bits set to 1 and the third bit set to 0 indicates a class C address. Out of the roughly 4 billion potential IP addresses, over 50% belong to class A, 25% belong to class B, and 12.5% belong to class C. Every class designates a specific amount of bits for the network portion of the address and reserves the remaining bits for the host portion. Class A networks consist of 7 bits for the network portion and 24 bits for the host portion. This means that there are only 126 available class A networks (excluding the reserved numbers 0 and 127). However, each of these networks can contain up to 16 million hosts (specifically, $224-2$ hosts, with two reserved values). Class B addresses allocate 14 bits for the network and 16 bits for the host, allowing each class B network to accommodate up to 65,534 hosts. Class C addresses comprise a host part consisting of 8 bits and a network part consisting of 21 bits. Hence, a class C network can accommodate a maximum of 256 distinct host identifiers, resulting in a limit of 254 connected hosts (with one host identification, 255, reserved for broadcast, and 0 being an invalid host number). Nevertheless, the addressing technique is capable of accommodating 221 class C networks.

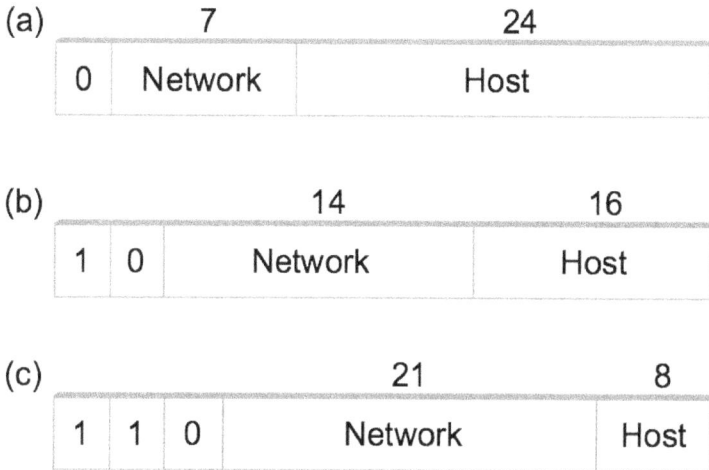

Figure 75. IP addresses: (a) class A; (b) class B; (c) class C.

At first glance, this addressing method offers significant flexibility, enabling networks of varying sizes to be efficiently accommodated. The initial concept was for the Internet to comprise a limited number of expansive wide area networks (designated as class A networks), a moderate number of site- or campus-sized networks (designated as class B networks), and a substantial number of local area networks (designated as class C networks). However, it proved to lack the necessary flexibility, as we would soon discover. Currently, IP addresses are typically "classless"; further explanation of this concept will be provided below. Prior to examining the utilization of IP addresses, it is necessary to consider certain pragmatic aspects, such as the proper method of recording them. IP addresses are often represented as a series of four decimal integers separated by dots, according to convention. Each integer corresponds to the decimal value stored in one byte of the address, beginning with the most significant byte. As an illustration, the IP address of the computer from which this sentence was typed is 171.69.210.245. It is crucial to avoid mixing up IP addresses and Internet domain names, as both have a hierarchical structure. Domain names typically consist of ASCII strings that are separated by dots, such as cs.princeton.edu. The crucial aspect of IP addresses is that they are contained within the headers of IP packets, and it is these addresses that are utilized in IP routers to determine how to forward the packets.

3.3.4 Datagram Forwarding in IP

We are now ready to look at the basic mechanism by which IP routers forward datagrams in an internetwork. Recall from an earlier section that forwarding is the process of taking a packet from an input and sending it out on the appropriate output, while routing is the process of building up the tables that allow the correct output for a packet to be determined. The discussion here focuses on forwarding; we take up routing in a later section.

The main points to bear in mind as we discuss the forwarding of IP datagrams are the following:

- ⊙ Every IP datagram contains the IP address of the destination host.

- ⊙ The network part of an IP address uniquely identifies a single physical network that is part of the larger Internet.

- ⊙ All hosts and routers that share the same network part of their address are connected to the same physical network and can thus communicate with each other by sending frames over that network.

- ⊙ Every physical network that is part of the Internet has at least one router that, by definition, is also connected to at least one other physical network; this router can exchange packets with hosts or routers on either network.

Forwarding IP datagrams can therefore be handled in the following way. A datagram is sent from a source host to a destination host, possibly passing through several routers along the way. Any node, whether it is a host or a router, first tries to establish whether it is connected to the same physical network as the destination. To do this, it compares the network part of the destination address with the network part of the address of each of its network interfaces. (Hosts normally have only one interface, while routers normally have two or more, since they are typically connected to two or more networks.) If a match occurs, then that means that the destination lies on the same physical network as the interface, and the packet can be directly delivered over that network. A later section explains some of the details of this process.

If the node is not connected to the same physical network as the destination node, then it needs to send the datagram to a router. In general, each node will have a choice of several routers, and so it needs to pick the best one, or at least one that has a reasonable chance of getting the datagram closer to its destination. The router that it chooses is known as the next hop router. The router finds the correct next hop by consulting its forwarding table. The forwarding table is conceptually just a list of (NetworkNum, NextHop) pairs. (As we will see below, forwarding tables in practice often contain some additional information related to the next hop.) Normally, there is also a default router that is used if none of the entries in the table matches the destination's network number. For a host, it may be quite acceptable to have a default router and nothing else—this means that all datagrams destined for hosts not on the physical network to which the sending host is attached will be sent out through the default router.

We can describe the datagram forwarding algorithm in the following way:

if (NetworkNum of destination = NetworkNum of one of my interfaces) then

    deliver packet to destination over that interface

else

    if (NetworkNum of destination is in my forwarding table) then

        deliver packet to NextHop router

    else

        deliver packet to default router

For a host with only one interface and only a default router in its forwarding table, this simplifies to

if (NetworkNum of destination = my NetworkNum) then

    deliver packet to destination directly

else

    deliver packet to default router

Let's see how this works in the example internetwork of Figure 70. First, suppose that H1 wants to send a datagram to H2. Since they are on the same physical network, H1 and H2 have the same network number in their IP address. Thus, H1 deduces that it can deliver the datagram directly to H2 over the Ethernet. The one issue that needs to be resolved is how H1 finds out the correct Ethernet address for H2—the resolution mechanism described in a later section addresses this issue.

Now suppose H5 wants to send a datagram to H8. Since these hosts are on different physical networks, they have different network numbers, so H5 deduces that it needs to send the datagram to a router. R1 is the only choice—the default router—so H1 sends the datagram over the wireless network to R1. Similarly, R1 knows that it cannot deliver a datagram directly to H8 because neither of R1's interfaces are on the same network as H8. Suppose R1's default router is R2; R1 then sends the datagram to R2 over the Ethernet. Assuming R2 has the forwarding table shown in Table 10, it looks up H8's network number (network 4) and forwards the datagram over the point-to-point network to R3. Finally, R3, since it is on the same network as H8, forwards the datagram directly to H8.

Table 10. Forwarding table for Router R2.

NetworkNum	NextHop
1	R1
4	R3

Note that it is possible to include the information about directly connected networks in the forwarding table. For example, we could label the network interfaces of router R2 as interface 0 for the point-to-point link (network 3) and interface 1 for the Ethernet (network 2). Then R2 would have the forwarding table shown in Table 11.

Table 11. Complete Forwarding table for Router R2.

NetworkNum	NextHop
1	R1
2	Interface 1
3	Interface 0
4	R3

Thus, for any network number that R2 encounters in a packet, it knows what to do. Either that network is directly connected to R2, in which case the packet can be delivered to its destination over that network, or the network is reachable via some next hop router that R2 can reach over a network to which it is connected. In either case, R2 will use ARP, described below, to find the MAC address of the node to which the packet is to be sent next.

The forwarding table used by R2 is simple enough that it could be manually configured. Usually, however, these tables are more complex and would be built up by running a routing protocol such as one of those described in a later section. Also note that, in practice, the network numbers are usually longer (e.g., 128.96).

We can now see how hierarchical addressing—splitting the address into network and host parts—has improved the scalability of a large network. Routers now contain forwarding tables that list only a set of network numbers rather than all the nodes in the network. In our simple example, that meant that R2 could store the information needed to reach all the hosts in the network (of which there were eight) in a four-entry table. Even if there were 100 hosts on each physical network, R2 would still only need those same four entries. This is a good first step (although by no means the last) in achieving scalability.

Key Takeaway

This illustrates one of the most important principles of building scalable networks: To achieve scalability, you need to reduce the amount of information that is stored in each node and that is exchanged between nodes. The most common way to do that is hierarchical aggregation. IP introduces a two-level hierarchy, with networks at the top level and nodes at the bottom level. We have aggregated information by letting routers deal only with reaching the right network; the information that a router needs to deliver a datagram to any node on a given network is represented by a single aggregated piece of information.

3.3.5 Subnetting and Classless Addressing

The original intent of IP addresses was that the network part would uniquely identify exactly one physical network. It turns out that this approach has a couple of drawbacks. Imagine a large campus that has lots of internal networks and decides to connect to the Internet. For every network, no matter how small, the site needs at least a class C network address. Even worse, for any network with more than 255 hosts, they need a class B address. This may not seem like a big deal, and indeed it wasn't when the Internet was first envisioned, but there are only a finite number of network numbers, and there are far fewer class B addresses than class Cs. Class B addresses tend to be in particularly high demand because you never know if your network might expand beyond 255 nodes, so it is easier to use a class B address from the start than to have to renumber every host when you run out of room on a class C network. The problem we observe here is address assignment inefficiency: A network with two nodes uses an entire class C network address, thereby wasting 253 perfectly useful addresses; a class B network with slightly more than 255 hosts wastes over 64,000 addresses.

Assigning one network number per physical network, therefore, uses up the IP address space potentially much faster than we would like. While we would need to connect over 4 billion hosts to use up all the valid addresses, we only need to connect 214 (about 16,000) class B networks before that part of the address space runs out. Therefore, we would like to find some way to use the network numbers more efficiently.

Assigning many network numbers has another drawback that becomes apparent when you think about routing. Recall that the amount of state that is stored in a node participating in a routing protocol is proportional to the number of other nodes, and that routing in an internet consists of building up forwarding tables that tell a router how to reach different networks. Thus, the more network numbers there are in use, the bigger the forwarding tables get. Big forwarding tables add costs to routers, and they are potentially slower to search than smaller tables for a given technology, so they degrade router performance. This provides another motivation for assigning network numbers carefully.

Subnetting provides a first step to reducing total number of network numbers that are assigned. The idea is to take a single IP network number and allocate the IP addresses with that network number to several physical networks, which are now referred to as subnets. Several things need to be done to make this work. First, the subnets should be close to each other. This is because from a distant point in the Internet, they will all look like a single network, having only one network number between them. This means that a router will only be able to select one route to reach any of the subnets, so they had better all be in the same general direction. A perfect situation in which to use subnetting is a large campus or corporation that has many physical networks. From outside the campus, all you need to know to reach any subnet inside the campus is where the campus connects to the rest of the Internet. This is often at a single point, so one entry in your forwarding table will suffice. Even if there are multiple points at which the campus is connected to the rest of the Internet, knowing how to get to one point in the campus network is still a good start.

The mechanism by which a single network number can be shared among multiple networks involves configuring all the nodes on each subnet with a subnet mask. With simple IP addresses, all hosts on the same network must have the same network number. The subnet mask enables us to introduce a subnet number; all hosts on the same physical network will have the same subnet number, which means that hosts may be on different physical networks but share a single network number. This concept is illustrated in Figure 76.

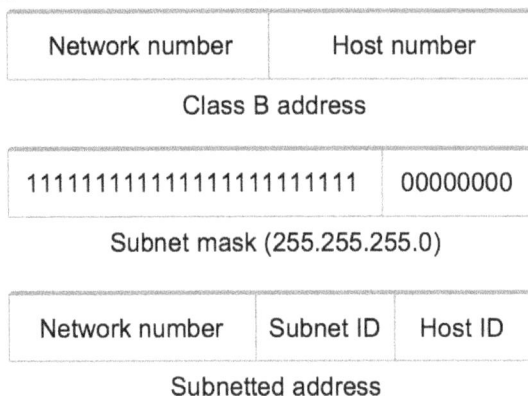

Network number	Host number

Class B address

1111111111111111111111111	00000000

Subnet mask (255.255.255.0)

Network number	Subnet ID	Host ID

Subnetted address

Figure 76. Subnet addressing.

What subnetting means to a host is that it is now configured with both an IP address and a subnet mask for the subnet to which it is attached. For example, host H1 in Figure 77 is configured with an address of 128.96.34.15 and a subnet mask of 255.255.255.128. (All hosts on a given subnet are configured with the same mask; that is, there is exactly one subnet mask per subnet.) The bitwise AND of these two numbers defines the subnet number of the host and of all other hosts on the same subnet. In this case, 128.96.34.15 AND 255.255.255.128 equals 128.96.34.0, so this is the subnet number for the topmost subnet in the figure.

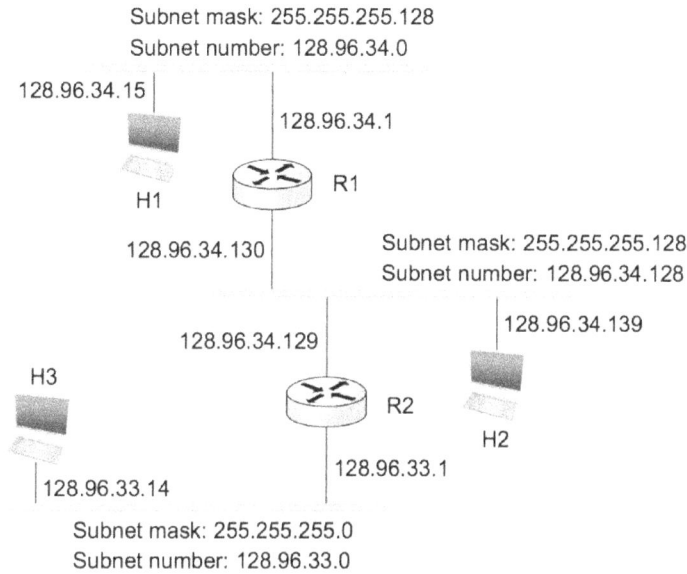

Subnet mask: 255.255.255.128
Subnet number: 128.96.34.0

128.96.34.15

128.96.34.1

H1

R1

128.96.34.130

Subnet mask: 255.255.255.128
Subnet number: 128.96.34.128

128.96.34.139

128.96.34.129

H3

R2

H2

128.96.33.1

128.96.33.14

Subnet mask: 255.255.255.0
Subnet number: 128.96.33.0

Figure 77. An example of subnetting.

When the host wants to send a packet to a certain IP address, the first thing it does is to perform a bitwise AND between its own subnet mask and the destination IP address. If the result equals the subnet number of the sending host, then it knows that the destination host is on the same subnet and the packet can be delivered directly over the subnet. If the results are not equal, the packet needs to be sent to a router to be forwarded to another subnet. For example, if H1 is sending to H2, then H1 ANDs its subnet mask (255.255.255.128) with the address for H2 (128.96.34.139) to obtain 128.96.34.128. This does not match the subnet number for H1 (128.96.34.0) so H1 knows that H2 is on a different subnet. Since H1 cannot deliver the packet to H2 directly over the subnet, it sends the packet to its default router R1.

The forwarding table of a router also changes slightly when we introduce subnetting. Recall that we previously had a forwarding table that consisted of entries of the form (NetworkNum, NextHop). To support subnetting, the table must now hold entries of the form (SubnetNumber, SubnetMask, NextHop). To find the right entry in the table, the router ANDs the packet's destination address with the SubnetMaskfor each entry in turn; if the result matches the SubnetNumber of the entry, then this is the right entry to use, and it forwards the packet to the next hop router indicated. In the example network of Figure 77, router R1 would have the entries shown in Table 12.

Table 12. Example Forwarding Table with Subnetting.

SubnetNumber	SubnetMask	NextHop
128.96.34.0	255.255.255.128	Interface 0
128.96.34.128	255.255.255.128	Interface 1
128.96.33.0	255.255.255.0	R2

Continuing with the example of a datagram from H1 being sent to H2, R1 would AND H2's address (128.96.34.139) with the subnet mask of the first entry (255.255.255.128) and compare the result (128.96.34.128) with the network number for that entry (128.96.34.0). Since this is not a match, it proceeds to the next entry. This time a match does occur, so R1 delivers the datagram to H2 using interface 1, which is the interface connected to the same network as H2.

We can now describe the datagram forwarding algorithm in the following way:

D = destination IP address

for each forwarding table entry (SubnetNumber, SubnetMask, NextHop)

    D1 = SubnetMask & D

    if D1 = SubnetNumber

        if NextHop is an interface

            deliver datagram directly to destination

        else

            deliver datagram to NextHop (a router)

Although not shown in this example, a default route would usually be included in the table and would be used if no explicit matches were found. Note that a naive implementation of this algorithm—one involving repeated ANDing of the destination address with a subnet mask that may not be different every time, and a linear table search—would be very inefficient.

An important consequence of subnetting is that different parts of the internet see the world differently. From outside our hypothetical campus, routers see a single network. In the example above, routers outside the campus see the collection of networks in Figure 77 as just the network 128.96, and they keep one entry in their forwarding tables to tell them how to reach it. Routers within the campus, however, need to be able to route packets to the right subnet. Thus, not all parts of the internet see exactly the same routing information. This is an example of an aggregation of routing information, which is fundamental to scaling of the routing system. The next section shows how aggregation can be taken to another level.

CLASSLESS ADDRESSING

Subnetting has a counterpart, sometimes called supernetting, but more often called Classless Interdomain Routing or CIDR, pronounced "cider." CIDR takes the subnetting idea to its logical conclusion by essentially doing away with address classes altogether. Why isn't subnetting alone sufficient? In essence, subnetting only allows us to split a classful address among multiple subnets, while CIDR allows us to coalesce several classful addresses into a single "supernet." This further tackles the address space inefficiency noted above, and does so in a way that keeps the routing system from being overloaded.

To see how the issues of address space efficiency and scalability of the routing system are coupled, consider the hypothetical case of a company whose network has 256 hosts on it. That is slightly too many for a Class C address, so you would be tempted to assign a class B. However, using up a chunk of address space that could address 65535 to address 256 hosts has an efficiency of only 256/65,535 = 0.39%. Even though subnetting can help us to assign addresses carefully, it does not get around the fact that any organization with more than 255 hosts, or an expectation of eventually having that many, wants a class B address.

The first way you might deal with this issue would be to refuse to give a class B address to any organization that requests one unless they can show a need for something close to 64K addresses, and instead giving them an appropriate number of class C addresses to cover the expected number of hosts. Since we would now be handing out address space in chunks of 256 addresses at a time, we could more accurately match the amount of address space consumed to the size of the organization. For any organization with at least 256 hosts, we can guarantee an address utilization of at least 50%, and typically much more. (Sadly, even if you can justify a request of a class B network number, don't bother, because they were all spoken for long ago.)

This solution, however, raises a problem that is at least as serious: excessive storage requirements at the routers. If a single site has, say, 16 class C network numbers assigned to it, that means every Internet backbone router needs 16 entries in its routing tables to direct packets to that site. This is true even if the path to every one of those networks is the same. If we had assigned a class B address to the site, the same routing information could be stored in one table entry. However, our address assignment efficiency would then be only 16 x 255 / 65,536 = 6.2%.

CIDR, therefore, tries to balance the desire to minimize the number of routes that a router needs to know against the need to hand out addresses efficiently. To do this, CIDR helps us to aggregate routes. That is, it lets us use a single entry in a forwarding table to tell us how to reach a lot of different networks. As noted above it does this by breaking the rigid boundaries between address classes. To understand how this works, consider our hypothetical organization with 16 class C network numbers. Instead of handing out 16 addresses at random, we can hand out a block of contiguous class C addresses. Suppose we assign the class C network numbers from 192.4.16 through 192.4.31. Observe that the top 20 bits of all the addresses in this range are the same (11000000 00000100 0001). Thus, what we have effectively created is a 20-bit network number—something that is between a class B network number and a class C number in terms of the number of hosts that it can support. In other words, we get both the high address efficiency of handing out addresses in chunks smaller than a class B network, and a single network prefix that can be used in forwarding tables. Observe that, for this scheme to work, we need to hand out blocks of class C addresses that share a common prefix, which means that each block must contain a number of class C networks that is a power of two.

CIDR requires a new type of notation to represent network numbers, or prefixes as they are known, because the prefixes can be of any length. The convention is to place a /X after the prefix, where X is the prefix length in bits. So, for the example above, the 20-bit prefix for all the networks 192.4.16 through 192.4.31 is represented as 192.4.16/20. By contrast, if we wanted to represent a single class C network number, which is 24 bits long, we would write it 192.4.16/24. Today, with CIDR being the norm, it is more common to hear people talk about "slash 24" prefixes than class C networks. Note that representing a network address in this way is similar to the(mask, value) approach used in subnetting, as long as masks consist of contiguous bits starting from the most significant bit (which in practice is almost always the case).

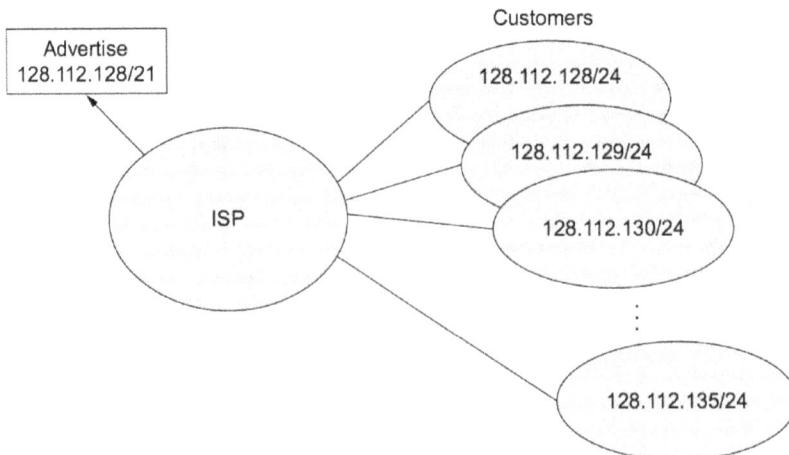

Figure 78. Route aggregation with CIDR.

The capacity to consolidate routes at the periphery of the network, as demonstrated before, is merely the initial phase. Envision a network operated by an Internet service provider that is primarily responsible for delivering

Internet connectivity to a multitude of organizations and campuses, which are its customers. To achieve a higher level of route aggregation, we can allocate prefixes to customers in a manner that allows several customer networks linked to the provider network to use a common, shorter address prefix. Examine the illustration depicted in Figure 78. Suppose that the provider network has issued neighboring 24-bit network prefixes to eight consumers. All of the prefixes have the same initial 21 bits. As all customers can be accessed through the same provider network, the network can promote a single route to all customers by advertising the shared 21-bit prefix that they have in common. Furthermore, the system can accomplish this task even if not all of the 24-bit prefixes have been distributed, as long as the provider retains the authority to distribute those prefixes to a client. An effective method to achieve this is to preallocate a segment of address space to the provider and subsequently allow the network provider to issue addresses from that space to its customers as required. It is important to mention that, unlike the basic example provided, there is no requirement for all customer prefixes to have the same length.

IP FORWARDING REVISITED

Throughout our previous discussions on IP forwarding, we have operated under the assumption that we could locate the network number within a packet and subsequently search for that number in a forwarding table. Nevertheless, now that CIDR has been introduced, it is necessary to reassess this premise. CIDR allows for the use of prefixes with a range of lengths, spanning from 2 to 32 bits. In addition, there are instances where the forwarding database can contain overlapping prefixes, meaning that certain addresses can match several prefixes. As an illustration, it is possible to encounter both 171.69 (a prefix with 16 bits) and 171.69.10 (a prefix with 24 bits) in the forwarding table of a single router. In this scenario, a transmission intended for the IP address 171.69.10.5 unequivocally corresponds to both prefixes. In this scenario, the rule is determined by the principle of "longest match". This means that the packet is matched with the prefix that is the longest, which in this example is 171.69.10. Conversely, if a packet is intended for 171.69.20.5, it would be considered a match for 171.69 and not 171.69.10. If there are no other matching entries in the routing table, 171.69 would be considered the longest match. Efficiently identifying the longest match between an IP address and the variable-length prefixes in a forwarding table has been a productive area of study for an extended period. The algorithm that is widely recognized utilizes a technique called a PATRICIA tree, which was originally created decades before CIDR.

3.3.6 Address Translation (ARP)

In the preceding section, we discussed the process of routing IP datagrams to the correct physical network. However, we did not delve into the matter of how to specifically direct a datagram to a particular host or router within that network. The primary concern is that IP datagrams include IP addresses, yet the physical interface hardware on the intended host or router only comprehends the addressing scheme specific to its network. Therefore, it is necessary to convert the IP address into a link-level address that is appropriate for this network, such as a 48-bit Ethernet address. Subsequently, we can enclose the IP datagram within a frame that includes the link-level address and transmit it to either the final destination or a router that guarantees to forward the datagram towards the final destination.

One simple way to map an IP address into a physical network address is to encode a host's physical address in the host part of its IP address. For example, a host with physical address 00100001 01010001 (which has the decimal value 33 in the upper byte and 81 in the lower byte) might be given the IP address 128.96.33.81. While this solution has been used on some networks, it is limited in that the network's physical addresses can be no more than 16 bits long in this example; they can be only 8 bits long on a class C network. This clearly will not work for 48-bit Ethernet addresses.

A more general solution would be for each host to maintain a table of address pairs; that is, the table would map IP addresses into physical addresses. While this table could be centrally managed by a system administrator and then copied to each host on the network, a better approach would be for each host to dynamically learn the contents of the table using the network. This can be accomplished using the Address Resolution Protocol (ARP). The goal of ARP is to enable each host on a network to build up a table of mappings between IP addresses and link-level addresses. Since these mappings may change over time (e.g., because an Ethernet card in a host breaks and is replaced by a new one with a new address), the entries are timed out periodically and removed. This happens on the order of every 15 minutes. The set of mappings currently stored in a host is known as the ARP cache or ARP table.

ARP takes advantage of the fact that many link-level network technologies, such as Ethernet, support broadcast. If a host wants to send an IP datagram to a host (or router) that it knows to be on the same network (i.e., the sending and receiving nodes have the same IP network number), it first checks for a mapping in the cache. If no mapping is found, it needs to invoke the Address Resolution Protocol over the network. It does this by broadcasting an ARP query onto the network. This query contains the IP address in question (the target IP address). Each host receives the query and checks to see if it matches its IP address. If it does match, the host sends a response message that contains its link-layer address back to the originator of the query. The originator adds the information contained in this response to its ARP table.

The query message also includes the IP address and link-layer address of the sending host. Thus, when a host broadcasts a query message, each host on the network can learn the sender's link-level and IP addresses and place that information in its ARP table. However, not every host adds this information to its ARP table. If the host already has an entry for that host in its table, it "refreshes" this entry; that is, it resets the length of time until it discards the entry. If that host is the target of the query, then it adds the information about the sender to its table, even if it did not already have an entry for that host. This is because there is a good chance that the source host is about to send it an application-level message, and it may eventually have to send a response or ACK back to the source; it will need the source's physical address to do this. If a host is not the target and does not already have an entry for the source in its ARP table, then it does not add an entry for the source. This is because there is no reason to believe that this host will ever need the source's link-level address; there is no need to clutter its ARP table with this information.

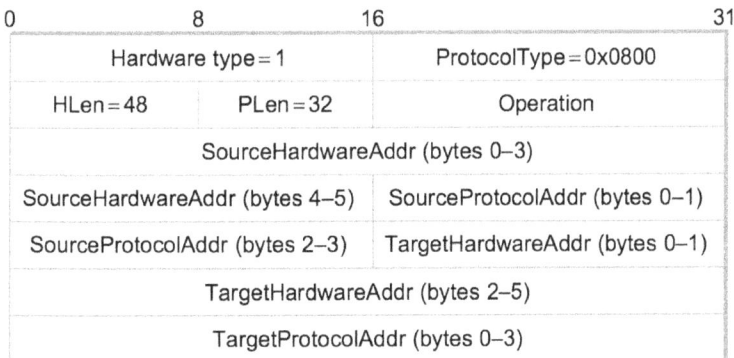

0	8	16	31
Hardware type = 1		ProtocolType = 0x0800	
HLen = 48	PLen = 32	Operation	
SourceHardwareAddr (bytes 0–3)			
SourceHardwareAddr (bytes 4–5)		SourceProtocolAddr (bytes 0–1)	
SourceProtocolAddr (bytes 2–3)		TargetHardwareAddr (bytes 0–1)	
TargetHardwareAddr (bytes 2–5)			
TargetProtocolAddr (bytes 0–3)			

Figure 79. ARP packet format for mapping IP addresses into Ethernet addresses.

Figure 79 shows the ARP packet format for IP-to-Ethernet address mappings. In fact, ARP can be used for lots of other kinds of mappings—the major differences are in the address sizes. In addition to the IP and link-layer addresses of both sender and target, the packet contains

- A HardwareType field, which specifies the type of physical network (e.g., Ethernet)

- A ProtocolType field, which specifies the higher-layer protocol (e.g., IP)

- HLen ("hardware" address length) and PLen ("protocol" address length) fields, which specify the length of the link-layer address and higher-layer protocol address, respectively

- An Operation field, which specifies whether this is a request or a response

- The source and target hardware (Ethernet) and protocol (IP) addresses

Note that the results of the ARP process can be added as an extra column in a forwarding table like the one in Table 10. Thus, for example, when R2 needs to forward a packet to network 2, it not only finds that the next hop is R1, but also finds the MAC address to place on the packet to send it to R1.

Key Takeaway

Thus far, we have observed the fundamental mechanisms that IP offers for managing both heterogeneity and scalability. Regarding heterogeneity, IP starts by establishing a best-effort service model that relies on faulty datagrams and makes few assumptions about the underlying networks. IP enhances the initial concept by introducing two significant elements: (1) a standardized packet structure that allows for effective transmission across networks with varying Maximum Transmission Units (MTUs) through fragmentation and reassembly, and (2) a universal addressing system that identifies all hosts globally, facilitated by the Address Resolution Protocol (ARP) to accommodate diverse physical addressing schemes. Regarding scale, IP employs hierarchical aggregation to minimize the information required for packet forwarding. IP addresses are divided into network and host components. When packets are sent, they are first directed towards the destination network and then delivered to the correct host on that network. [Next]

3.3.7 Host Configuration (DHCP)

The network adaptor is preconfigured with Ethernet addresses by the manufacturer, and this procedure is carefully overseen to guarantee that these addresses are universally distinct. This condition is plainly enough to guarantee that any group of hosts linked to a single Ethernet (even an extended LAN) will possess distinct addresses. Moreover, we just require Ethernet addresses to possess the quality of being one-of-a-kind. Unlike other elements, IP addresses need to be both unique within a certain internetwork and also need to represent the organization of the internetwork. As previously mentioned, IP addresses consist of a network portion and a host portion, with the network portion needing to be same for all hosts inside the same network. Therefore, it is not feasible for the IP address to be pre-set in a host during its manufacturing process, as this would need the manufacturer to have knowledge of the specific networks each host will be connected to. Additionally, it would restrict a host from being able to switch to a different network after being initially attached. Therefore, it is necessary to have the ability to reconfigure IP addresses. Aside from an IP address, a host must possess some additional pieces of information in order to initiate the transmission of packets. One important example is the default router's address, which is where packets are sent when their destination address is not on the same network as the sender host. Many host operating systems offer a method for a system administrator or user to manually set up the necessary IP information for a host. However, this approach has clear disadvantages. One reason is that configuring all the hosts in a big network directly requires a significant amount of effort, particularly considering that these hosts cannot be accessed over a network until they are configured. Furthermore, the configuration process is highly susceptible to errors, as it requires meticulous attention to assigning the correct network number to each host and ensuring that no two hosts are assigned the same IP address. Therefore, it is necessary to employ automated configuration procedures for these specific reasons. The main approach employs a protocol called the Dynamic Host Configuration Protocol (DHCP). DHCP depends on the presence of a DHCP server, which is responsible for supplying configuration information to hosts. There exists a minimum of one Dynamic Host Configuration Protocol (DHCP) server for an administrative domain. At its most basic level, the DHCP server serves as a centralized storage for host configuration information. Let's take into account, for instance, the issue of managing addresses in the internetwork of a sizable corporation. DHCP eliminates the need for network managers to physically visit each host in the firm, armed with a list of addresses and network layout, and manually configure each host. Alternatively, the configuration data for each computer could be saved in the DHCP server and subsequently downloaded by each host upon booting or connecting to the network. Nevertheless, the administrator would continue to select the address for each host to receive, but would simply keep it in the server. The configuration information for each host in this approach is maintained in a database that is indexed by a unique client identification, usually the hardware address (such as the Ethernet address of the network adaptor). An advanced implementation of DHCP eliminates the need for network administrators to manually issue addresses to each individual host. In this arrangement, the DHCP server manages a reservoir of accessible addresses that it distributes to hosts as needed. This significantly decreases the configuration workload for administrators, since they now just need to assign a range of IP addresses (all sharing the same network number) to each network. As the primary objective of DHCP is to reduce the need for human configuration in order for a host to operate, it would be counterproductive if each host had to be manually configured with the address of a DHCP server. Therefore, the initial challenge encountered by DHCP is the issue of server discovery. In order to establish communication with a DHCP server, a host that has just been booted or connected sends a DHCPDISCOVER message to an IP address (255.255.255.255) that serves as a broadcast address. This implies that it will be received by every host and router within that network. (Routers refrain from forwarding these packets to other networks, so preventing their dissemination to the full Internet.) In the most basic scenario, one of these nodes functions as the DHCP server for the network. The server would subsequently respond to the host that initiated the discovery message (while disregarding it from all other nodes). Nevertheless, mandating a DHCP server for each network is not very advantageous, as it results in a potentially significant number of servers that must be accurately and uniformly setup. Therefore, DHCP utilizes the notion of a relay agent. Each network has at least one relay agent, which is setup with a single piece of information: the IP address of the DHCP server. Upon receiving a DHCPDISCOVER message, a relay agent forwards it to the DHCP server over unicast communication and waits for the response. Once received, the relay agent sends the response back to the client that made the initial request. Figure 80 illustrates the procedure of transmitting a message from a host to a distant DHCP server.

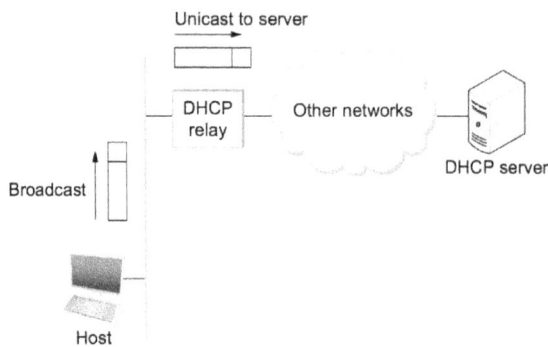

Figure 80. A DHCP relay agent receives a broadcast DHCPDISCOVER message from a host and sends a unicast DHCPDISCOVER to the DHCP server.

Figure 81 below shows the format of a DHCP message. The message is actually sent using a protocol called the User Datagram Protocol (UDP) that runs over IP. UDP is discussed in detail in the next chapter, but the only interesting thing it does in this context is to provide a demultiplexing key that says, "This is a DHCP packet."

Figure 81. DHCP packet format.

DHCP is derived from an earlier protocol called BOOTP, and some of the packet fields are thus not strictly relevant to host configuration. When trying to obtain configuration information, the client puts its hardware address (e.g., its Ethernet address) in the chaddr field. The DHCP server replies by filling in the yiaddr ("your" IP address) field and sending it to the client. Other information such as the default router to be used by this client can be included in the options field.

In the case where DHCP dynamically assigns IP addresses to hosts, it is clear that hosts cannot keep addresses indefinitely, as this would eventually cause the server to exhaust its address pool. At the same time, a host cannot be depended upon to give back its address, since it might have crashed, been unplugged from the network, or been turned off. Thus, DHCP allows addresses to be leased for some period of time. Once the lease expires, the server is free to return that address to its pool. A host with a leased address clearly needs to renew the lease periodically if in fact it is still connected to the network and functioning correctly.

Key Takeaway

DHCP illustrates an important aspect of scaling: the scaling of network management. While discussions of scaling often focus on keeping the state in network devices from growing too fast, it is important to pay attention to the growth of network management complexity. By allowing network managers to configure a range of IP addresses per network rather than one IP address per host, DHCP improves the manageability of a network.

Note that DHCP may also introduce some more complexity into network management, since it makes the binding between physical hosts and IP addresses much more dynamic. This may make the network manager's job more difficult if, for example, it becomes necessary to locate a malfunctioning host.

3.3.8 Error Reporting (ICMP)

The next issue is how the Internet treats errors. While IP is perfectly willing to drop datagrams when the going gets tough—for example, when a router does not know how to forward the datagram or when one fragment of a datagram fails to arrive at the destination—it does not necessarily fail silently. IP is always configured with a companion protocol, known as the Internet Control Message Protocol (ICMP), that defines a collection of error messages that are sent back to the source host whenever a router or host is unable to process an IP datagram successfully. For example, ICMP defines error messages indicating that the destination host is unreachable (perhaps due to a link failure), that the reassembly process failed, that the TTL had reached 0, that the IP header checksum failed, and so on.

ICMP also defines a handful of control messages that a router can send back to a source host. One of the most useful control messages, called an ICMP-Redirect, tells the source host that there is a better route to the destination. ICMP-Redirects are used in the following situation. Suppose a host is connected to a network that has two routers attached to it, called R1 and R2, where the host uses R1 as its default router. Should R1 ever receive a datagram from the host, where based on its forwarding table it knows that R2 would have been a better choice for a particular destination address, it sends an ICMP-Redirect back to the host, instructing it to use R2 for all future datagrams addressed to that destination. The host then adds this new route to its forwarding table.

ICMP also provides the basis for two widely used debugging tools, ping and traceroute. Ping uses ICMP echo messages to determine if a node is reachable and alive. traceroute uses a slightly non-intuitive technique to determine the set of routers along the path to a destination, which is the topic for one of the exercises at the end of this chapter.

3.3.9 Virtual Networks and Tunnels

We conclude our introduction to IP by considering an issue you might not have anticipated, but one that is increasingly important. Our discussion up to this point has focused on making it possible for nodes on different networks to communicate with each other in an unrestricted way. This is usually the goal in the Internet—everybody wants to be able to send email to everybody, and the creator of a new website wants to reach the widest possible audience. However, there are many situations where more controlled connectivity is required. An important example of such a situation is the virtual private network (VPN).

The term VPN is heavily overused and definitions vary, but intuitively we can define a VPN by considering first the idea of a private network. Corporations with many sites often build private networks by leasing circuits from the phone companies and using those lines to interconnect sites. In such a network, communication is restricted to take place only among the sites of that corporation, which is often desirable for security reasons. To make a private network virtual, the leased transmission lines—which are not shared with any other corporations—would be replaced by some sort of shared network. A virtual circuit (VC) is a very reasonable replacement for a leased line because it still provides a logical point-to-point connection between the corporation's sites. For example, if corporation X has a VC from site A to site B, then clearly it can send packets between sites A and B. But there is no way that corporation Y can get its packets delivered to site B without first establishing its own virtual circuit to site B, and the establishment of such a VC can be administratively prevented, thus preventing unwanted connectivity between corporation X and corporation Y.

Figure 82(a) shows two private networks for two separate corporations. In Figure 82(b) they are both migrated to a virtual circuit network. The limited connectivity of a real private network is maintained, but since the private networks now share the same transmission facilities and switches we say that two virtual private networks have been created.

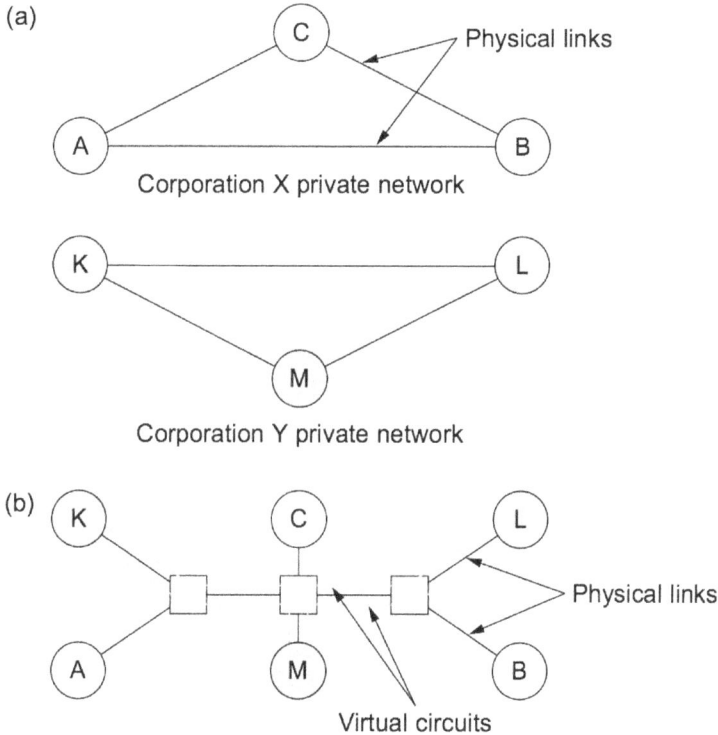

Figure 82. An example of virtual private networks: (a) two separate private networks; (b) two virtual private networks sharing common switches.

In Figure 82, a virtual circuit network (using ATM, for example) is used to provide the controlled connectivity among sites. It is also possible to provide a similar function using an IP network to provide the connectivity. However, we cannot just connect the various corporations' sites to a single internetwork because that would provide connectivity between corporation X and corporation Y, which we wish to avoid. To solve this problem, we need to introduce a new concept, the IP tunnel.

We can think of an IP tunnel as a virtual point-to-point link between a pair of nodes that are actually separated by an arbitrary number of networks. The virtual link is created within the router at the entrance to the tunnel by providing it with the IP address of the router at the far end of the tunnel. Whenever the router at the entrance of the tunnel wants to send a packet over this virtual link, it encapsulates the packet inside an IP datagram. The destination address in the IP header is the address of the router at the far end of the tunnel, while the source address is that of the encapsulating router.

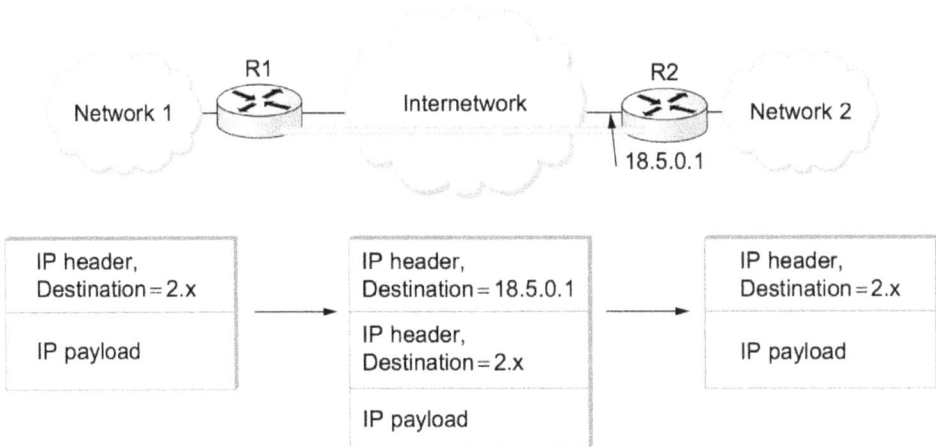

Figure 83. A tunnel through an internetwork. 18.5.0.1 is the address of R2 that can be reached from R1 across the internetwork.

Within the forwarding table of the router located at the entrance of the tunnel, this virtual link appears similar to a regular link. Take into account, as an illustration, the network depicted in Figure 83. A tunnel has been established between R1 and R2, with a virtual interface number of 0 assigned to it. The forwarding table in R1 may resemble Table 13.

Table 13. Forwarding Table for Router R1.

NetworkNum	NextHop
1	Interface 0
2	Virtual interface 0
Default	Interface 1

R1 has two physical interfaces. Interface 0 connects to network 1; interface 1 connects to a large internetwork and is thus the default for all traffic that does not match something more specific in the forwarding table. In addition, R1 has a virtual interface, which is the interface to the tunnel. Suppose R1 receives a packet from network 1 that contains an address in network 2. The forwarding table says this packet should be sent out virtual interface 0. In order to send a packet out this interface, the router takes the packet, adds an IP header addressed to R2, and then proceeds to forward the packet as if it had just been received. R2's address is 18.5.0.1; since the network number of this address is 18, not 1 or 2, a packet destined for R2 will be forwarded out the default interface into the internetwork.

Once the packet leaves R1, it looks to the rest of the world like a normal IP packet destined to R2, and it is forwarded accordingly. All the routers in the internetwork forward it using normal means, until it arrives at R2. When R2 receives the packet, it finds that it carries its own address, so it removes the IP header and looks at the payload of the packet. What it finds is an inner IP packet whose destination address is in network 2. R2 now processes this packet like any other IP packet it receives. Since R2 is directly connected to network 2, it forwards the packet on to that network. Figure 83 shows the change in encapsulation of the packet as it moves across the network.

While R2 is acting as the endpoint of the tunnel, there is nothing to prevent it from performing the normal functions of a router. For example, it might receive some packets that are not tunneled, but that are addressed to networks that it knows how to reach, and it would forward them in the normal way.

You might wonder why anyone would want to go to all the trouble of creating a tunnel and changing the encapsulation of a packet as it goes across an internetwork. One reason is security. Supplemented with encryption, a tunnel can become a very private sort of link across a public network. Another reason may be that R1 and R2 have some capabilities that are not widely available in the intervening networks, such as multicast routing. By connecting these routers with a tunnel, we can build a virtual network in which all the routers with this capability appear to be directly connected. A third reason to build tunnels is to carry packets from protocols other than IP across an IP network. As long as the routers at either end of the tunnel know how to handle these other protocols, the IP tunnel looks to them like a point-to-point link over which they can send non-IP packets. Tunnels also provide a mechanism by which we can force a packet to be delivered to a particular place even if its original header—the one that gets encapsulated inside the tunnel header—might suggest that it should go somewhere else. Thus, we see that tunneling is a powerful and quite general technique for building virtual links across internetworks. So general, in fact, that the technique recurses, with the most common use case being to tunnel IP over IP.

Tunneling does have its downsides. One is that it increases the length of packets; this might represent a significant waste of bandwidth for short packets. Longer packets might be subject to fragmentation, which has its own set of drawbacks. There may also be performance implications for the routers at either end of the tunnel, since they need to do more work than normal forwarding as they add and remove the tunnel header. Finally, there is a management cost for the administrative entity that is responsible for setting up the tunnels and making sure they are correctly handled by the routing protocols.

3.4 Routing

Up until this point in the chapter, we have made the assumption that the switches and routers had sufficient understanding of the network architecture to make informed decisions about which port to use for each packet's output. For virtual circuits, routing is just a concern for the initial connection request packet. All following packets will follow the exact same path as the request. In datagram networks, such as IP networks, routing is a concern for each every packet. Regardless of the scenario, a switch or router must have the capability to examine a destination address and thereafter determine the optimal output port for transmitting a packet to that address. As previously demonstrated, the switch determines this outcome by referring to a forwarding table. The primary issue in routing is the acquisition of information in the forwarding tables of switches and routers.

Key Takeaway

We restate an important distinction, which is often neglected, between forwarding and routing. Forwarding consists of receiving a packet, looking up its destination address in a table, and sending the packet in a direction determined by that table. We saw several examples of forwarding in the preceding section. It is a simple and well-defined process performed locally at each node, and is often referred to as the network's data plane. Routing is the process by which forwarding tables are built. It depends on complex distributed algorithms, and is often referred to as the network's control plane.

While the terms forwarding table and routing table are sometimes used interchangeably, we will make a distinction between them here. The forwarding table is used when a packet is being forwarded and so must contain enough information to accomplish the forwarding function. This means that a row in the forwarding table contains the mapping from a network prefix to an outgoing interface and some MAC information, such as the Ethernet address of the next hop. The routing table, on the other hand, is the table that is built up by the routing algorithms as a precursor to building the forwarding table. It generally contains mappings from network prefixes to next hops. It may also contain information about how this information was learned, so that the router will be able to decide when it should discard some information.

Whether the routing table and forwarding table are actually separate data structures is something of an implementation choice, but there are numerous reasons to keep them separate. For example, the forwarding table needs to be structured to optimize the process of looking up an address when forwarding a packet, while the routing table needs to be optimized for the purpose of calculating changes in topology. In many cases, the forwarding table may even be implemented in specialized hardware, whereas this is rarely if ever done for the routing table.

Table 14 gives an example of a row from a routing table, which tells us that network prefix 18/8 is to be reached by a next hop router with the IP address 171.69.245.10

Table 14. Example row from a routing table.

Prefix/Length	Next Hop
18/8	171.69.245.10

In contrast, Table 15 gives an example of a row from a forwarding table, which contains the information about exactly how to forward a packet to that next hop: Send it out interface number 0 with a MAC address of 8:0:2b:e4:b:1:2. Note that the last piece of information is provided by the Address Resolution Protocol.

Table 15. Example row from a forwarding table.

Prefix/Length	Interface	MAC Address
18/8	if0	8:0:2b:e4:b:1:2

Before getting into the details of routing, we need to remind ourselves of the key question we should be asking anytime we try to build a mechanism for the Internet: "Does this solution scale?" The answer for the algorithms and protocols described in this section is "not so much." They are designed for networks of fairly modest size—up to a few hundred nodes, in practice. However, the solutions we describe do serve as a building block for a hierarchical routing infrastructure that is used in the Internet today. Specifically, the protocols described in this section are collectively known as intradomain routing protocols, or interior gateway protocols (IGPs). To understand these terms, we need to define a routing domain. A good working definition is an internetwork in which all the routers are under the same administrative control (e.g., a single university campus, or the network of a single Internet Service Provider). The relevance of this definition will become apparent in the next chapter when we look at interdomain routing protocols. For now, the important thing to keep in mind is that we are considering the problem of routing in the context of small to midsized networks, not for a network the size of the Internet.

3.4.1 Network as a Graph

Routing is, in essence, a problem of graph theory. Figure 84 shows a graph representing a network. The nodes of the graph, labeled A through F, may be hosts, switches, routers, or networks. For our initial discussion, we will focus on the case where the nodes are routers. The edges of the graph correspond to the network links. Each edge has an associated cost, which gives some indication of the desirability of sending traffic over that link. A discussion of how edge costs are assigned is given in a later section.

Note that the example networks (graphs) used throughout this chapter have undirected edges that are assigned a single cost. This is actually a slight simplification. It is more accurate to make the edges directed, which typically means that there would be a pair of edges between each node—one flowing in each direction, and each with its own edge cost.

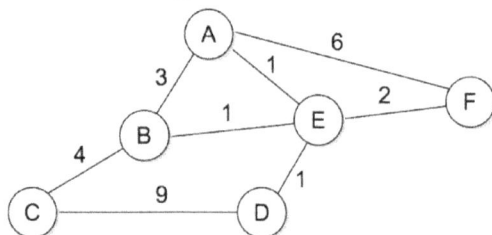

Figure 84. Network represented as a graph.

The basic problem of routing is to find the lowest-cost path between any two nodes, where the cost of a path equals the sum of the costs of all the edges that make up the path. For a simple network like the one in Figure 84, you could imagine just calculating all the shortest paths and loading them into some nonvolatile storage on each node. Such a static approach has several shortcomings:

⊙ It does not deal with node or link failures.

⊙ It does not consider the addition of new nodes or links.

⊙ It implies that edge costs cannot change, even though we might reasonably wish to have link costs change over time (e.g., assigning high cost to a link that is heavily loaded).

For these reasons, routing is achieved in most practical networks by running routing protocols among the nodes. These protocols provide a distributed, dynamic way to solve the problem of finding the lowest cost path in the presence of link and node failures and changing edge costs. Note the word distributed in the previous sentence; it is difficult to make centralized solutions scalable, so all the widely used routing protocols use distributed algorithms.

The distributed nature of routing algorithms is one of the main reasons why this has been such a rich field of research and development—there are a lot of challenges in making distributed algorithms work well. For example, distributed algorithms raise the possibility that two routers will at one instant have different ideas about the shortest path to some destination. In fact, each one may think that the other one is closer to the destination and decide to send packets to the other one. Clearly, such packets will be stuck in a loop until the discrepancy between the two routers is resolved, and it would be good to resolve it as soon as possible. This is just one example of the type of problem routing protocols must address.

To begin our analysis, we assume that the edge costs in the network are known. We will examine the two main classes of routing protocols: distance vector and link state. In a later section, we return to the problem of calculating edge costs in a meaningful way.

3.4 2 Distance-Vector (RIP)

The idea behind the distance-vector algorithm is suggested by its name. (The other common name for this class of algorithm is Bellman-Ford, after its inventors.) Each node constructs a one-dimensional array (a vector) containing the "distances" (costs) to all other nodes and distributes that vector to its immediate neighbors. The starting assumption for distance-vector routing is that each node knows the cost of the link to each of its directly connected neighbors. These costs may be provided when the router is configured by a network manager. A link that is down is assigned an infinite cost.

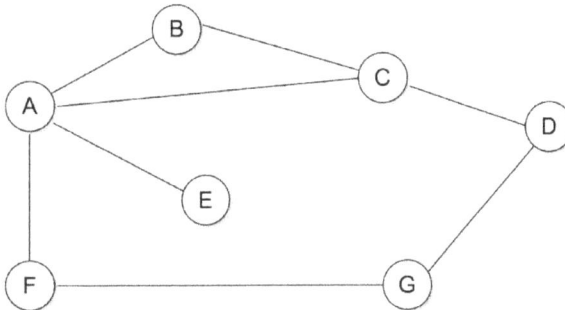

Figure 85. Distance-vector routing: an example network.

Table 16. Initial Distances Stored at Each Node (Global View).

	A	B	C	D	E	F	G
A	0	1	1	∞	1	1	∞
B	1	0	1	∞	∞	∞	∞
C	1	1	0	1	∞	∞	∞
D	∞	∞	1	0	∞	∞	1
E	1	∞	∞	∞	0	∞	∞
F	1	∞	∞	∞	∞	0	1
G	∞	∞	∞	1	∞	1	0

To see how a distance-vector routing algorithm works, it is easiest to consider an example like the one depicted in Figure 85. In this example, the cost of each link is set to 1, so that a least-cost path is simply the one with the fewest hops. (Since all edges have the same cost, we do not show the costs in the graph.) We can represent each node's knowledge about the distances to all other nodes as a table like Table 16. Note that each node knows only the information in one row of the table (the one that bears its name in the left column). The global view that is presented here is not available at any single point in the network.

We may consider each row in Table 16 as a list of distances from one node to all other nodes, representing the current beliefs of that node. Initially, each node sets a cost of 1 to its directly connected neighbors and ∞ to all other nodes. Thus, A initially believes that it can reach B in one hop and that D is unreachable. The routing table stored at A reflects this set of beliefs and includes the name of the next hop that A would use to reach any reachable node. Initially, then, A's routing table would look like Table 17.

Table 17. Initial Routing Table at Node A.

Destination	Cost	NextHop
B	1	B
C	1	C
D	∞	—
E	1	E
F	1	F
G	∞	—

The next step in distance-vector routing is that every node sends a message to its directly connected neighbors containing its personal list of distances. For example, node F tells node A that it can reach node G at a cost of 1; A also knows it can reach F at a cost of 1, so it adds these costs to get the cost of reaching G by means of F. This total cost of 2 is less than the current cost of infinity, so A records that it can reach G at a cost of 2 by going through F. Similarly, A learns from C that D can be reached from C at a cost of 1; it adds this to the cost of reaching C (1) and decides that D can be reached via C at a cost of 2, which is better than the old cost of infinity. At the same time, A learns from C that B can be reached from C at a cost of 1, so it concludes that the cost of reaching B via C is 2. Since this is worse than the current cost of reaching B (1), this new information is ignored. At this point, A can update its routing table with costs and next hops for all nodes in the network. The result is shown in Table 18.

Table 18. Final Routing Table at Node A.

Destination	Cost	NextHop
B	1	B
C	1	C
D	2	C
E	1	E
F	1	F
G	2	F

In the absence of any topology changes, it takes only a few exchanges of information between neighbors before each node has a complete routing table. The process of getting consistent routing information to all the nodes is called convergence. Table 19 shows the final set of costs from each node to all other nodes when routing has converged. We must stress that there is no one node in the network that has all the information in this table—each node only knows about the contents of its own routing table. The beauty of a distributed algorithm like this is that it enables all nodes to achieve a consistent view of the network in the absence of any centralized authority.

Table 19. Final Distances Stored at Each Node (Global View).

	A	B	C	D	E	F	G
A	0	1	1	2	1	1	2
B	1	0	1	2	2	2	3
C	1	1	0	1	2	2	2
D	2	2	1	0	3	2	1
E	1	2	2	3	0	2	3
F	1	2	2	2	2	0	1
G	2	3	2	1	3	1	0

There are a few details to fill in before our discussion of distance-vector routing is complete. First we note that there are two different circumstances under which a given node decides to send a routing update to its neighbors. One of these circumstances is the periodic update. In this case, each node automatically sends an update message every so often, even if nothing has changed. This serves to let the other nodes know that this node is still running. It also makes sure that they keep getting information that they may need if their current routes become unviable. The frequency of these periodic updates varies from protocol to protocol, but it is typically on the order of several seconds to several minutes. The second mechanism, sometimes called a triggered update, happens whenever a node notices a link failure or receives an update from one of its neighbors that causes it to change one of the routes in its routing table. Whenever a node's routing table changes, it sends an update to its neighbors, which may lead to a change in their tables, causing them to send an update to their neighbors.

Now consider what happens when a link or node fails. The nodes that notice first send new lists of distances to their neighbors, and normally the system settles down fairly quickly to a new state. As to the question of how a node detects a failure, there are a couple of different answers. In one approach, a node continually tests the link to another node by sending a control packet and seeing if it receives an acknowledgment. In another approach, a node determines that the link (or the node at the other end of the link) is down if it does not receive the expected periodic routing update for the last few update cycles.

To understand what happens when a node detects a link failure, consider what happens when F detects that its link to G has failed. First, F sets its new distance to G to infinity and passes that information along to A. Since A knows that its 2-hop path to G is through F, A would also set its distance to G to infinity. However, with the next update from C, A would learn that C has a 2-hop path to G. Thus, A would know that it could reach G in 3 hops through C, which is less than infinity, and so A would update its table accordingly. When it advertises this to F, node F would learn that it can reach G at a cost of 4 through A, which is less than infinity, and the system would again become stable.

Unfortunately, slightly different circumstances can prevent the network from stabilizing. Suppose, for example, that the link from A to E goes down. In the next round of updates, A advertises a distance of infinity to E, but B and C advertise a distance of 2 to E. Depending on the exact timing of events, the following might happen: Node B, upon hearing that E can be reached in 2 hops from C, concludes that it can reach E in 3 hops and advertises this to A; node A concludes that it can reach E in 4 hops and advertises this to C; node C concludes that it can reach E in 5 hops; and so on. This cycle stops only when the distances reach some number that is large enough to be considered infinite. In the meantime, none of the nodes actually knows that E is unreachable, and the routing tables for the network do not stabilize. This situation is known as the count to infinity problem.

There are several partial solutions to this problem. The first one is to use some relatively small number as an approximation of infinity. For example, we might decide that the maximum number of hops to get across a certain network is never going to be more than 16, and so we could pick 16 as the value that represents infinity. This at least bounds the amount of time that it takes to count to infinity. Of course, it could also present a problem if our network grew to a point where some nodes were separated by more than 16 hops.

One technique to improve the time to stabilize routing is called split horizon. The idea is that when a node sends a routing update to its neighbors, it does not send those routes it learned from each neighbor back to that neighbor. For example, if B has the route (E, 2, A) in its table, then it knows it must have learned this route from A, and so whenever B sends a routing update to A, it does not include the route (E, 2) in that update. In a stronger variation of split horizon, called split horizon with poison reverse, B actually sends that route back to A, but it puts negative information in the route to ensure that A will not eventually use B to get to E. For example, B sends the route (E, ∞) to A. The problem with both of these techniques is that they only work for routing loops that involve two nodes. For larger routing loops, more drastic measures are called for. Continuing the above example, if B and C had waited for a while after hearing of the link failure from A before advertising routes to E, they would have found that neither of them really had a route to E. Unfortunately, this approach delays the convergence of the protocol; speed of convergence is one of the key advantages of its competitor, link-state routing, the subject of a later section.

Implementation

The code that implements this algorithm is very straightforward; we give only some of the basics here. Structure Route defines each entry in the routing table, and constant MAX_TTL specifies how long an entry is kept in the table before it is discarded.

```
#define MAX_ROUTES    128    /* maximum size of routing table */
#define MAX_TTL       120    /* time (in seconds) until route expires */


typedef struct {
   NodeAddr  Destination;   /* address of destination */
   NodeAddr  NextHop;       /* address of next hop */
   int       Cost;       /* distance metric */
   u_short   TTL;         /* time to live */
} Route;


int     numRoutes = 0;
Route   routingTable[MAX_ROUTES];
```

The routine that updates the local node's routing table based on a new route is given by mergeRoute. Although not shown, a timer function periodically scans the list of routes in the node's routing table, decrements the TTL (time to live) field of each route, and discards any routes that have a time to live of 0. Notice, however, that the TTL field is reset to MAX_TTL any time the route is reconfirmed by an update message from a neighboring node.

```
void
mergeRoute (Route *new)
{
   int i;

   for (i = 0; i < numRoutes; ++i)
   {
```

```
  if (new->Destination == routingTable[i].Destination)
  {
    if (new->Cost + 1 < routingTable[i].Cost)
    {
      /* found a better route: */
      break;
    } else if (new->NextHop == routingTable[i].NextHop) {
      /* metric for current next-hop may have changed: */
      break;
    } else {
      /* route is uninteresting---just ignore it */
      return;
    }
  }
}
if (i == numRoutes)
{
  /* this is a completely new route; is there room for it? */
  if (numRoutes < MAXROUTES)
  {
    ++numRoutes;
  } else {
    /* can`t fit this route in table so give up */
    return;
  }
}
routingTable[i] = *new;
/* reset TTL */
routingTable[i].TTL = MAX_TTL;
/* account for hop to get to next node */
++routingTable[i].Cost;
```

```
}
```

Finally, the procedure updateRoutingTable is the main routine that calls mergeRoute to incorporate all the routes contained in a routing update that is received from a neighboring node.

```
void

updateRoutingTable (Route *newRoute, int numNewRoutes)

{

    int i;


    for (i=0; i < numNewRoutes; ++i)

    {

        mergeRoute(&newRoute[i]);

    }

}
```

ROUTING INFORMATION PROTOCOL (RIP)

One of the more widely used routing protocols in IP networks is the Routing Information Protocol (RIP). Its widespread use in the early days of IP was due in no small part to the fact that it was distributed along with the popular Berkeley Software Distribution (BSD) version of Unix, from which many commercial versions of Unix were derived. It is also extremely simple. RIP is the canonical example of a routing protocol built on the distance-vector algorithm just described.

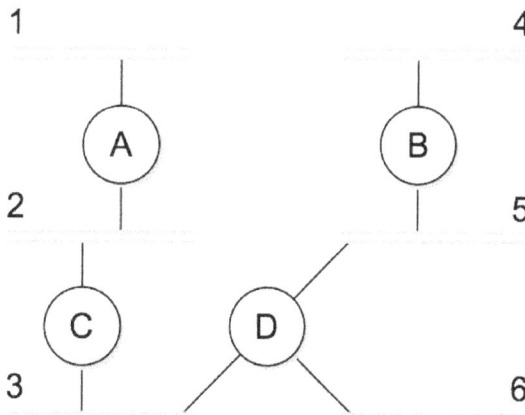

Figure 86. Example network running RIP.

Routing protocols in internetworks differ very slightly from the idealized graph model described above. In an internetwork, the goal of the routers is to learn how to forward packets to various networks. Thus, rather than advertising the cost of reaching other routers, the routers advertise the cost of reaching networks. For example, in Figure 86, router C would advertise to router A the fact that it can reach networks 2 and 3 (to which it is directly connected) at a cost of 0, networks 5 and 6 at cost 1, and network 4 at cost 2.

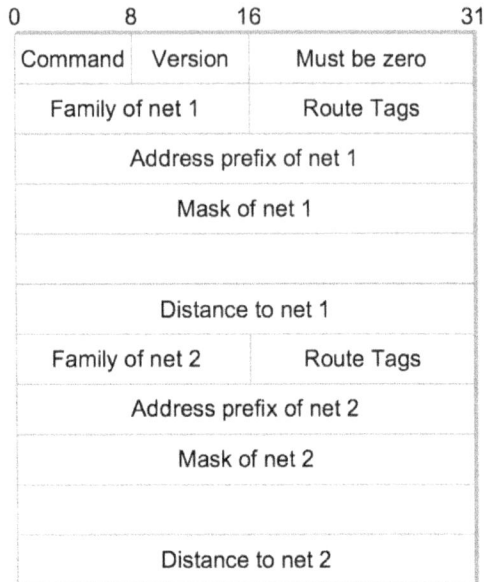

0	8	16	31
Command	Version	Must be zero	
Family of net 1		Route Tags	
Address prefix of net 1			
Mask of net 1			
Distance to net 1			
Family of net 2		Route Tags	
Address prefix of net 2			
Mask of net 2			
Distance to net 2			

Figure 87. RIPv2 packet format.

We can see evidence of this in the RIP (version 2) packet format in Figure 87. The majority of the packet is taken up with (address, mask, distance) triples. However, the principles of the routing algorithm are just the same. For example, if router A learns from router B that network X can be reached at a lower cost via B than via the existing next hop in the routing table, A updates the cost and next hop information for the network number accordingly.

RIP is in fact a fairly straightforward implementation of distance-vector routing. Routers running RIP send their advertisements every 30 seconds; a router also sends an update message whenever an update from another router causes it to change its routing table. One point of interest is that it supports multiple address families, not just IP—that is the reason for the Family part of the advertisements. RIP version 2 (RIPv2) also introduced the subnet masks described in an earlier section, whereas RIP version 1 worked with the old classful addresses of IP.

As we will see below, it is possible to use a range of different metrics or costs for the links in a routing protocol. RIP takes the simplest approach, with all link costs being equal to 1, just as in our example above. Thus, it always tries to find the minimum hop route. Valid distances are 1 through 15, with 16 representing infinity. This also limits RIP to running on fairly small networks—those with no paths longer than 15 hops.

3.4.3 Link State (OSPF)

Link-state routing is the second major class of intradomain routing protocol. The starting assumptions for link-state routing are rather similar to those for distance-vector routing. Each node is assumed to be capable of finding out the state of the link to its neighbors (up or down) and the cost of each link. Again, we want to provide each node with enough information to enable it to find the least-cost path to any destination. The basic idea behind link-state protocols is very simple: Every node knows how to reach its directly connected neighbors, and if we make sure that the totality of this knowledge is disseminated to every node, then every node will have enough knowledge of the network to build a complete map of the network. This is clearly a sufficient condition (although not a necessary one) for finding the shortest path to any point in the network. Thus, link-state routing protocols rely on two mechanisms: reliable dissemination of link-state information, and the calculation of routes from the sum of all the accumulated link-state knowledge.

RELIABLE FLOODING

Reliable flooding is the process of making sure that all the nodes participating in the routing protocol get a copy of the link-state information from all the other nodes. As the term flooding suggests, the basic idea is for a node to send its link-state information out on all of its directly connected links; each node that receives this information then forwards it out on all of its links. This process continues until the information has reached all the nodes in the network.

More precisely, each node creates an update packet, also called a link-state packet (LSP), which contains the following information:

- ◉ The ID of the node that created the LSP
- ◉ A list of directly connected neighbors of that node, with the cost of the link to each one
- ◉ A sequence number
- ◉ A time to live for this packet

The first two items are needed to enable route calculation; the last two are used to make the process of flooding the packet to all nodes reliable. Reliability includes making sure that you have the most recent copy of the information, since there may be multiple, contradictory LSPs from one node traversing the network. Making the flooding reliable has proven to be quite difficult. (For example, an early version of link-state routing used in the ARPANET caused that network to fail in 1981.)

Flooding works in the following way. First, the transmission of LSPs between adjacent routers is made reliable using acknowledgments and retransmissions just as in the reliable link-layer protocol. However, several more steps are necessary to reliably flood an LSP to all nodes in a network.

Consider a node X that receives a copy of an LSP that originated at some other node Y. Note that Y may be any other router in the same routing domain as X. X checks to see if it has already stored a copy of an LSP from Y. If not, it stores the LSP. If it already has a copy, it compares the sequence numbers; if the new LSP has a larger sequence number, it is assumed to be the more recent, and that LSP is stored, replacing the old one. A smaller (or equal) sequence number would imply an LSP older (or not newer) than the one stored, so it would be discarded and no further action would be needed. If the received LSP was the newer one, X then sends a copy of that LSP to all of its neighbors except the neighbor from which the LSP was just received. The fact that the LSP is not sent back to the node from which it was received helps to bring an end to the flooding of an LSP. Since X passes the LSP on to all its neighbors, who then turn around and do the same thing, the most recent copy of the LSP eventually reaches all nodes.

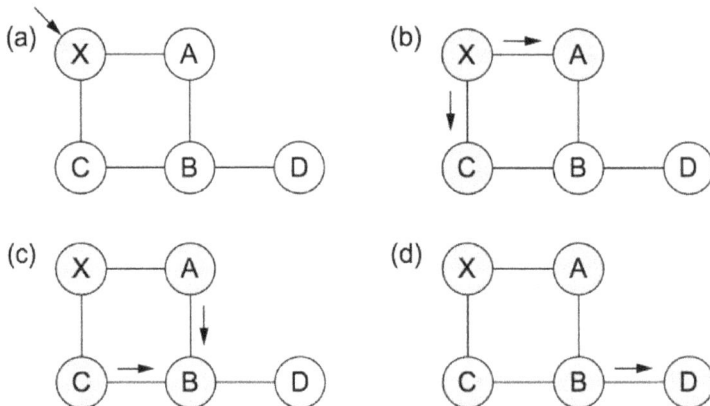

Figure 88. Flooding of link-state packets: (a) LSP arrives at node X; (b) X floods LSP to A and C; (c) A and C flood LSP to B (but not X); (d) flooding is complete.

Figure 88 shows an LSP being flooded in a small network. Each node becomes shaded as it stores the new LSP. In Figure 88(a) the LSP arrives at node X, which sends it to neighbors A and C in Figure 88(b). A and C do not send it back to X, but send it on to B. Since B receives two identical copies of the LSP, it will accept whichever arrived first and ignore the second as a duplicate. It then passes the LSP onto D, which has no neighbors to flood it to, and the process is complete.

Just as in RIP, each node generates LSPs under two circumstances. Either the expiry of a periodic timer or a change in topology can cause a node to generate a new LSP. However, the only topology-based reason for a node to generate an LSP is if one of its directly connected links or immediate neighbors has gone down. The failure of a link can be detected in some cases by the link-layer protocol. The demise of a neighbor or loss of connectivity to that neighbor can be detected using periodic "hello" packets. Each node sends these to its immediate neighbors at defined intervals. If a sufficiently long time passes without receipt of a "hello" from a neighbor, the link to that neighbor will be declared down, and a new LSP will be generated to reflect this fact.

One of the important design goals of a link-state protocol's flooding mechanism is that the newest information must be flooded to all nodes as quickly as possible, while old information must be removed from the network and not allowed to circulate. In addition, it is clearly desirable to minimize the total amount of routing traffic that is sent around the network; after all, this is just overhead from the perspective of those who actually use the network for their applications. The next few paragraphs describe some of the ways that these goals are accomplished.

One easy way to reduce overhead is to avoid generating LSPs unless absolutely necessary. This can be done by using very long timers—often on the order of hours—for the periodic generation of LSPs. Given that the flooding protocol is truly reliable when topology changes, it is safe to assume that messages saying "nothing has changed" do not need to be sent very often.

To make sure that old information is replaced by newer information, LSPs carry sequence numbers. Each time a node generates a new LSP, it increments the sequence number by 1. Unlike most sequence numbers used in protocols, these sequence numbers are not expected to wrap, so the field needs to be quite large (say, 64 bits). If a node goes down and then comes back up, it starts with a sequence number of 0. If the node was down for a long time, all the old LSPs for that node will have timed out (as described below); otherwise, this node will eventually receive a copy of its own LSP with a higher sequence number, which it can then increment and use as its own sequence number. This will ensure that its new LSP replaces any of its old LSPs left over from before the node went down.

LSPs also carry a time to live. This is used to ensure that old link-state information is eventually removed from the network. A node always decrements the TTL of a newly received LSP before flooding it to its neighbors. It also "ages" the LSP while it is stored in the node. When the TTL reaches 0, the node refloods the LSP with a TTL of 0, which is interpreted by all the nodes in the network as a signal to delete that LSP.

ROUTE CALCULATION

Once a given node has a copy of the LSP from every other node, it is able to compute a complete map for the topology of the network, and from this map it is able to decide the best route to each destination. The question, then, is exactly how it calculates routes from this information. The solution is based on a well-known algorithm from graph theory—Dijkstra's shortest-path algorithm.

We first define Dijkstra's algorithm in graph-theoretic terms. Imagine that a node takes all the LSPs it has received and constructs a graphical representation of the network, in which N denotes the set of nodes in the graph, $l(i,j)$ denotes the nonnegative cost (weight) associated with the edge between nodes i, j in N and $l(i, j) = \infty$ if no edge connects i and j. In the following description, we let s in N denote this node, that is, the node executing the algorithm to find the shortest path to all the other nodes in N. Also, the algorithm maintains the following two variables: M denotes the set of nodes incorporated so far by the algorithm, and $C(n)$ denotes the cost of the path from s to each node n. Given these definitions, the algorithm is defined as follows:

M = {s}

for each n in N - {s}

  C(n) = l(s,n)

while (N != M)

  M = M + {w} such that C(w) is the minimum for all w in (N-M)

  for each n in (N-M)

  C(n) = MIN(C(n), C(w)+l(w,n))

Basically, the algorithm works as follows. We start with M containing this node s and then initialize the table of costs (the array $C(n)$) to other nodes using the known costs to directly connected nodes. We then look for the node that is reachable at the lowest cost (w) and add it to M. Finally, we update the table of costs by considering the cost of reaching nodes through w. In the last line of the algorithm, we choose a new route to node n that goes through node w if the total cost of going from the source to w and then following the link from w to n is less than the old route we had to n. This procedure is repeated until all nodes are incorporated in M.

In practice, each switch computes its routing table directly from the LSPs it has collected using a realization of Dijkstra's algorithm called the forward search algorithm. Specifically, each switch maintains two lists, known as Tentative and Confirmed. Each of these lists contains a set of entries of the form (Destination, Cost, NextHop). The algorithm works as follows:

⊙ Initialize the Confirmed list with an entry for myself; this entry has a cost of 0.

⊙ For the node just added to the Confirmed list in the previous step, call it node Next and select its LSP.

⊙ For each neighbor (Neighbor) of Next, calculate the cost (Cost) to reach this Neighbor as the sum of the cost from myself to Next and from Next to Neighbor.

- If Neighbor is currently on neither the Confirmed nor the Tentative list, then add (Neighbor, Cost, NextHop) to the Tentative list, where NextHop is the direction I go to reach Next.

- If Neighbor is currently on the Tentative list, and the Cost is less than the currently listed cost for Neighbor, then replace the current entry with (Neighbor, Cost, NextHop), where NextHop is the direction I go to reach Next.

- If the Tentative list is empty, stop. Otherwise, pick the entry from the Tentative list with the lowest cost, move it to the Confirmed list, and return to step 2.

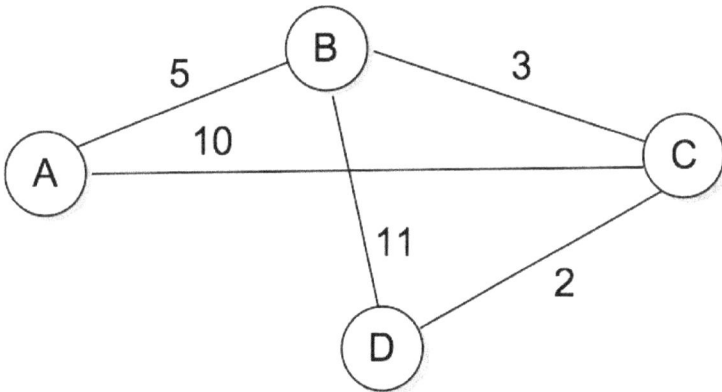

Figure 89. Link-state routing: an example network.

This will become a lot easier to understand when we look at an example. Consider the network depicted in Figure 89. Note that, unlike our previous example, this network has a range of different edge costs. Table 20 traces the steps for building the routing table for node D. We denote the two outputs of D by using the names of the nodes to which they connect, B and C. Note the way the algorithm seems to head off on false leads (like the 11-unit cost path to B that was the first addition to the Tentative list) but ends up with the least-cost paths to all nodes.

Table 20. Steps for Building Routing Table for Node D.

Step	Confirmed	Tentative	Comments
1	(D,0,–)		Since D is the only new member of the confirmed list, look at its LSP.
2	(D,0,–)	(B,11,B) (C,2,C)	D's LSP says we can reach B through B at cost 11, which is better than anything else on either list, so put it on Tentative list; same for C.
3	(D,0,–) (C,2,C)	(B,11,B)	Put lowest-cost member of Tentative (C) onto Confirmed list. Next, examine LSP of newly confirmed member (C).
4	(D,0,–) (C,2,C)	(B,5,C) (A,12,C)	Cost to reach B through C is 5, so replace (B,11,B). C's LSP tells us that we can reach A at cost 12.

Step	Confirmed	Tentative	Comments
5	(D,0,–) (C,2,C) (B,5,C)	(A,12,C)	Move lowest-cost member of Tentative (B) to Confirmed, then look at its LSP.
6	(D,0,–) (C,2,C) (B,5,C)	(A,10,C)	Since we can reach A at cost 5 through B, replace the Tentative entry.
7	(D,0,–) (C,2,C) (B,5,C) (A,10,C)		Move lowest-cost member of Tentative (A) to Confirmed, and we are all done.

The link-state routing algorithm has many nice properties: It has been proven to stabilize quickly, it does not generate much traffic, and it responds rapidly to topology changes or node failures. On the downside, the amount of information stored at each node (one LSP for every other node in the network) can be quite large. This is one of the fundamental problems of routing and is an instance of the more general problem of scalability. Some solutions to both the specific problem (the amount of storage potentially required at each node) and the general problem (scalability) will be discussed in the next section.

Key Takeaway

Distance-vector and link-state are both distributed routing algorithms, but they adopt different strategies. In distance-vector, each node talks only to its directly connected neighbors, but it tells them everything it has learned (i.e., distance to all nodes). In link-state, each node talks to all other nodes, but it tells them only what it knows for sure (i.e., only the state of its directly connected links). In contrast to both of these algorithms, we will consider a more centralized approach to routing in Section 3.5 when we introduce Software Defined Networking (SDN).

THE OPEN SHORTEST PATH FIRST PROTOCOL (OSPF)

One of the most widely used link-state routing protocols is OSPF. The first word, "Open," refers to the fact that it is an open, nonproprietary standard, created under the auspices of the Internet Engineering Task Force (IETF). The "SPF" part comes from an alternative name for link-state routing. OSPF adds quite a number of features to the basic link-state algorithm described above, including the following:

- ⊙ **Authentication of routing messages**—One feature of distributed routing algorithms is that they disperse information from one node to many other nodes, and the entire network can thus be impacted by bad information from one node. For this reason, it's a good idea to be sure that all the nodes taking part in the protocol can be trusted. Authenticating routing messages helps achieve this. Early versions of OSPF used a simple 8-byte password for authentication. This is not a strong enough form of authentication to prevent dedicated malicious users, but it alleviates some problems caused by misconfiguration or casual attacks. (A similar form of authentication was added to RIP in version 2.) Strong cryptographic authentication was later added.

⊙ **Additional hierarchy**—Hierarchy is one of the fundamental tools used to make systems more scalable. OSPF introduces another layer of hierarchy into routing by allowing a domain to be partitioned into areas. This means that a router within a domain does not necessarily need to know how to reach every network within that domain—it may be able to get by knowing only how to get to the right area. Thus, there is a reduction in the amount of information that must be transmitted to and stored in each node.

⊙ **Load balancing**—OSPF allows multiple routes to the same place to be assigned the same cost and will cause traffic to be distributed evenly over those routes, thus making better use of the available network capacity.

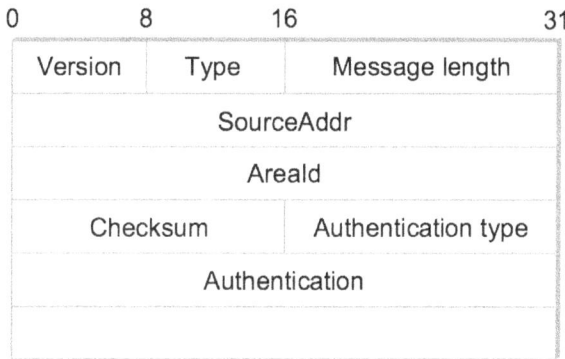

0	8	16	31
Version	Type	Message length	
SourceAddr			
AreaId			
Checksum		Authentication type	
Authentication			

Figure 90. OSPF header format.

There are several different types of OSPF messages, but all begin with the same header, as shown in Figure 90. The Version field is currently set to 2, and the Type field may take the values 1 through 5. The SourceAddr identifies the sender of the message, and the AreaId is a 32-bit identifier of the area in which the node is located. The entire packet, except the authentication data, is protected by a 16-bit checksum using the same algorithm as the IP header. The Authentication type is 0 if no authentication is used; otherwise, it may be 1, implying that a simple password is used, or 2, which indicates that a cryptographic authentication checksum is used. In the latter cases, the Authentication field carries the password or cryptographic checksum.

Of the five OSPF message types, type 1 is the "hello" message, which a router sends to its peers to notify them that it is still alive and connected as described above. The remaining types are used to request, send, and acknowledge the receipt of link-state messages. The basic building block of link-state messages in OSPF is the link-state advertisement (LSA). One message may contain many LSAs. We provide a few details of the LSA here.

Like any internetwork routing protocol, OSPF must provide information about how to reach networks. Thus, OSPF must provide a little more information than the simple graph-based protocol described above. Specifically, a router running OSPF may generate link-state packets that advertise one or more of the networks that are directly connected to that router. In addition, a router that is connected to another router by some link must advertise the cost of reaching that router over the link. These two types of advertisements are necessary to enable all the routers in a domain to determine the cost of reaching all networks in that domain and the appropriate next hop for each network.

LS Age		Options	Type = 1
Link-state ID			
Advertising router			
LS sequence number			
LS checksum		Length	
0	Flags	0	Number of links
Link ID			
Link data			
Link type	Num_TOS	Metric	
Optional TOS information			
More links			

Figure 91. OSPF link-state advertisement.

Figure 91 shows the packet format for a type 1 link-state advertisement. Type 1 LSAs advertise the cost of links between routers. Type 2 LSAs are used to advertise networks to which the advertising router is connected, while other types are used to support additional hierarchy as described in the next section. Many fields in the LSA should be familiar from the preceding discussion. The LS Age is the equivalent of a time to live, except that it counts up and the LSA expires when the age reaches a defined maximum value. The Type field tells us that this is a type 1 LSA.

In a type 1 LSA, the Link state ID and the Advertising router field are identical. Each carries a 32-bit identifier for the router that created this LSA. While a number of assignment strategies may be used to assign this ID, it is essential that it be unique in the routing domain and that a given router consistently uses the same router ID. One way to pick a router ID that meets these requirements would be to pick the lowest IP address among all the IP addresses assigned to that router. (Recall that a router may have a different IP address on each of its interfaces.)

The LS sequence number is used exactly as described above to detect old or duplicate LSAs. The LS checksum is similar to others we have seen in other protocols; it is, of course, used to verify that data has not been corrupted. It covers all fields in the packet except LS Age, so it is not necessary to recompute a checksum every time LS Age is incremented. Length is the length in bytes of the complete LSA.

Now we get to the actual link-state information. This is made a little complicated by the presence of TOS (type of service) information. Ignoring that for a moment, each link in the LSA is represented by a Link ID, some Link Data, and a metric. The first two of these fields identify the link; a common way to do this would be to use the router ID of the router at the far end of the link as the Link ID and then use the Link Data to disambiguate among multiple parallel links if necessary. The metric is of course the cost of the link. Type tells us something about the link—for example, if it is a point-to-point link.

The TOS information is present to allow OSPF to choose different routes for IP packets based on the value in their TOS field. Instead of assigning a single metric to a link, it is possible to assign different metrics depending on the TOS value of the data. For example, if we had a link in our network that was very good for delay-sensitive traffic, we could give it a low metric for the TOS value representing low delay and a high metric for everything else. OSPF would then pick a different shortest path for those packets that had their TOS field set to that value. It is worth noting that, at the time of writing, this capability has not been widely deployed.

3.4.4 Metrics

The preceding discussion assumes that link costs, or metrics, are known when we execute the routing algorithm. In this section, we look at some ways to calculate link costs that have proven effective in practice. One example that we have seen already, which is quite reasonable and very simple, is to assign a cost of 1 to all links—the least-cost route will then be the one with the fewest hops. Such an approach has several drawbacks, however. First, it does not distinguish between links on a latency basis. Thus, a satellite link with 250-ms latency looks just as attractive to the routing protocol as a terrestrial link with 1-ms latency. Second, it does not distinguish between routes on a capacity basis, making a 1-Mbps link look just as good as a 10-Gbps link. Finally, it does not distinguish between links based on their current load, making it impossible to route around overloaded links. It turns out that this last problem is the hardest because you are trying to capture the complex and dynamic characteristics of a link in a single scalar cost.

The ARPANET was the testing ground for a number of different approaches to link-cost calculation. (It was also the place where the superior stability of link-state over distance-vector routing was demonstrated; the original mechanism used distance vector while the later version used link state.) The following discussion traces the evolution of the ARPANET routing metric and, in so doing, explores the subtle aspects of the problem.

The original ARPANET routing metric measured the number of packets that were queued waiting to be transmitted on each link, meaning that a link with 10 packets queued waiting to be transmitted was assigned a larger cost weight than a link with 5 packets queued for transmission. Using queue length as a routing metric did not work well, however, since queue length is an artificial measure of load—it moves packets toward the shortest queue rather than toward the destination, a situation all too familiar to those of us who hop from line to line at the grocery store. Stated more precisely, the original ARPANET routing mechanism suffered from the fact that it did not take either the bandwidth or the latency of the link into consideration.

A second version of the ARPANET routing algorithm took both link bandwidth and latency into consideration and used delay, rather than just queue length, as a measure of load. This was done as follows. First, each incoming packet was timestamped with its time of arrival at the router (ArrivalTime); its departure time from the router (DepartTime) was also recorded. Second, when the link-level ACK was received from the other side, the node computed the delay for that packet as

Delay = (DepartTime - ArrivalTime) + TransmissionTime + Latency

where TransmissionTime and Latency were statically defined for the link and captured the link's bandwidth and latency, respectively. Notice that in this case, Depart Time - Arrival Time represents the amount of time the packet was delayed (queued) in the node due to load. If the ACK did not arrive, but instead the packet timed out, then DepartTime was reset to the time the packet was retransmitted. In this case, DepartTime - ArrivalTime captures the reliability of the link—the more frequent the retransmission of packets, the less reliable the link, and the more we want to avoid it. Finally, the weight assigned to each link was derived from the average delay experienced by the packets recently sent over that link.

Although an improvement over the original mechanism, this approach also had a lot of problems. Under light load, it worked reasonably well, since the two static factors of delay dominated the cost. Under heavy load, however, a congested link would start to advertise a very high cost. This caused all the traffic to move off that link, leaving it idle, so then it would advertise a low cost, thereby attracting back all the traffic, and so on. The effect of this instability was that, under heavy load, many links would in fact spend a great deal of time being idle, which is the last thing you want under heavy load.

Another problem was that the range of link values was much too large. For example, a heavily loaded 9.6-kbps link could look 127 times more costly than a lightly loaded 56-kbps link. (Keep in mind, we're talking about the ARPANET circa 1975.) This means that the routing algorithm would choose a path with 126 hops of lightly loaded 56-kbps links in preference to a 1-hop 9.6-kbps path. While shedding some traffic from an overloaded line is a good idea, making it look so unattractive that it loses all its traffic is excessive. Using 126 hops when 1 hop will do is in general a bad use of network resources. Also, satellite links were unduly penalized, so that an idle 56-kbps satellite link looked considerably more costly than an idle 9.6-kbps terrestrial link, even though the former would give better performance for high-bandwidth applications.

A third approach addressed these problems. The major changes were to compress the dynamic range of the metric considerably, to account for the link type, and to smooth the variation of the metric with time.

The smoothing was achieved by several mechanisms. First, the delay measurement was transformed to a link utilization, and this number was averaged with the last reported utilization to suppress sudden changes. Second, there was a hard limit on how much the metric could change from one measurement cycle to the next. By smoothing the changes in the cost, the likelihood that all nodes would abandon a route at once is greatly reduced.

The compression of the dynamic range was achieved by feeding the measured utilization, the link type, and the link speed into a function that is shown graphically in Figure 92. below. Observe the following:

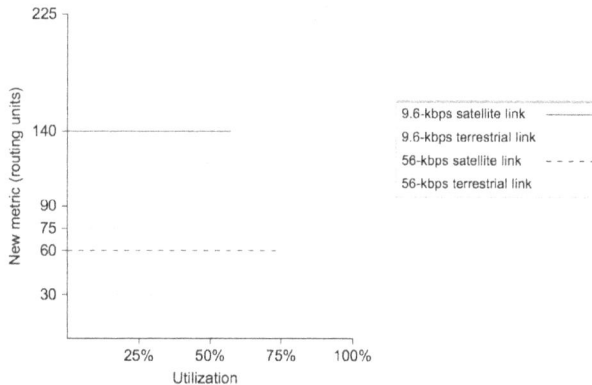

Figure 92. Revised ARPANET routing metric versus link utilization.

- A highly loaded link never shows a cost of more than three times its cost when idle.

- The most expensive link is only seven times the cost of the least expensive.

- A high-speed satellite link is more attractive than a low-speed terrestrial link.

- Cost is a function of link utilization only at moderate to high loads.

All of these factors mean that a link is much less likely to be universally abandoned, since a threefold increase in cost is likely to make the link unattractive for some paths while letting it remain the best choice for others. The slopes, offsets, and breakpoints for the curves in Figure 92 were arrived at by a great deal of trial and error, and they were carefully tuned to provide good performance. Despite all these improvements, it turns out that in the majority of real-world network deployments, metrics change rarely if at all and only under the control of a network administrator, not automatically as described above. The reason for this is partly that conventional wisdom now holds that dynamically changing metrics are too unstable, even though this probably need not be true. Perhaps more significantly, many networks today lack the great disparity of link speeds and latencies that prevailed in the ARPANET. Thus, static metrics are the norm. One common approach to setting metrics is to use a constant multiplied by (1/ link_bandwidth).

Key Takeaway

Why do we still tell the story about a decades old algorithm that's no longer in use? Because it perfectly illustrates two valuable lessons. The first is that computer systems are often designed iteratively based on experience. We seldom get it right the first time, so it's important to deploy a simple solution sooner rather than later, and expect to improve it over time. Staying stuck in the design phase indefinitely is usually not a good plan. The second is the well-know KISS principle: Keep it Simple, Stupid. When building a complex system, less is often more. Opportunities to invent sophisticated optimizations are plentiful, and it's a tempting opportunity to pursue. While such optimizations sometimes have short-term value, it is shocking how often a simple approach proves best over time. This is because when a system has many moving parts, as the Internet most certainly does, keeping each part as simple as possible is usually the best approach. [Next]

3.5 Implementation

Up until now, we have discussed the necessary functions of switches and routers without delving into the specific methods they employ to carry out these tasks. There is a direct and uncomplicated method to construct a switch or router: Purchase a versatile CPU and install various network interfaces on it. A device equipped with appropriate software can receive packets through one of its interfaces, execute any of the switching or forwarding functions outlined in this chapter, and transmit packets through another interface. The architecture of several commercial mid- to low-end network devices closely resembles that of this software switch.Two Implementations that achieve superior performance often leverage supplementary hardware acceleration. These are commonly known as hardware switches, although it is important to note that both methods use a combination of hardware and software. This section provides a summary of software-centric and hardware-centric designs. However, it is important to mention that when it comes to switches versus routers, the difference is not significant. The implementation of switches and routers have many similarities, allowing network administrators to purchase a single forwarding box and configure it to function as either an L2 switch, an L3 router, or a combination of both. Due to the similarities in their internal architecture, we will use the term "switch" to refer to both types in this section, thereby avoiding the need to repeatedly mention "switch or router". When necessary, we will highlight the distinctions between the two.

3.5.1 Software Switch

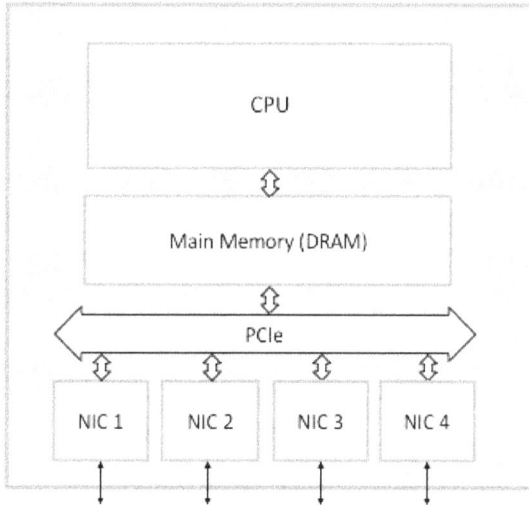

Figure 93. A general-purpose processor used as a software switch.

Figure 93 shows a software switch built using a general-purpose processor with four network interface cards (NICs). The path for a typical packet that arrives on, say, NIC 1 and is forwarded out on NIC 2 is straightforward: as NIC 1 receives the packet it copies its bytes directly into the main memory over the I/O bus (PCIe in this example) using a technique called direct memory access (DMA). Once the packet is in memory, the CPU examines its header to determine which interface the packet should be sent out on, and instructs NIC 2 to transmit the packet, again directly out of main memory using DMA. The important take-away is that the packet is buffered in main memory (this is the "store" half of store-and-forward), with the CPU reading only the necessary header fields into its internal registers for processing.

There are two potential bottlenecks with this approach, one or both of which limits the aggregate packet forwarding capacity of the software switch.

The first problem is that performance is limited by the fact that all packets must pass into and out of main memory. Your mileage will vary based on how much you are willing to pay for hardware, but as an example, a machine limited by a 1333-MHz, 64-bit-wide memory bus can transmit data at a peak rate of a little over 100 Gbps—enough to build a switch with a handful of 10-Gbps Ethernet ports, but hardly enough for a high-end router in the core of the Internet.

Moreover, this upper bound assumes that moving data is the only problem. This is a fair approximation for long packets but a bad one when packets are short, which is the worst-case situation switch designers have to plan for. With minimum-sized packets, the cost of processing each packet—parsing its header and deciding which output link to transmit it on—is likely to dominate, and potentially become a bottleneck. Suppose, for example, that a processor can perform all the necessary processing to switch 40 million packets each second. This is sometimes called the packet per second (pps) rate. If the average packet is 64 bytes, this would imply that is, a throughput of about 20 Gbps—fast, but substantially below the range users are demanding from their switches today. Bear in mind that this 20 Gbps would be shared by all users connected to the switch, just as the bandwidth of a single (unswitched) Ethernet segment is shared among all users connected to the shared medium. Thus, for example, a 16-port switch with this aggregate throughput would only be able to cope with an average data rate of about 1 Gbps on each port.[3]

$$\text{Throughput} = \text{pps} \times \text{BitsPerPacket}$$

$$= 40 \times 10^6 \times 64 \times 8$$

$$= 2048 \times 10^7$$

One final consideration is important to understand when evaluating switch implementations. The non-trivial algorithms discussed in this chapter—the spanning tree algorithm used by learning bridges, the distance-vector algorithm used by RIP, and the link-state algorithm used by OSPF—are not directly part of the per-packet forwarding decision. They run periodically in the background, but switches do not have to execute, say, OSPF code for every packet it forwards. The most costly routine the CPU is likely to execute on a per-packet basis is a table lookup, for example, looking up a VCI number in a VC table, an IP address in an L3 forwarding table, or an Ethernet address in an L2 forwarding table.

Key Takeaway

The distinction between these two kinds of processing is important enough to give it a name: the control plane corresponds to the background processing required to "control" the network (e.g., running OSPF, RIP, or the BGP protocol described in the next chapter) and the data plane corresponds to the per-packet processing required to move packets from input port to output port. For historical reasons, this distinction is called control plane and user plane in cellular access networks, but the idea is the same, and in fact, the 3GPP standard defines CUPS (Control/User Plane Separation) as an architectural principle.

These two kinds of processing are easy to conflate when both run on the same CPU, as is the case in software switch depicted in Figure 93, but performance can be dramatically improved by optimizing how the data plane is implemented, and correspondingly, specifying a well-defined interface between the control and data planes.

3.5.2 Hardware Switch

Throughout much of the Internet's history, high-performance switches and routers have been specialized devices, built with Application-Specific Integrated Circuits (ASICs). While it was possible to build low-end routers and switches using commodity servers running C programs, ASICs were required to achieve the required throughput rates.

The problem with ASICs is that hardware takes a long time to design and fabricate, meaning the delay for adding new features to a switch is usually measured in years, not the days or weeks today's software industry is accustomed to. Ideally, we'd like to benefit from the performance of ASICs and the agility of software.

Fortunately, recent advances in domain specific processors (and other commodity components) have made this possible. Just as importantly, the full architectural specification for switches that take advantage of these new processors is now available online—the hardware equivalent of open source software. This means anyone can build a high-performance switch by pulling the blueprint off the web (see the Open Compute Project, OCP, for examples) in the same way it is possible to build your own PC. In both cases you still need software to run on the hardware, but just as Linux is available to run on your home-built PC, there are now open source L2 and L3 stacks available on GitHub to run on your home-built switch. Alternatively, you can simply buy a pre-built switch from a commodity switch manufacturer and then load your own software onto it. The following describes these open bare-metal switches, so called to contrast them with closed devices, in which hardware and software are tightly bundled, that have historically dominated the industry.

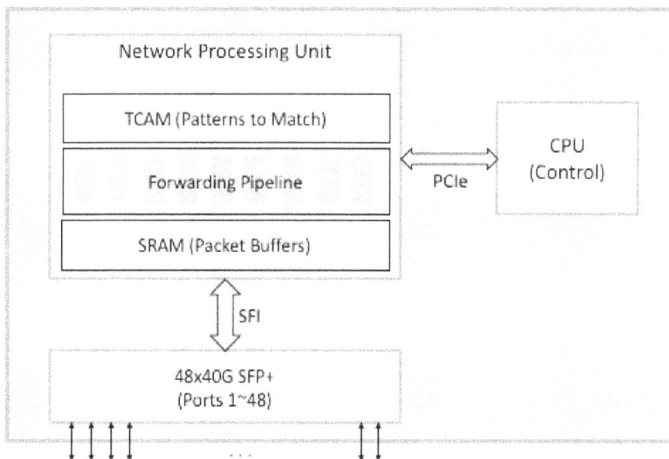

Figure 94. Bare-metal switch using a Network Processing Unit.

Figure 94 is a simplified depiction of a bare-metal switch. The key difference from the earlier implementation on a general-purpose processor is the addition of a Network Processor Unit (NPU), a domain-specific processor with an architecture and instruction set that has been optimized for processing packet headers (i.e., for implementing the data plane). NPUs are similar in spirit to GPUs that have an architecture optimized for rendering computer graphics, but in this case, the NPU is optimized for parsing packet headers and making a forwarding decision. NPUs are able to process packets (input, make a forwarding decision, and output) at rates measured in Terabits per second (Tbps), easily fast enough to keep up with 32x100-Gbps ports, or the 48x40-Gbps ports shown in the diagram.

NETWORK PROCESSING UNITS

Our use of the term NPU is a bit non-standard. Historically, NPU was the name given more narrowly-defined network processing chips used, for example, to implement intelligent firewalls or deep packet inspection. They were not as general-purpose as the NPUs we're discussing here; nor were they as high-performance. It seems likely that the current approach will make purpose-built network processors obsolete, but in any case, we prefer the NPU nomenclature because it is consistent with the trend to build programmable domain-specific processors, including GPUs for graphics and TPUs (Tensor Processing Units) for AI.

The beauty of this new switch design is that a given bare-metal switch can now be programmed to be an L2 switch, an L3 router, or a combination of both, just by a matter of programming. The exact same control plane software stack used in a software switch still runs on the control CPU, but in addition, data plane "programs" are loaded onto the NPU to reflect the forwarding decisions made by the control plane software. Exactly how one "programs" the NPU depends on the chip vendor, of which there are currently several. In some cases, the forwarding pipeline is fixed and the control processor merely loads the forwarding table into the NPU (by fixed we mean the NPU only knows how to process certain headers, like Ethernet and IP), but in other cases, the forwarding pipeline is itself programmable. P4 is a new programming language that can be used to program such NPU-based forwarding pipelines. Among other things, P4 tries to hide many of the differences in the underlying NPU instruction sets.

Internally, an NPU takes advantage of three technologies. First, a fast SRAM-based memory buffers packets while they are being processed. SRAM (Static Random Access Memory), is roughly an order of magnitude faster than the DRAM (Dynamic Random Access Memory) that is used by main memory. Second, a TCAM-based memory stores bit patterns to be matched in the packets being processed. The "CAM" in TCAM stands for "Content Addressable Memory," which means that the key you want to look up in a table can effectively be used as the address into the memory that implements the table. The "T" stands for "Ternary" which is a fancy way to say the key you want to look up can have wildcards in it (e.g, key 10*1 matches both 1001 and 1011). Finally, the processing involved to forward each packet is implemented by a forwarding pipeline. This pipeline is implemented by an ASIC, but when well-designed, the pipeline's forwarding behavior can be modified by changing the program it runs. At a high level, this program is expressed as a collection of (Match, Action) pairs: if you match such-and-such field in the header, then execute this-or-that action.

The relevance of packet processing being implemented by a multi-stage pipeline rather than a single-stage processor is that forwarding a single packet likely involves looking at multiple header fields. Each stage can be programmed to look at a different combination of fields. A multi-stage pipeline adds a little end-to-end latency to each packet (measured in nanoseconds), but also means that multiple packets can be processed at the same time. For example, Stage 2 can be making a second lookup on packet A while Stage 1 is doing an initial lookup on packet B, and so on. This means the NPU as a whole is able to keep up with line speeds. As of this writing, the state of the art is 25.6 Tbps.

Finally, Figure 94 includes other commodity components that make this all practical. In particular, it is now possible to buy pluggable transceiver modules that take care of all the media access details—be it Gigabit Ethernet, 10-Gigabit Ethernet, or SONET—as well as the optics. These transceivers all conform to standardized form factors, such as SFP+, that can in turn be connected to other components over a standardized bus (e.g., SFI). Again, the key takeaway is that the networking industry is just now entering into the same commoditized world that the computing industry has enjoyed for the last two decades.

3.5.3 Software Defined Networks

With switches becoming increasingly commoditized, attention is rightfully shifting to the software that controls them. This puts us squarely in the middle of a trend to build Software Defined Networks (SDN), an idea that started to germinate about ten years ago. In fact, it was the early stages of SDN that triggered the networking industry to move towards bare-metal switches.

The fundamental idea of SDN is one we've already discussed: to decouple the network control plane (i.e., where routing algorithms like RIP, OSPF, and BGP run) from the network data plane (i.e., where packet forwarding decisions get made), with the former moved into software running on commodity servers and the latter implemented by bare-metal switches. The key enabling idea behind SDN was to take this decoupling a step further, and to define a standard interface between the control plane and the data plane. Doing so allows any implementation of the control plane to talk to any implementation of the data plane; this breaks the dependency on any one vendor's bundled solution. The original interface is called OpenFlow, and this idea of decoupling the control and data planes came to be known as disaggregation. (The P4 language mentioned in the previous subsection is a second-generation attempt to define this interface by generalizing OpenFlow.)

Another important aspect of disaggregation is that a logically centralized control plane can be used to control a distributed network data plane. We say logically centralized because while the state collected by the control plane is maintained in a global data structure, such as a Network Map, the implementation of this data structure could still be distributed over multiple servers. For example, it could run in a cloud. This is important for both scalability and availability, where the key is that the two planes are configured and scaled independent of each other. This idea took off quickly in the cloud, where today's cloud providers run SDN-based solutions both within their datacenters and across the backbone networks that interconnect their datacenters.

One consequence of this design that isn't immediately obvious is that a logically centralized control plane doesn't just manage a network of physical (hardware) switches that interconnects physical servers, but it also manages a network of virtual (software) switches that interconnect virtual servers (e.g., Virtual Machines and containers). If you're counting "switch ports" (a good measure of all the devices connected to your network) then the number of virtual ports in the Internet rocketed past the number of physical ports in 2012.

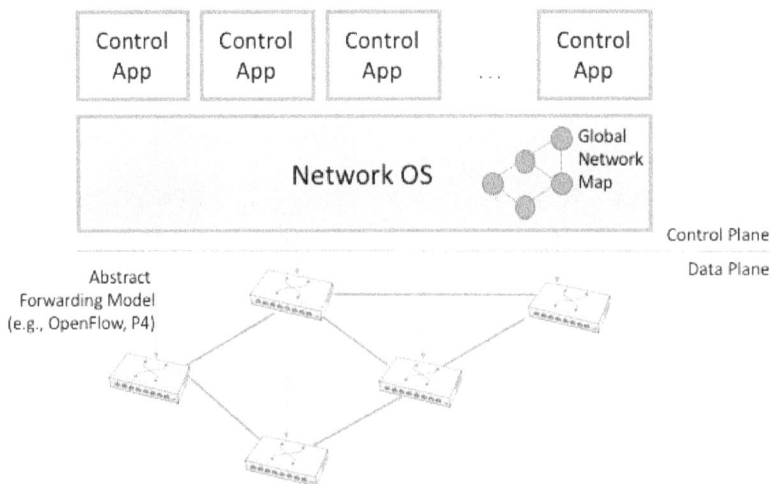

Figure 95. Network Operating System (NOS) hosting a set of control applications and providing a logically centralized point of control for an underlying network data plane.

One of other key enablers for SDN's success, as depicted in Figure 95, is the Network Operating System (NOS). Like a server operating system (e.g., Linux, iOS, Android, Windows) that provides a set of high-level abstractions that make it easier to implement applications (e.g., you can read and write files instead of directly accessing disk drives), a NOS makes it easier to implement network control functionality, otherwise known as Control Apps. A good NOS abstracts the details of the network switches and provides a Network Map abstraction to the application developer. The NOS detects changes in the underlying network (e.g., switches, ports, and links going up-and-down) and the control application simply implements the behavior it wants on this abstract graph. This means the NOS takes on the burden of collecting network state (the hard part of distributed algorithms like Link-State and Distance-Vector algorithms) and the app is free to simply implement the shortest path algorithm and load the forwarding rules into the underlying switches. By centralizing this logic, the goal is to come up with a globally optimized solution. The published evidence from cloud providers that have embraced this approach confirms this advantage.

Key Takeaway

It is important to understand that SDN is an implementation strategy. It does not magically make fundamental problems like needing to compute a forwarding table go away. But instead of burdening the switches with having to exchange messages with each other as part of a distributed routing algorithm, the logically centralized SDN controller is charged with collecting link and port status information from the individual switches, constructing a global view of the network graph, and making that graph available to the control apps. From the control application's perspective, all the information it needs to compute the forwarding table is locally available. Keeping in mind that the SDN Controller is logically centralized but physically replicated on multiple servers—for both scalable performance and high availability—it is still a hotly contested question whether the centralized or distributed approach is best. [Next]

As much of an advantage as the cloud providers have been able to get out of SDN, its adoption in enterprises and Telcos has been much slower. This is partly about the ability of different markets to manage their networks. The Googles, Microsofts, and Amazons of the world have the engineers and DevOps skills needed to take advantage of this technology, whereas others still prefer pre-packaged and integrated solutions that support the management and command line interfaces they are familiar with.

PERSPECTIVE: VIRTUAL NETWORKS ALL THE WAY DOWN

For almost as long as there have been packet-switched networks, there have been ideas about how to virtualize them, starting with virtual circuits. But what exactly does it mean to virtualize a network?

Virtual memory is a helpful example. Virtual memory creates an abstraction of a large and private pool of memory, even though the underlying physical memory may be shared by many applications and considerably smaller that the apparent pool of virtual memory. This abstraction enables programmers to operate under the illusion that there is plenty of memory and that no-one else is using it, while under the covers the memory management system takes care of things like mapping the virtual memory to physical resources and avoiding conflict between users.

Similarly, server virtualization presents the abstraction of a virtual machine (VM), which has all the features of a physical machine. Again, there may be many VMs supported on a single physical server, and the operating system and users on the virtual machine are happily unaware that the VM is being mapped onto physical resources.

A key point is the virtualization of computing resources preserves the abstractions and interfaces that existed before they were virtualized. This is important because it means that users of those abstractions don't need to change— they see a faithful reproduction of the resource being virtualized. Virtualization also means that the different users (sometimes called tenants) cannot interfere with each other. So what happens when we try to virtualize a network?

VPNs, as described in Section 3.3, were one early success for virtual networking. They allowed carriers to present corporate customers with the illusion that they had their own private network, even though in reality they were sharing underlying links and switches with many other users. VPNs, however, only virtualize a few resources, notably addressing and routing tables. Network virtualization as commonly understood today goes further, virtualizing every aspect of networking. That means that a virtual network should support all the basic abstractions of a physical network. In this sense, they are analogous to the virtual machine, with its support of all the resources of a server: CPU, storage, I/O, and so on.

To this end, VLANs, as described in Section 3.2, are how we typically virtualize an L2 network. VLANs proved to be quite useful to enterprises that wanted to isolate different internal groups (e.g., departments, labs), giving each of them the appearance of having their own private LAN. VLANs were also seen as a promising way to virtualize L2 networks in cloud datacenters, making it possible to give each tenant their own L2 network so as to isolate their traffic from the traffic of all other tenants. But there was a problem: the 4096 possible VLANs was not sufficient to account for all the tenants that a cloud might host, and to complicate matters, in a cloud the network needs to connect virtual machines rather than the physical machines that those VMs run on. To address this problem, another standard called Virtual Extensible LAN (VXLAN) was introduced. Unlike the original approach, which effectively encapsulated a virtualized ethernet frame inside another ethernet frame, VXLAN encapsulates a virtual ethernet frame inside a UDP packet. This means a VXLAN-based virtual network (which is often referred to as an overlay network) runs on top of an IP-based network, which in turn runs on an underlying ethernet (or perhaps in just one VLAN of the underlying ethernet). VXLAN also makes it possible for one cloud tenant to have multiple VLANs of their own, which allows them to segregate their own internal traffic. This means it is ultimately possible to have a VLAN encapsulated in a VXLAN overlay encapsulated in a VLAN.

The powerful thing about virtualization is that when done right, it should be possible to nest one virtualized resource inside another virtualized resource, since after all, a virtual resource should behave just like a physical resources and we know how to virtualize physical resources! Said another way, being able to virtualize a virtual resource is the best proof that you have done a good job of virtualizing the original physical resource. To re-purpose the mythology of the World Turtle: It's virtual networks all the way down.

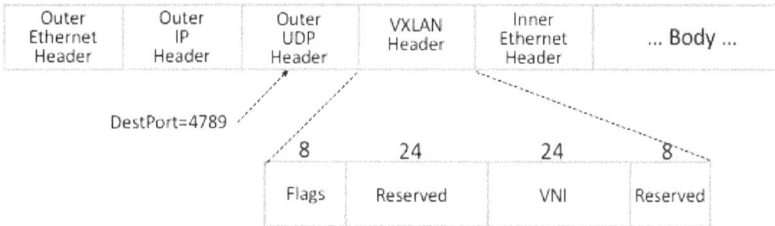

Figure 96. VXLAN Header encapsulated in a UDP/IP packet.

The current VXLAN header is straightforward, as depicted in Figure 96. The 24-bit Virtual Network Id (VNI) is accompanied with flag and reserved bits. Furthermore, it indicates a specific configuration of the UDP source and destination port fields (see to Section 5.1), where the destination port 4789 is officially designated for VXLANs. Identifying virtual LANs (VLAN tags) and virtual networks (VXLAN VIDs) is a straightforward task. The reason for this is that encapsulation serves as the fundamental basis for virtualization. It only requires the inclusion of an identification that indicates the specific user to whom this encapsulated packet belongs, among numerous potential users. The challenging aspect involves comprehending the concept of virtual networks being nested (encapsulated) within other virtual networks, which might be likened to recursion in the field of networking. Another obstacle lies in comprehending the process of automating the establishment, administration, transfer, and removal of virtual networks. In this regard, there is still ample scope for enhancement. Mastering this difficulty will be crucial for networking in the next decade. While part of this work will probably occur in proprietary settings, there are open source network virtualization technologies, such as the Linux Foundation's Tungsten Fabric project, that are taking the lead.

BROADER PERSPECTIVE

To continue reading about the cloudification of the Internet, see Perspective: The Cloud is Eating the Internet.

To learn more about the maturation of virtual networks, we recommend:

- ⊙ Network Heresy, 2012.
- ⊙ Tungsten Fabric, 2018.

CHAPTER-4
ADVANCED INTERNETWORKING

PROBLEM: SCALING TO BILLIONS

We have now seen how to build an internetwork that consists of a number of networks of Various categories. In other words, we have successfully addressed the issue of heterogeneity. The second crucial issue in internetworking, which might be considered the fundamental challenge for all networking, is scalability. In order to comprehend the issue of scaling a network, it is valuable to examine the expansion of the Internet, which has approximately doubled in magnitude annually for a period of 30 years. This type of expansion compels us to confront certain obstacles. One of the main challenges is how to construct a routing system capable of managing a large number of networks, numbering in the hundreds of thousands, and a vast amount of end nodes, reaching into the billions. In this chapter, we shall see that the majority of methods for addressing the scalability of routing rely on the implementation of a hierarchical structure. Hierarchy can be implemented by dividing a domain into several parts. Additionally, hierarchy is utilized to expand the routing system across multiple domains. BGP is the interdomain routing protocol that has facilitated the Internet's expansion to its present magnitude. We will examine the functioning of BGP and analyze the difficulties encountered by BGP as the Internet expands. The issue of addressing is closely linked to the scalability of routing. It was evident twenty years ago that the 32-bit addressing scheme of IP version 4 would not be sustainable in the long term. As a result, a new iteration of IP called version 6 was introduced, as version 5 had already been utilized in a previous experiment. IPv6 largely increases the capacity for addresses, while also introducing several new functionalities, some of which have been adapted for use with IPv4. As the Internet expands, it must also adapt and improve its capabilities. The last portions of this chapter discuss notable improvements to the Internet's functionalities. The first service, multicast, is an improved version of the fundamental service model. In this paper, we present the integration of multicast, which enables efficient delivery of identical packets to multiple receivers, into an internet infrastructure. Additionally, we discuss various routing methods that have been specifically designed to facilitate multicast functionality. Multiprotocol Label Switching (MPLS) is a modification to the forwarding mechanism of IP networks, resulting in an enhanced performance. This update has facilitated alterations in the manner in which IP routing is executed and in the services provided by IP networks. Lastly, we examine the impact of mobility on routing and outline several improvements to IP that facilitate the functioning of mobile hosts and routers. Scalability remains a significant concern for each of these improvements.

4.1 Global Internet

Thus far, we have observed the process of linking many networks of different types to form an internetwork, as well as utilizing the basic structure of IP addresses to enable more efficient routing inside an internet. We use the term "somewhat" scalable because, although each router does not require knowledge of all the hosts connected to the internet, it does need to know about all the networks connected to the internet in the current architecture. The present-day Internet encompasses a multitude of networks, numbering in the hundreds of thousands or even more, depending on the method of enumeration. Routing protocols, like the ones we just spoke about, are not capable of handling large volumes of data efficiently. This section examines a range of strategies that significantly enhance scalability and have facilitated the Internet's extensive growth.

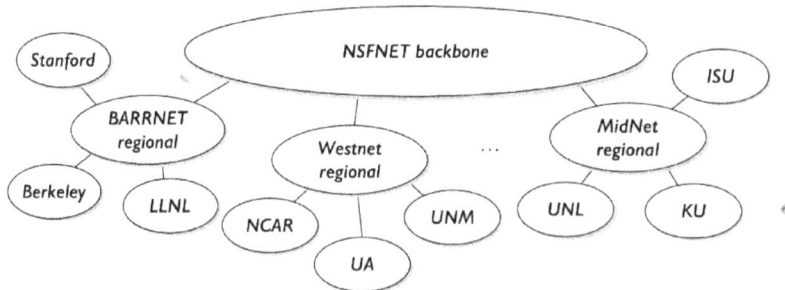

Figure 97. The tree structure of the Internet in 1990.

Prior to delving into these strategies, it is essential to establish a comprehensive understanding of the overall structure and composition of the worldwide Internet. It is not a haphazard interconnection of Ethernets, but rather it assumes a configuration that mirrors its interaction with several other organizations. Figure 97 provides a basic representation of the condition of the Internet in 1990. Since then, the structure of the Internet has become somewhat more intricate than what is depicted in this diagram. We will provide a little more precise representation of the modern Internet in a subsequent section, but for now, this diagram will suffice. An important characteristic of this architecture is that it comprises of end-user sites, such as Stanford University, that are connected to service provider networks.

For example, BARRNET was a provider network that served sites in the San Francisco Bay Area. During the year 1990, numerous service providers operated inside a restricted geographical area and were hence referred to as regional networks. The regional networks were interconnected via a countrywide backbone. The National Science Foundation (NSF) funded the backbone in 1990, hence it was named the NSFNET backbone.

NSFNET gave way to Internet2, which still runs a backbone on behalf of Research and Education institutions in the US (there are similar R&E networks in other countries), but of course most people get their Internet connectivity from commercial providers. Although the detail is not shown in the figure, today the largest provider networks (they are called tier-1) are typically built from dozens of high-end routers located in major metropolitan areas (colloquially referred to as "NFL cities") connected by point-to-point links (often with 100 Gbps capacity). Similarly, each end-user site is typically not a single network but instead consists of multiple physical networks connected by switches and routers.

Notice that each provider and end-user is likely to be an administratively independent entity. This has some significant consequences on routing. For example, it is quite likely that different providers will have different ideas about the best routing protocol to use within their networks and on how metrics should be assigned to links in their network. Because of this independence, each provider's network is usually a single autonomous system (AS). We will define this term more precisely in a later section, but for now it is adequate to think of an AS as a network that is administered independently of other ASs.

The fact that the Internet has a discernible structure can be used to our advantage as we tackle the problem of scalability. In fact, we need to deal with two related scaling issues. The first is the scalability of routing. We need to find ways to minimize the number of network numbers that get carried around in routing protocols and stored in the routing tables of routers. The second is address utilization—that is, making sure that the IP address space does not get consumed too quickly.

Throughout this book, we see the principle of hierarchy used again and again to improve scalability. We saw in the previous chapter how the hierarchical structure of IP addresses, especially with the flexibility provided by Classless Interdomain Routing (CIDR) and subnetting, can improve the scalability of routing. In the next two sections, we'll see further uses of hierarchy (and its partner, aggregation) to provide greater scalability, first in a single domain and then between domains. Our final subsection looks at IP version 6, the invention of which was largely the result of scalability concerns.

4.1.1 Routing Areas

As a first example of using hierarchy to scale up the routing system, we'll examine how link-state routing protocols (such as OSPF and IS-IS) can be used to partition a routing domain into subdomains called areas. (The terminology varies somewhat among protocols—we use the OSPF terminology here.) By adding this extra level of hierarchy, we enable single domains to grow larger without overburdening the routing protocols or resorting to the more complex interdomain routing protocols described later.

An area is a set of routers that are administratively configured to exchange link-state information with each other. There is one special area—the backbone area, also known as area 0. An example of a routing domain divided into areas is shown in Figure 98 . Routers R1, R2, and R3 are members of the backbone area. They are also members of at least one nonbackbone area; R1 is actually a member of both area 1 and area 2. A router that is a member of both the backbone area and a nonbackbone area is an area border router (ABR). Note that these are distinct from the routers that are at the edge of an AS, which are referred to as AS border routers for clarity.

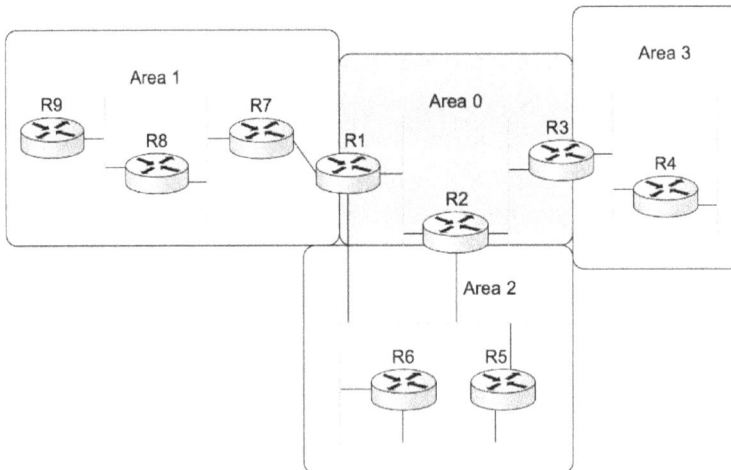

Figure 98. A domain divided into areas.

Routing within a single area is exactly as described in the previous chapter. All the routers in the area send link-state advertisements to each other and thus develop a complete, consistent map of the area. However, the link-state advertisements of routers that are not area border routers do not leave the area in which they originated. This has the effect of making the flooding and route calculation processes considerably more scalable. For example, router R4 in area 3 will never see a link-state advertisement from router R8 in area 1. As a consequence, it will know nothing about the detailed topology of areas other than its own.

How, then, does a router in one area determine the right next hop for a packet destined to a network in another area? The answer to this becomes clear if we imagine the path of a packet that has to travel from one nonbackbone area to another as being split into three parts. First, it travels from its source network to the backbone area, then it crosses the backbone, then it travels from the backbone to the destination network. To make this work, the area border routers summarize routing information that they have learned from one area and make it available in their advertisements to other areas. For example, R1 receives link-state advertisements from all the routers in area 1 and can thus determine the cost of reaching any network in area 1. When R1 sends link-state advertisements into area 0, it advertises the costs of reaching the networks in area 1 much as if all those networks were directly connected to R1. This enables all the area 0 routers to learn the cost to reach all networks in area 1. The area border routers then summarize this information and advertise it into the nonbackbone areas. Thus, all routers learn how to reach all networks in the domain.

Note that, in the case of area 2, there are two ABRs and that routers in area 2 will thus have to make a choice as to which one they use to reach the backbone. This is easy enough, since both R1 and R2 will be advertising costs to various networks, so it will become clear which is the better choice as the routers in area 2 run their shortest-path algorithm. For example, it is pretty clear that R1 is going to be a better choice than R2 for destinations in area 1.

When partitioning a domain into areas, the network administrator must balance between the scalability and the efficiency of routing. Utilizing regions compels all packets that are moving from one area to another to pass via the backbone area, regardless of the possibility of a shorter route. For instance, even if R4 and R5 were physically linked, data packets would not be transmitted between them due to their placement in separate nonbackbone locations. The requirement for scalability frequently takes precedence over the requirement for utilizing the most concise route.

Key Takeaway

This exemplifies a crucial aspect in network architecture. Scalability often involves sacrificing some form of optimality. Introducing hierarchy in a network results in the concealment of information from certain nodes, hence impeding their capacity to make optimal decisions. Information concealing is crucial for scaling a solution since it prevents the need for all nodes to possess global knowledge. In big networks, prioritizing scalability over finding the ideal path is consistently true [Next]

Additionally, it is worth mentioning that network administrators have a method to strategically choose the placement of routers in area 0 with greater flexibility. This technique employs the concept of a virtual connection between routers. A virtual link is established by configuring a router, which is not directly linked to area 0, to communicate backbone routing information with a connected router. As an illustration, a virtual connection might be established from R8 to R1, thereby integrating R8 into the backbone network. R8 will now engage in link-state advertisement flooding with the other routers in area 0. The cost of the virtual link between R8 and R1 is defined by the exchange of routing information that occurs in region 1. This strategy can enhance the efficiency of routing.

4.1.2 Interdomain Routing (BGP)

At the beginning of this chapter, we introduced the notion that the Internet is organized as autonomous systems, each of which is under the control of a single administrative entity. A corporation's complex internal network might be a single AS, as may the national network of any single Internet Service Provider (ISP). Figure 99 shows a simple network with two autonomous systems.

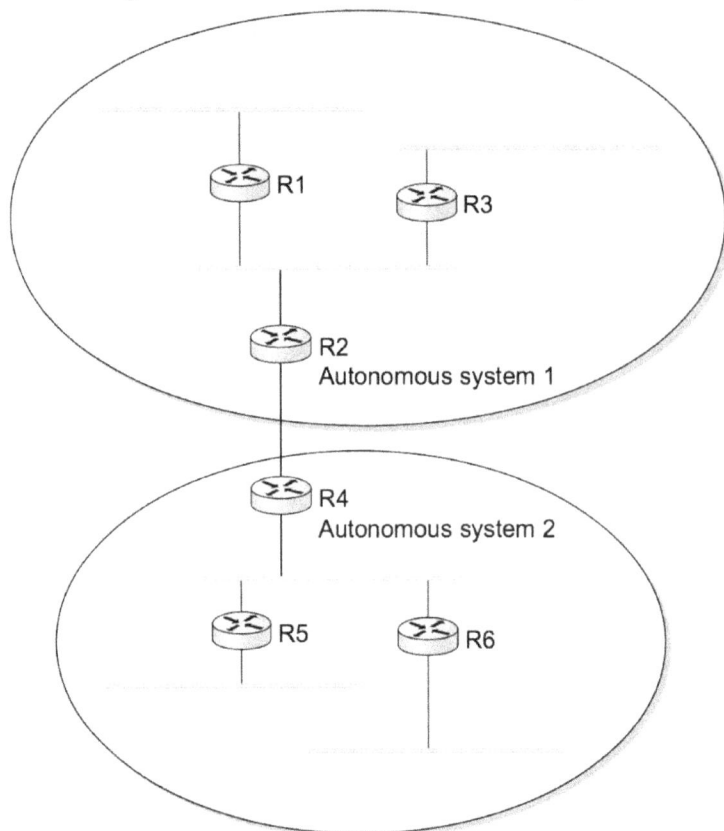

Figure 99. A network with two autonomous systems.

The fundamental concept underlying autonomous systems is to offer an extra method for hierarchically consolidating routing information in a vast internet, hence enhancing scalability. The routing problem is now divided into two distinct parts: intra-autonomous system routing and inter-autonomous system routing. Autonomous systems in the Internet, also known as routing domains, are divided into two parts for the routing problem: interdomain routing and intradomain routing. The AS concept not only enhances scalability but also separates the intradomain routing inside one AS from that in another AS. Therefore, any Autonomous System (AS) has the freedom to implement any intradomain routing protocols of its choice. It has the capability to utilize static routes or various protocols, if preferred. The interdomain routing problem involves the sharing of reachability information between multiple Autonomous Systems (ASs). This information consists of descriptions of the set of IP addresses that can be accessed through a specific AS.

CHALLENGES IN INTERDOMAIN ROUTING

Perhaps the most important challenge of interdomain routing today is the need for each AS to determine its own routing policies. A simple example routing policy implemented at a particular AS might look like this: "Whenever possible, I prefer to send traffic via AS X than via AS Y, but I'll use AS Y if it is the only path, and I never want to carry traffic from AS X to AS Y or vice versa." Such a policy would be typical when I have paid money to both AS X and AS Y to connect my AS to the rest of the Internet, and AS X is my preferred provider of connectivity, with AS Y being the fallback. Because I view both AS X and AS Y as providers (and presumably I paid them to play this role), I don't expect to help them out by carrying traffic between them across my network (this is called transit traffic). The more autonomous systems I connect to, the more complex policies I might have, especially when you consider backbone providers, who may interconnect with dozens of other providers and hundreds of customers and have different economic arrangements (which affect routing policies) with each one.

A key design goal of interdomain routing is that policies like the example above, and much more complex ones, should be supported by the interdomain routing system. To make the problem harder, I need to be able to implement such a policy without any help from other autonomous systems, and in the face of possible misconfiguration or malicious behavior by other autonomous systems. Furthermore, there is often a desire to keep the policies private, because the entities that run the autonomous systems—mostly ISPs—are often in competition with each other and don't want their economic arrangements made public.

There have been two major interdomain routing protocols in the history of the Internet. The first was the Exterior Gateway Protocol (EGP), which had a number of limitations, perhaps the most severe of which was that it constrained the topology of the Internet rather significantly. EGP was designed when the Internet had a treelike topology, such as that illustrated in Figure 97, and did not allow for the topology to become more general. Note that in this simple treelike structure there is a single backbone, and autonomous systems are connected only as parents and children and not as peers.

The replacement for EGP was the Border Gateway Protocol (BGP), which has iterated through four versions (BGP-4). BGP is often regarded as one of the more complex parts of the Internet. We'll cover some of its high points here.

Unlike its predecessor EGP, BGP makes virtually no assumptions about how autonomous systems are interconnected—they form an arbitrary graph. This model is clearly general enough to accommodate non-tree-structured internetworks, like the simplified picture of a multi-provider Internet shown in Figure 100. (It turns out there is still some sort of structure to the Internet, as we'll see below, but it's nothing like as simple as a tree, and BGP makes no assumptions about such structure.)

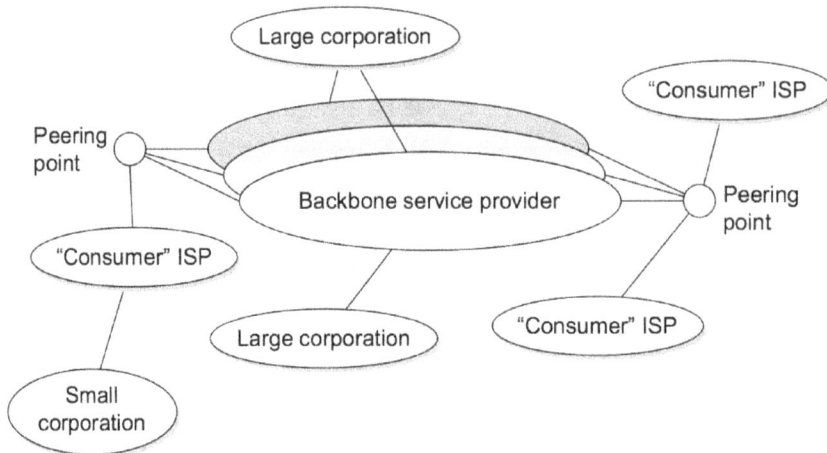

Figure 100. A simple multi-provider Internet.

Unlike the simple tree-structured Internet shown in Figure 97, or even the fairly simple picture in Figure 100, today's Internet consists of a richly interconnected set of networks, mostly operated by private companies (ISPs) rather than governments. Many Internet Service Providers (ISPs) exist mainly to provide service to "consumers" (i.e., individuals with computers in their homes), while others offer something more like the old backbone service, interconnecting other providers and sometimes larger corporations. Often, many providers arrange to interconnect with each other at a single peering point.

To get a better sense of how we might manage routing among this complex interconnection of autonomous systems, we can start by defining a few terms. We define local traffic as traffic that originates at or terminates on nodes within an AS, and transit traffic as traffic that passes through an AS. We can classify autonomous systems into three broad types:

- ◉ **Stub AS**—an AS that has only a single connection to one other AS; such an AS will only carry local traffic. The small corporation in Figure 100 is an example of a stub AS.

- ◉ **Multihomed AS**—an AS that has connections to more than one other AS but that refuses to carry transit traffic, such as the large corporation at the top of Figure 100.

- ◉ **Transit AS**—an AS that has connections to more than one other AS and that is designed to carry both transit and local traffic, such as the backbone providers in Figure 100.

Whereas the discussion of routing in the previous chapter focused on finding optimal paths based on minimizing some sort of link metric, the goals of interdomain routing are rather more complex. First, it is necessary to find some path to the intended destination that is loop free. Second, paths must be compliant with the policies of the various autonomous systems along the path—and, as we have already seen, those policies might be almost arbitrarily complex. Thus, while intradomain focuses on a well-defined problem of optimizing the scalar cost of the path, interdomain focuses on finding a non-looping, policy-compliant path—a much more complex optimization problem.

There are additional factors that make interdomain routing hard. The first is simply a matter of scale. An Internet backbone router must be able to forward any packet destined anywhere in the Internet. That means having a routing table that will provide a match for any valid IP address. While CIDR has helped to control the number of distinct prefixes that are carried in the Internet's backbone routing, there is inevitably a lot of routing information to pass around—roughly 700,000 prefixes in mid-2018.

A further challenge in interdomain routing arises from the autonomous nature of the domains. Note that each domain may run its own interior routing protocols and use any scheme it chooses to assign metrics to paths. This means that it is impossible to calculate meaningful path costs for a path that crosses multiple autonomous systems. A cost of 1000 across one provider might imply a great path, but it might mean an unacceptably bad one from another provider. As a result, interdomain routing advertises only reachability. The concept of reachability is basically a statement that "you can reach this network through this AS." This means that for interdomain routing to pick an optimal path is essentially impossible.

The autonomous nature of interdomain raises issue of trust. Provider A might be unwilling to believe certain advertisements from provider B for fear that provider B will advertise erroneous routing information. For example, trusting provider B when he advertises a great route to anywhere in the Internet can be a disastrous choice if provider B turns out to have made a mistake configuring his routers or to have insufficient capacity to carry the traffic.

The issue of trust is also related to the need to support complex policies as noted above. For example, I might be willing to trust a particular provider only when he advertises reachability to certain prefixes, and thus I would have a policy that says, "Use AS X to reach only prefixes p and q, if and only if AS X advertises reachability to those prefixes."

BASICS OF BGP

Each AS has one or more border routers through which packets enter and leave the AS. In our simple example in Figure 99, routers R2 and R4 would be border routers. (Over the years, routers have sometimes also been known as gateways, hence the names of the protocols BGP and EGP). A border router is simply an IP router that is charged with the task of forwarding packets between autonomous systems.

Each AS that participates in BGP must also have at least one BGP speaker, a router that "speaks" BGP to other BGP speakers in other autonomous systems. It is common to find that border routers are also BGP speakers, but that does not have to be the case.

BGP does not belong to either of the two main classes of routing protocols, distance-vector or link-state. Unlike these protocols, BGP advertises complete paths as an enumerated list of autonomous systems to reach a particular network. It is sometimes called a path-vector protocol for this reason. The advertisement of complete paths is necessary to enable the sorts of policy decisions described above to be made in accordance with the wishes of a particular AS. It also enables routing loops to be readily detected.

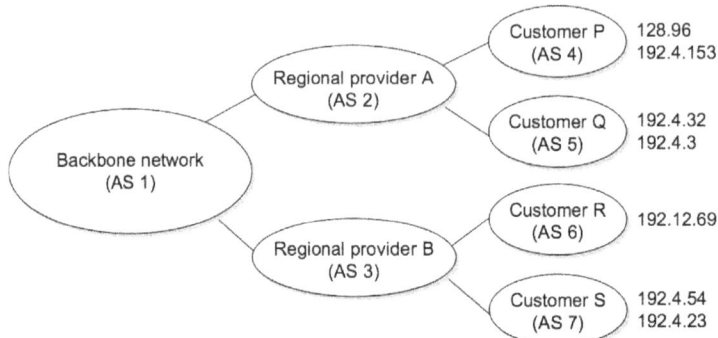

Figure 101. Example of a network running BGP.

To see how this works, consider the very simple example network in Figure 101. Assume that the providers are transit networks, while the customer networks are stubs. A BGP speaker for the AS of provider A (AS 2) would be able to advertise reachability information for each of the network numbers assigned to customers P and Q. Thus, it would say, in effect, "The networks 128.96, 192.4.153, 192.4.32, and 192.4.3 can be reached directly from AS 2." The backbone network, on receiving this advertisement, can advertise, "The networks 128.96, 192.4.153, 192.4.32, and 192.4.3 can be reached along the path (AS 1, AS 2)." Similarly, it could advertise, "The networks 192.12.69, 192.4.54, and 192.4.23 can be reached along the path (AS 1, AS 3)."

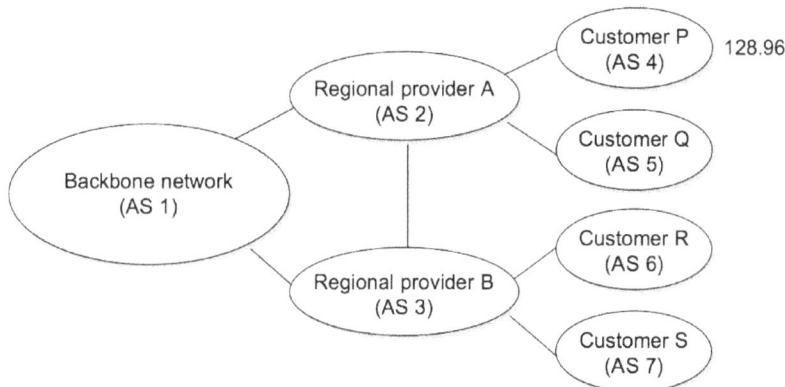

Figure 102. Example of loop among autonomous systems.

An important job of BGP is to prevent the establishment of looping paths. For example, consider the network illustrated in Figure 102. It differs from Figure 101 only in the addition of an extra link between AS 2 and AS 3, but the effect now is that the graph of autonomous systems has a loop in it. Suppose AS 1 learns that it can reach network 128.96 through AS 2, so it advertises this fact to AS 3, who in turn advertises it back to AS 2. In the absence of any loop prevention mechanism, AS 2 could now decide that AS 3 was the preferred route for packets destined for 128.96. If AS 2 starts sending packets addressed to 128.96 to AS 3, AS 3 would send them to AS 1; AS 1 would send them back to AS 2; and they would loop forever. This is prevented by carrying the complete AS path in the routing messages. In this case, the advertisement for a path to 128.96 received by AS 2 from AS 3 would contain an AS path of (AS 3, AS 1, AS 2, AS 4). AS 2 sees itself in this path, and thus concludes that this is not a useful path for it to use.

In order for this loop prevention technique to work, the AS numbers carried in BGP clearly need to be unique. For example, AS 2 can only recognize itself in the AS path in the above example if no other AS identifies itself in the same way. AS numbers are now 32-bits long, and they are assigned by a central authority to assure uniqueness.

A given AS will only advertise routes that it considers good enough for itself. That is, if a BGP speaker has a choice of several different routes to a destination, it will choose the best one according to its own local policies, and then that will be the route it advertises. Furthermore, a BGP speaker is under no obligation to advertise any route to a destination, even if it has one. This is how an AS can implement a policy of not providing transit—by refusing to advertise routes to prefixes that are not contained within that AS, even if it knows how to reach them.

Given that links fail and policies change, BGP speakers need to be able to cancel previously advertised paths. This is done with a form of negative advertisement known as a withdrawn route. Both positive and negative reachability information are carried in a BGP update message, the format of which is shown in Figure 103. (Note that the fields in this figure are multiples of 16 bits, unlike other packet formats in this chapter.)

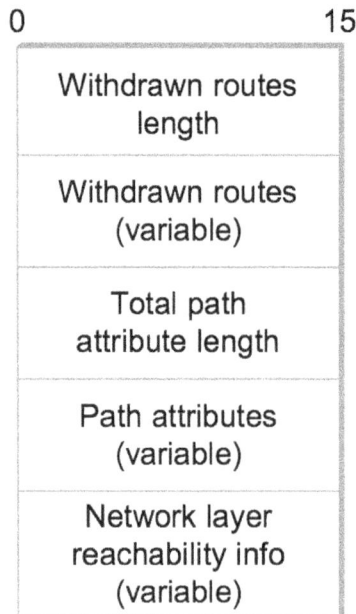

0	15
Withdrawn routes length	
Withdrawn routes (variable)	
Total path attribute length	
Path attributes (variable)	
Network layer reachability info (variable)	

Figure 103. BGP-4 update packet format.

Unlike the routing protocols described in the previous chapter, BGP is defined to run on top of TCP, the reliable transport protocol. Because BGP speakers can count on TCP to be reliable, this means that any information that has been sent from one speaker to another does not need to be sent again. Thus, as long as nothing has changed, a BGP speaker can simply send an occasional keepalive message that says, in effect, "I'm still here and nothing has changed." If that router were to crash or become disconnected from its peer, it would stop sending the keepalives, and the other routers that had learned routes from it would assume that those routes were no longer valid.

COMMON AS RELATIONSHIPS AND POLICIES

Having said that policies may be arbitrarily complex, there turn out to be a few common ones, reflecting common relationships between autonomous systems. The most common relationships are illustrated in Figure 104. The three common relationships and the policies that go with them are as follows:

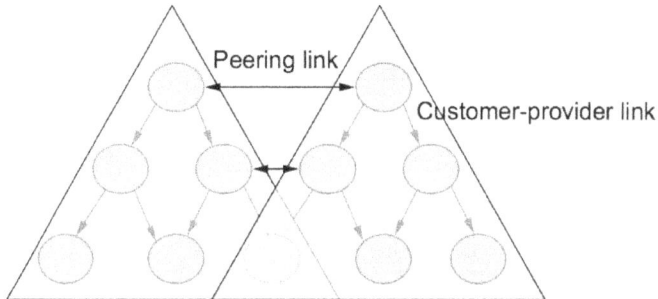

Figure 104. Common AS relationships.

- **Provider-Customer**—Providers are in the business of connecting their customers to the rest of the Internet. A customer might be a corporation, or it might be a smaller ISP (which may have customers of its own). So the common policy is to advertise all the routes I know about to my customer, and advertise routes I learn from my customer to everyone.

- **Customer-Provider**—In the other direction, the customer wants to get traffic directed to him (and his customers, if he has them) by his provider, and he wants to be able to send traffic to the rest of the Internet through his provider. So the common policy in this case is to advertise my own prefixes and routes learned from my customers to my provider, advertise routes learned from my provider to my customers, but don't advertise routes learned from one provider to another provider. That last part is to make sure the customer doesn't find himself in the business of carrying traffic from one provider to another, which isn't in his interests if he is paying the providers to carry traffic for him.

- **Peer**—The third option is a symmetrical peering between autonomous systems. Two providers who view themselves as equals usually peer so that they can get access to each other's customers without having to pay another provider. The typical policy here is to advertise routes learned from my customers to my peer, advertise routes learned from my peer to my customers, but don't advertise routes from my peer to any provider or vice versa.

One thing to note about this figure is the way it has brought back some structure to the apparently unstructured Internet. At the bottom of the hierarchy we have the stub networks that are customers of one or more providers, and as we move up the hierarchy we see providers who have other providers as their customers. At the top, we have providers who have customers and peers but are not customers of anyone. These providers are known as the Tier-1 providers.

Key Takeaway

Let's return to the real question: How does all this help us to build scalable networks? First, the number of nodes participating in BGP is on the order of the number of autonomous systems, which is much smaller than the number of networks. Second, finding a good interdomain route is only a matter of finding a path to the right border router, of which there are only a few per AS. Thus, we have neatly subdivided the routing problem into manageable parts, once again using a new level of hierarchy to increase scalability. The complexity of interdomain routing is now on the order of the number of autonomous systems, and the complexity of intradomain routing is on the order of the number of networks in a single AS.

INTEGRATING INTERDOMAIN AND INTRADOMAIN ROUTING

While the preceding discussion illustrates how a BGP speaker learns interdomain routing information, the question still remains as to how all the other routers in a domain get this information. There are several ways this problem can be addressed.

Let's start with a very simple situation, which is also very common. In the case of a stub AS that only connects to other autonomous systems at a single point, the border router is clearly the only choice for all routes that are outside the AS. Such a router can inject a default route into the intradomain routing protocol. In effect, this is a statement that any network that has not been explicitly advertised in the intradomain protocol is reachable through the border router. Recall from the discussion of IP forwarding in the previous chapter that the default entry in the forwarding table comes after all the more specific entries, and it matches anything that failed to match a specific entry.

The next step up in complexity is to have the border routers inject specific routes they have learned from outside the AS. Consider, for example, the border router of a provider AS that connects to a customer AS. That router could learn that the network prefix 192.4.54/24 is located inside the customer AS, either through BGP or because the information is configured into the border router. It could inject a route to that prefix into the routing protocol running inside the provider AS. This would be an advertisement of the sort, "I have a link to 192.4.54/24 of cost X." This would cause other routers in the provider AS to learn that this border router is the place to send packets destined for that prefix.

The final level of complexity comes in backbone networks, which learn so much routing information from BGP that it becomes too costly to inject it into the intradomain protocol. For example, if a border router wants to inject 10,000 prefixes that it learned about from another AS, it will have to send very big link-state packets to the other routers in that AS, and their shortest-path calculations are going to become very complex. For this reason, the routers in a backbone network use a variant of BGP called interior BGP (iBGP) to effectively redistribute the information that is learned by the BGP speakers at the edges of the AS to all the other routers in the AS. (The other variant of BGP, discussed above, runs between autonomous systems and is called exterior BGP, or eBGP). iBGP enables any router in the AS to learn the best border router to use when sending a packet to any address. At the same time, each router in the AS keeps track of how to get to each border router using a conventional intradomain protocol with no injected information. By combining these two sets of information, each router in the AS is able to determine the appropriate next hop for all prefixes.

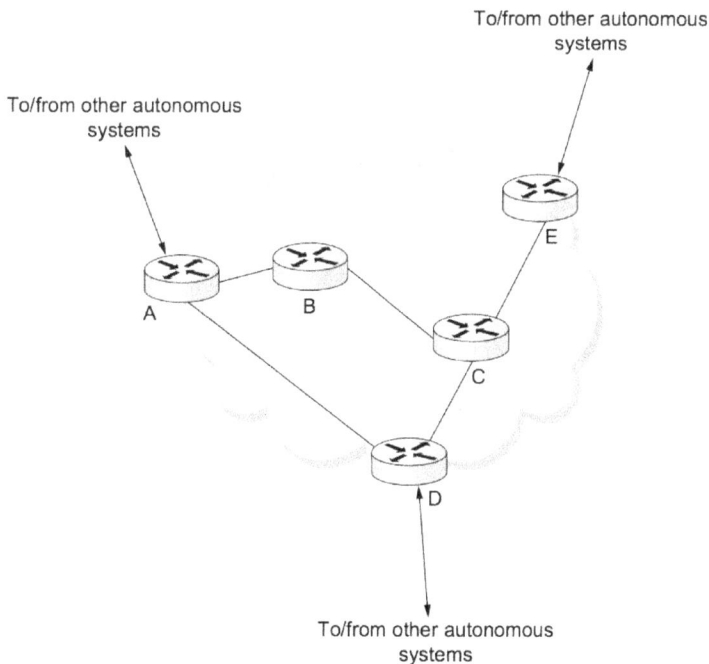

Figure 105. Example of interdomain and intradomain routing. All routers run iBGP and an intradomain routing protocol. Border routers A, D, and E also run eBGP to other autonomous systems.

To see how this all works, consider the simple example network, representing a single AS, in Figure 105. The three border routers, A, D, and E, speak eBGP to other autonomous systems and learn how to reach various prefixes. These three border routers communicate with each other and with the interior routers B and C by building a mesh of iBGP sessions among all the routers in the AS. Let's now focus in on how router B builds up its complete view of how to forward packets to any prefix. Look at the top left of Figure 106, which shows the information that router

B learns from its iBGP sessions. It learns that some prefixes are best reached via router A, some via D, and some via E. At the same time, all the routers in the AS are also running some intradomain routing protocol such as Routing Information Protocol (RIP) or Open Shortest Path First (OSPF). (A generic term for intradomain protocols is an interior gateway protocol, or IGP.) From this completely separate protocol, B learns how to reach other nodes inside the domain, as shown in the top right table. For example, to reach router E, B needs to send packets toward router C. Finally, in the bottom table, B puts the whole picture together, combining the information about external prefixes learned from iBGP with the information about interior routes to the border routers learned from the IGP. Thus, if a prefix like 18.0/16 is reachable via border router E, and the best interior path to E is via C, then it follows that any packet destined for 18.0/16 should be forwarded toward C. In this way, any router in the AS can build up a complete routing table for any prefix that is reachable via some border router of the AS.

Prefix	BGP Next Hop
18.0/16	E
12.5.5/24	A
128.34/16	D
128.69./16	A

BGP table for the AS

Router	IGP Path
A	A
C	C
D	C
E	C

IGP table for router B

Prefix	IGP Path
18.0/16	C
12.5.5/24	A
128.34/16	C
128.69./16	A

Combined table for router B

Figure 106. BGP routing table, IGP routing table, and combined table at router B.

4.2 IP Version 6

The rationale behind the development of a new iteration of IP is straightforward: to address the issue of IP address space depletion. CIDR significantly aided in limiting the rate at which the Internet address space was being depleted and also facilitated the management of routing table information required by the Internet's routers. Nevertheless, these strategies are now insufficient. Specifically, attaining a 100% address use efficiency is practically unattainable, resulting in the depletion of the address space well before the connection of the 4 billionth host to the Internet. Although the utilization of all 4 billion addresses is possible, it has become evident that IP addresses must now be allocated to a wider range of devices outside conventional computers, such as smartphones, televisions, household appliances, and drones. In retrospect, a 32-bit address space is significantly limited.

4.2.1 Historical Perspective

In 1991, the IETF initiated an examination of the issue of increasing the IP address space, and multiple alternatives were put up. Due to the fact that the IP address is included in the header of each IP packet, every increase in the address size necessitates a modification in the packet header. This entails the development of a fresh iteration of the Internet Protocol, which in turn necessitates the creation of novel software for each host and router within the Internet. This is undeniably a significant issue that requires meticulous consideration. The endeavor to establish a fresh iteration of IP was initially referred to as IP Next Generation, or IPng. As the work advanced, an official IP version number was designated, so IPng was renamed as IPv6. It is important to mention that the IP version described in this chapter is specifically version 4, also known as IPv4. The observed discrepancy in numbering can be attributed to the utilization of version number 5 for an experimental protocol conducted several years ago. The transition to a new version of IP had a profound impact that led to a chain reaction. The prevailing sentiment among network designers was that if one were to undertake such a significant upgrade, it would be prudent to address as many other issues in IP as feasible concurrently. As a result, the IETF requested white papers from individuals interested in contributing, seeking opinion on the needed characteristics for a potential future version of IP.

In addition to the need to accommodate scalable routing and addressing, some of the other wish list items for IPng included:

- Support for real-time services

- Security support

- Autoconfiguration (i.e., the ability of hosts to automatically configure themselves with such information as their own IP address and domain name)

- Enhanced routing functionality, including support for mobile hosts

It is interesting to note that, while many of these features were absent from IPv4 at the time IPv6 was being designed, support for all of them has made its way into IPv4 in recent years, often using similar techniques in both protocols. It can be argued that the freedom to think of IPv6 as a clean slate facilitated the design of new capabilities for IP that were then retrofitted into IPv4.

Aside from the desired features, it was imperative for IPv6 to have a transition strategy that would facilitate the migration from the existing IP version (version 4) to the new version. Given the vastness of the Internet and its lack of centralized authority, it would be utterly unfeasible to implement a "flag day" where all sites and routers are shut down and a new version of IP is deployed. The developers anticipated a prolonged transitional phase during which certain addresses and routers would exclusively use IPv4, some would utilize both IPv4 and IPv6, and others would solely rely on IPv6. They probably did not expect that the changeover period would last for almost 30 years.

4.2.2 Addresses and Routing

First and foremost, IPv6 provides a 128-bit address space, as opposed to the 32 bits of version 4. Thus, while version 4 can potentially address 4 billion nodes if address assignment efficiency reaches 100%, IPv6 can address 3.4×1038 nodes, again assuming 100% efficiency. As we have seen, though, 100% efficiency in address assignment is not likely. Some analysis of other addressing schemes, such as those of the French and U.S. telephone networks, as well as that of IPv4, have turned up some empirical numbers for address assignment efficiency. Based on the most pessimistic estimates of efficiency drawn from this study, the IPv6 address space is predicted to provide over 1500 addresses per square foot of the Earth's surface, which certainly seems like it should serve us well even when toasters on Venus have IP addresses.

Address Space Allocation

Drawing on the effectiveness of CIDR in IPv4, IPv6 addresses are also classless, but the address space is still subdivided in various ways based on the leading bits. Rather than specifying different address classes, the leading bits specify different uses of the IPv6 address. The current assignment of prefixes is listed in Table 21.

Table 21. Address Prefix Assignments for IPv6.

Prefix	Use
00...0 (128 bits)	Unspecified
00...1 (128 bits)	Loopback
1111 1111	Multicast addresses
1111 1110 10	Link-local unicast
Everything else	Global Unicast

This allocation of the address space warrants a little discussion. First, the entire functionality of IPv4's three main address classes (A, B, and C) is contained inside the "everything else" range. Global Unicast Addresses, as we will see shortly, are a lot like classless IPv4 addresses, only much longer. These are the main ones of interest at this point, with over 99% of the total IPv6 address space available to this important form of address. (At the time of writing, IPv6 unicast addresses are being allocated from the block that begins 001, with the remaining address space—about 87%—being reserved for future use.)

The multicast address space is (obviously) for multicast, thereby serving the same role as class D addresses in IPv4. Note that multicast addresses are easy to distinguish—they start with a byte of all 1s. We will see how these addresses are used in a later section.

The idea behind link-local use addresses is to enable a host to construct an address that will work on the network to which it is connected without being concerned about the global uniqueness of the address. This may be useful for autoconfiguration, as we will see below. Similarly, the site-local use addresses are intended to allow valid addresses to be constructed on a site (e.g., a private corporate network) that is not connected to the larger Internet; again, global uniqueness need not be an issue.

Within the global unicast address space are some important special types of addresses. A node may be assigned an IPv4-compatible IPv6 address by zero-extending a 32-bit IPv4 address to 128 bits. A node that is only capable of understanding IPv4 can be assigned an IPv4-mapped IPv6 address by prefixing the 32-bit IPv4 address with 2 bytes of all 1s and then zero-extending the result to 128 bits. These two special address types have uses in the IPv4-to-IPv6 transition (see the sidebar on this topic).

ADDRESS NOTATION

Just as with IPv4, there is some special notation for writing down IPv6 addresses. The standard representation is x:x:x:x:x:x:x:x, where each x is a hexadecimal representation of a 16-bit piece of the address. An example would be

47CD:1234:4422:AC02:0022:1234:A456:0124

Any IPv6 address can be written using this notation. Since there are a few special types of IPv6 addresses, there are some special notations that may be helpful in certain circumstances. For example, an address with a large number of contiguous 0s can be written more compactly by omitting all the 0 fields. Thus,

47CD:0000:0000:0000:0000:0000:A456:0124

could be written

47CD::A456:0124

Clearly, this form of shorthand can only be used for one set of contiguous 0s in an address to avoid ambiguity.

The two types of IPv6 addresses that contain an embedded IPv4 address have their own special notation that makes extraction of the IPv4 address easier. For example, the IPv4-mapped IPv6 address of a host whose IPv4 address was 128.96.33.81 could be written as:

:FFFF:128.96.33.81

That is, the last 32 bits are written in IPv4 notation, rather than as a pair of hexadecimal numbers separated by a colon. Note that the double colon at the front indicates the leading 0s.

GLOBAL UNICAST ADDRESSES

By far the most important sort of addressing that IPv6 must provide is plain old unicast addressing. It must do this in a way that supports the rapid rate of addition of new hosts to the Internet and that allows routing to be done in a scalable way as the number of physical networks in the Internet grows. Thus, at the heart of IPv6 is the unicast address allocation plan that determines how unicast addresses will be assigned to service providers, autonomous systems, networks, hosts, and routers.

In fact, the address allocation plan that is proposed for IPv6 unicast addresses is extremely similar to that being deployed with CIDR in IPv4. To understand how it works and how it provides scalability, it is helpful to define some new terms. We may think of a nontransit AS (i.e., a stub or multihomed AS) as a subscriber, and we may think of a transit AS as a provider. Furthermore, we may subdivide providers into direct and indirect. The former are directly connected to subscribers. The latter primarily connect other providers, are not connected directly to subscribers, and are often known as backbone networks.

With this set of definitions, we can see that the Internet is not just an arbitrarily interconnected set of autonomous systems; it has some intrinsic hierarchy. The difficulty lies in making use of this hierarchy without inventing mechanisms that fail when the hierarchy is not strictly observed, as happened with EGP. For example, the distinction between direct and indirect providers becomes blurred when a subscriber connects to a backbone or when a direct provider starts connecting to many other providers.

As with CIDR, the goal of the IPv6 address allocation plan is to provide aggregation of routing information to reduce the burden on intradomain routers. Again, the key idea is to use an address prefix—a set of contiguous bits at the most significant end of the address—to aggregate reachability information to a large number of networks and even to a large number of autonomous systems. The main way to achieve this is to assign an address prefix to a direct provider and then for that direct provider to assign longer prefixes that begin with that prefix to its subscribers. Thus, a provider can advertise a single prefix for all of its subscribers.

Of course, the drawback is that if a site decides to change providers, it will need to obtain a new address prefix and renumber all the nodes in the site. This could be a colossal undertaking, enough to dissuade most people from ever changing providers. For this reason, there is ongoing research on other addressing schemes, such as geographic addressing, in which a site's address is a function of its location rather than the provider to which it attaches. At present, however, provider-based addressing is necessary to make routing work efficiently.

Note that while IPv6 address assignment is essentially equivalent to the way address assignment has happened in IPv4 since the introduction of CIDR, IPv6 has the significant advantage of not having a large installed base of assigned addresses to fit into its plans.

One question is whether it makes sense for hierarchical aggregation to take place at other levels in the hierarchy. For example, should all providers obtain their address prefixes from within a prefix allocated to the backbone to which they connect? Given that most providers connect to multiple backbones, this probably doesn't make sense. Also, since the number of providers is much smaller than the number of sites, the benefits of aggregating at this level are much fewer.

One place where aggregation may make sense is at the national or continental level. Continental boundaries form natural divisions in the Internet topology. If all addresses in Europe, for example, had a common prefix, then a great deal of aggregation could be done, and most routers in other continents would only need one routing table entry for all networks with the Europe prefix. Providers in Europe would all select their prefixes such that they began with the European prefix. Using this scheme, an IPv6 address might look like Figure 107. The RegistryID might be an identifier assigned to a European address registry, with different IDs assigned to other continents or countries. Note that prefixes would be of different lengths under this scenario. For example, a provider with few customers could have a longer prefix (and thus less total address space available) than one with many customers.

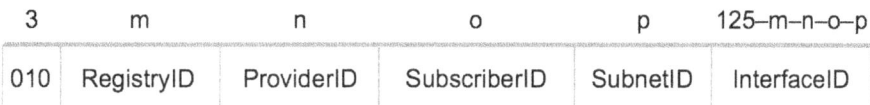

3	m	n	o	p	125–m–n–o–p
010	RegistryID	ProviderID	SubscriberID	SubnetID	InterfaceID

Figure 107. An IPv6 provider-based unicast address.

One tricky situation could occur when a subscriber is connected to more than one provider. Which prefix should the subscriber use for his or her site? There is no perfect solution to the problem. For example, suppose a subscriber is connected to two providers, X and Y. If the subscriber takes his prefix from X, then Y has to advertise a prefix that has no relationship to its other subscribers and that as a consequence cannot be aggregated. If the subscriber numbers part of his AS with the prefix of X and part with the prefix of Y, he runs the risk of having half his site become unreachable if the connection to one provider goes down. One solution that works fairly well if X and Y have a lot of subscribers in common is for them to have three prefixes between them: one for subscribers of X only, one for subscribers of Y only, and one for the sites that are subscribers of both X and Y.

4.2.3 Packet Format

Despite the fact that IPv6 extends IPv4 in several ways, its header format is actually simpler. This simplicity is due to a concerted effort to remove unnecessary functionality from the protocol. Figure 108 shows the result.

As with many headers, this one starts with a Version field, which is set to 6 for IPv6. The Version field is in the same place relative to the start of the header as IPv4's Version field so that header-processing software can immediately decide which header format to look for. The TrafficClass and FlowLabel fields both relate to quality of service issues.

The PayloadLen field gives the length of the packet, excluding the IPv6 header, measured in bytes. The NextHeader field cleverly replaces both the IP options and the Protocol field of IPv4. If options are required, then they are carried in one or more special headers following the IP header, and this is indicated by the value of the NextHeader field. If there are no special headers, the NextHeader field is the demux key identifying the higher-level protocol running over IP (e.g., TCP or UDP); that is, it serves the same purpose as the IPv4 Protocol field. Also, fragmentation is now handled as an optional header, which means that the fragmentation-related fields of IPv4 are not included in the IPv6 header. The HopLimit field is simply the TTL of IPv4, renamed to reflect the way it is actually used.

Finally, the bulk of the header is taken up with the source and destination addresses, each of which is 16 bytes (128 bits) long. Thus, the IPv6 header is always 40 bytes long. Considering that IPv6 addresses are four times longer than those of IPv4, this compares quite well with the IPv4 header, which is 20 bytes long in the absence of options.

0	4	12	16	24	31

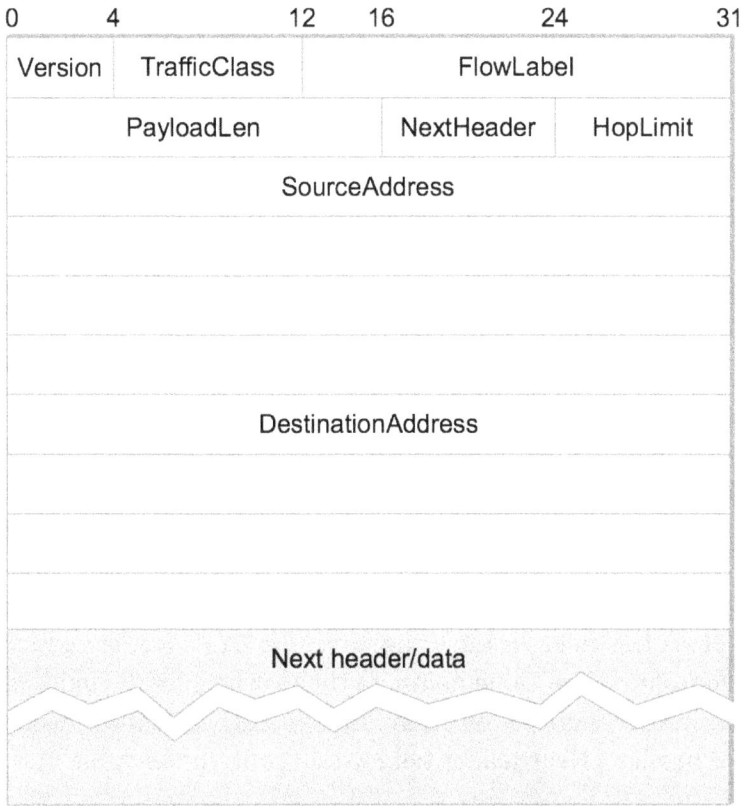

Figure 108. IPv6 packet header.

The way that IPv6 handles options is quite an improvement over IPv4. In IPv4, if any options were present, every router had to parse the entire options field to see if any of the options were relevant. This is because the options were all buried at the end of the IP header, as an unordered collection of '(type, length, value)' tuples. In contrast, IPv6 treats options as extension headers that must, if present, appear in a specific order. This means that each router can quickly determine if any of the options are relevant to it; in most cases, they will not be. Usually this can be determined by just looking at the NextHeader field. The end result is that option processing is much more efficient in IPv6, which is an important factor in router performance. In addition, the new formatting of options as extension headers means that they can be of arbitrary length, whereas in IPv4 they were limited to 44 bytes at most. We will see how some of the options are used below.

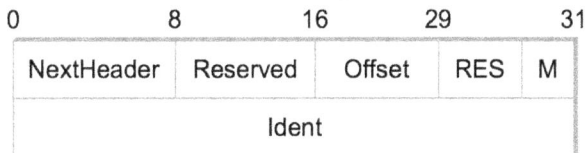

Figure 109. IPv6 fragmentation extension header.

Each option has its own type of extension header. The type of each extension header is identified by the value of the NextHeader field in the header that precedes it, and each extension header contains a NextHeader field to identify the header following it. The last extension header will be followed by a transport-layer header (e.g., TCP) and in this case the value of the NextHeader field is the same as the value of the Protocol field would be in an IPv4 header. Thus, the NextHeader field does double duty; it may either identify the type of extension header to follow, or, in the last extension header, it serves as a demux key to identify the higher-layer protocol running over IPv6.

Consider the example of the fragmentation header, shown in Figure 109. This header provides functionality similar to the fragmentation fields in the IPv4 header, but it is only present if fragmentation is necessary. Assuming it is the only extension header present, then the NextHeader field of the IPv6 header would contain the value 44, which is the value assigned to indicate the fragmentation header. The NextHeader field of the fragmentation header itself contains a value describing the header that follows it. Again, assuming no other extension headers are present, then the next header might be the TCP header, which results in NextHeader containing the value 6, just as the Protocol field would in IPv4. If the fragmentation header were followed by, say, an authentication header, then the fragmentation header's NextHeader field would contain the value 51.

4.2.4 Advanced Capabilities

As mentioned at the beginning of this section, the primary motivation behind the development of IPv6 was to support the continued growth of the Internet. Once the IP header had to be changed for the sake of the addresses, however, the door was open for a wide variety of other changes, two of which we describe below. But IPv6 includes several additional features, most of which are covered elsewhere in this book; e.g., mobility, security, quality-of-service. It is interesting to note that, in most of these areas, the IPv4 and IPv6 capabilities have become virtually indistinguishable, so that the main driver for IPv6 remains the need for larger addresses.

AUTOCONFIGURATION

While the Internet's growth has been impressive, one factor that has inhibited faster acceptance of the technology is the fact that getting connected to the Internet has typically required a fair amount of system administration expertise. In particular, every host that is connected to the Internet needs to be configured with a certain minimum amount of information, such as a valid IP address, a subnet mask for the link to which it attaches, and the address of a name server. Thus, it has not been possible to unpack a new computer and connect it to the Internet without some preconfiguration. One goal of IPv6, therefore, is to provide support for autoconfiguration, sometimes referred to as plug-and-play operation.

As we saw in the previous chapter, autoconfiguration is possible for IPv4, but it depends on the existence of a server that is configured to hand out addresses and other configuration information to Dynamic Host Configuration Protocol (DHCP) clients. The longer address format in IPv6 helps provide a useful, new form of autoconfiguration called stateless autoconfiguration, which does not require a server.

Recall that IPv6 unicast addresses are hierarchical, and that the least significant portion is the interface ID. Thus, we can subdivide the autoconfiguration problem into two parts:

⦿ Obtain an interface ID that is unique on the link to which the host is attached.

⦿ Obtain the correct address prefix for this subnet.

The first part turns out to be rather easy, since every host on a link must have a unique link-level address. For example, all hosts on an Ethernet have a unique 48-bit Ethernet address. This can be turned into a valid link-local use address by adding the appropriate prefix from Table 21 (1111 1110 10) followed by enough 0s to make up 128 bits. For some devices—for example, printers or hosts on a small routerless network that do not connect to any other networks—this address may be perfectly adequate. Those devices that need a globally valid address depend on a router on the same link to periodically advertise the appropriate prefix for the link. Clearly, this requires that the router be configured with the correct address prefix, and that this prefix be chosen in such a way that there is enough space at the end (e.g., 48 bits) to attach an appropriate link-level address.

The ability to embed link-level addresses as long as 48 bits into IPv6 addresses was one of the reasons for choosing such a large address size. Not only does 128 bits allow the embedding, but it leaves plenty of space for the multilevel hierarchy of addressing that we discussed above.

SOURCE-DIRECTED ROUTING

Another of IPv6's extension headers is the routing header. In the absence of this header, routing for IPv6 differs very little from that of IPv4 under CIDR. The routing header contains a list of IPv6 addresses that represent nodes or topological areas that the packet should visit en route to its destination. A topological area may be, for example, a backbone provider's network. Specifying that packets must visit this network would be a way of implementing provider selection on a packet-by-packet basis. Thus, a host could say that it wants some packets to go through a provider that is cheap, others through a provider that provides high reliability, and still others through a provider that the host trusts to provide security.

To provide the ability to specify topological entities rather than individual nodes, IPv6 defines an anycast address. An anycast address is assigned to a set of interfaces, and packets sent to that address will go to the "nearest" of those interfaces, with nearest being determined by the routing protocols. For example, all the routers of a backbone provider could be assigned a single anycast address, which would be used in the routing header.

4.3 Multicast

Multi-access networks, such as Ethernet, utilize hardware to implement multicast. Nevertheless, there are certain applications that require a more extensive multicasting capacity that is capable of functioning well on the Internet's large scale. When a radio station is streamed over the Internet, the identical data needs to be transmitted to all the hosts where a user is connected to that station. In that particular example, the mode of communication is characterized by a one-to-many relationship. Additional instances of one-to-many applications encompass the dissemination of identical news, real-time stock prices, software upgrades, or television channels to numerous recipients. The second case is frequently referred to as IPTV. Additionally, there are applications that facilitate communication among several participants, known as many-to-many communication. Examples of such applications include multimedia teleconferencing, online multiplayer gaming, and distributed simulations. In such instances, individuals within a collective receive information from several transmitters, usually from one another. All recipients receive identical data from a certain sender.

Normal IP communication, in which each packet must be addressed and sent to a single host, is not well suited to such applications. If an application has data to send to a group, it would have to send a separate packet with the identical data to each member of the group. This redundancy consumes more bandwidth than necessary. Furthermore, the redundant traffic is not distributed evenly but rather is focused around the sending host, and may easily exceed the capacity of the sending host and the nearby networks and routers.

To better support many-to-many and one-to-many communication, IP provides an IP-level multicast analogous to the link-level multicast provided by multi-access networks like Ethernet. Now that we are introducing the concept of multicast for IP, we also need a term for the traditional one-to-one service of IP that has been described so far: That service is referred to as unicast.

The basic IP multicast model is a many-to-many model based on multicast groups, where each group has its own IP multicast address. The hosts that are members of a group receive copies of any packets sent to that group's multicast address. A host can be in multiple groups, and it can join and leave groups freely by telling its local router using a protocol that we will discuss shortly. Thus, while we think of unicast addresses as being associated with a node or an interface, multicast addresses are associated with an abstract group, the membership of which changes dynamically over time. Further, the original IP multicast service model allows any host to send multicast traffic to a group; it doesn't have to be a member of the group, and there may be any number of such senders to a given group.

Using IP multicast to send the identical packet to each member of the group, a host sends a single copy of the packet addressed to the group's multicast address. The sending host doesn't need to know the individual unicast IP address of each member of the group because, as we will see, that knowledge is distributed among the routers in the internetwork. Similarly, the sending host doesn't need to send multiple copies of the packet because the routers will make copies whenever they have to forward the packet over more than one link. Compared to using unicast IP to deliver the same packets to many receivers, IP multicast is more scalable because it eliminates the redundant traffic (packets) that would have been sent many times over the same links, especially those near to the sending host.

IP's original many-to-many multicast has been supplemented with support for a form of one-to-many multicast. In this model of one-to-many multicast, called Source-Specific Multicast (SSM), a receiving host specifies both a multicast group and a specific sending host. The receiving host would then receive multicasts addressed to the specified group, but only if they are from the specified sender. Many Internet multicast applications (e.g., radio broadcasts) fit the SSM model. To contrast it with SSM, IP's original many-to-many model is sometimes referred to as Any Source Multicast (ASM).

A host signals its desire to join or leave a multicast group by communicating with its local router using a special protocol for just that purpose. In IPv4, that protocol is the Internet Group Management Protocol (IGMP); in IPv6, it is Multicast Listener Discovery (MLD). The router then has the responsibility for making multicast behave correctly with regard to that host. Because a host may fail to leave a multicast group when it should (after a crash or other failure, for example), the router periodically polls the network to determine which groups are still of interest to the attached hosts.

4.3.1 Multicast Addresses

IP has a subrange of its address space reserved for multicast addresses. In IPv4, these addresses are assigned in the class D address space, and IPv6 also has a portion of its address space reserved for multicast group addresses. Some subranges of the multicast ranges are reserved for intradomain multicast, so they can be reused independently by different domains.

There are thus 28 bits of possible multicast address in IPv4 when we ignore the prefix shared by all multicast addresses. This presents a problem when attempting to take advantage of hardware multicasting on a local area network (LAN). Let's take the case of Ethernet. Ethernet multicast addresses have only 23 bits when we ignore their shared prefix. In other words, to take advantage of Ethernet multicasting, IP has to map 28-bit IP multicast addresses into 23-bit Ethernet multicast addresses. This is implemented by taking the low-order 23 bits of any IP multicast address to use as its Ethernet multicast address and ignoring the high-order 5 bits. Thus, 32 (2^5) IP addresses map into each one of the Ethernet addresses.

In this section we use Ethernet as a canonical example of a networking technology that supports multicast in hardware, but the same is also true of PON (Passive Optical Networks), which is the access network technology often used to deliver fiber-to-the-home. In fact, IP Multicast over PON is now a common way to deliver IPTV to homes.

When a host on an Ethernet joins an IP multicast group, it configures its Ethernet interface to receive any packets with the corresponding Ethernet multicast address. Unfortunately, this causes the receiving host to receive not only the multicast traffic it desired but also traffic sent to any of the other 31 IP multicast groups that map to the same Ethernet address, if they are routed to that Ethernet. Therefore, IP at the receiving host must examine the IP header of any multicast packet to determine whether the packet really belongs to the desired group. In summary, the mismatch of multicast address sizes means that multicast traffic may place a burden on hosts that are not even interested in the group to which the traffic was sent. Fortunately, in some switched networks (such as switched Ethernet) this problem can be mitigated by schemes wherein the switches recognize unwanted packets and discard them.

One perplexing question is how senders and receivers learn which multicast addresses to use in the first place. This is normally handled by out-of-band means, and there are some quite sophisticated tools to enable group addresses to be advertised on the Internet.

4.3.2 Multicast Routing (DVMRP, PIM, MSDP)

A router's unicast forwarding tables indicate, for any IP address, which link to use to forward the unicast packet. To support multicast, a router must additionally have multicast forwarding tables that indicate, based on multicast address, which links—possibly more than one—to use to forward the multicast packet (the router duplicates the packet if it is to be forwarded over multiple links). Thus, where unicast forwarding tables collectively specify a set of paths, multicast forwarding tables collectively specify a set of trees: multicast distribution trees. Furthermore, to support Source-Specific Multicast (and, it turns out, for some types of Any Source Multicast), the multicast forwarding tables must indicate which links to use based on the combination of multicast address and the (unicast) IP address of the source, again specifying a set of trees.

Multicast routing is the process by which the multicast distribution trees are determined or, more concretely, the process by which the multicast forwarding tables are built. As with unicast routing, it is not enough that a multicast routing protocol "work"; it must also scale reasonably well as the network grows, and it must accommodate the autonomy of different routing domains.

DVMRP

Distance-vector routing used in unicast can be extended to support multicast. The resulting protocol is called Distance Vector Multicast Routing Protocol, or DVMRP. DVMRP was the first multicast routing protocol to see widespread use.

Recall that, in the distance-vector algorithm, each router maintains a table of Destination, Cost, NextHop tuples, and exchanges a list of (Destination, Cost) pairs with its directly connected neighbors. Extending this algorithm to support multicast is a two-stage process. First, we create a broadcast mechanism that allows a packet to be forwarded to all the networks on the internet. Second, we need to refine this mechanism so that it prunes back networks that do not have hosts that belong to the multicast group. Consequently, DVMRP is one of several multicast routing protocols described as flood-and-prune protocols.

Given a unicast routing table, each router knows that the current shortest path to a given destination goes through NextHop. Thus, whenever it receives a multicast packet from source S, the router forwards the packet on all outgoing links (except the one on which the packet arrived) if and only if the packet arrived over the link that is on the shortest path to S (i.e., the packet came from the NextHop associated with S in the routing table). This strategy effectively floods packets outward from S but does not loop packets back toward S.

There are two major shortcomings to this approach. The first is that it truly floods the network; it has no provision for avoiding LANs that have no members in the multicast group. We address this problem below. The second limitation is that a given packet will be forwarded over a LAN by each of the routers connected to that LAN. This is due to the forwarding strategy of flooding packets on all links other than the one on which the packet arrived, without regard to whether or not those links are part of the shortest-path tree rooted at the source.

The solution to this second limitation is to eliminate the duplicate broadcast packets that are generated when more than one router is connected to a given LAN. One way to do this is to designate one router as the parent router for each link, relative to the source, where only the parent router is allowed to forward multicast packets from that source over the LAN. The router that has the shortest path to source S is selected as the parent; a tie between two routers would be broken according to which router has the smallest address. A given router can learn if it is the parent for the LAN (again relative to each possible source) based upon the distance-vector messages it exchanges with its neighbors.

Notice that this refinement requires that each router keep, for each source, a bit for each of its incident links indicating whether or not it is the parent for that source/link pair. Keep in mind that in an internet setting, a source is a network, not a host, since an internet router is only interested in forwarding packets between networks. The resulting mechanism is sometimes called Reverse Path Broadcast (RPB) or Reverse Path Forwarding (RPF). The path is reverse because we are considering the shortest path toward the source when making our forwarding decisions, as compared to unicast routing, which looks for the shortest path to a given destination.

The RPB mechanism just described implements shortest-path broadcast. We now want to prune the set of networks that receives each packet addressed to group G to exclude those that have no hosts that are members of G. This can be accomplished in two stages. First, we need to recognize when a leaf network has no group members. Determining that a network is a leaf is easy—if the parent router as described above is the only router on the network, then the network is a leaf. Determining if any group members reside on the network is accomplished by having each host that is a member of group G periodically announce this fact over the network, as described in our earlier description of link-state multicast. The router then uses this information to decide whether or not to forward a multicast packet addressed to G over this LAN.

The second stage is to propagate this "no members of G here" information up the shortest-path tree. This is done by having the router augment the (Destination, Cost) pairs it sends to its neighbors with the set of groups for which the leaf network is interested in receiving multicast packets. This information can then be propagated from router to router, so that for each of its links a given router knows for what groups it should forward multicast packets.

Note that including all of this information in the routing update is a fairly expensive thing to do. In practice, therefore, this information is exchanged only when some source starts sending packets to that group. In other words, the strategy is to use RPB, which adds a small amount of overhead to the basic distance-vector algorithm, until a particular multicast address becomes active. At that time, routers that are not interested in receiving packets addressed to that group speak up, and that information is propagated to the other routers.

PIM-SM

Protocol Independent Multicast, or PIM, was developed in response to the scaling problems of earlier multicast routing protocols. In particular, it was recognized that the existing protocols did not scale well in environments where a relatively small proportion of routers want to receive traffic for a certain group. For example, broadcasting traffic to all routers until they explicitly ask to be removed from the distribution is not a good design choice if most routers don't want to receive the traffic in the first place. This situation is sufficiently common that PIM divides the problem space into sparse mode and dense mode, where sparse and dense refer to the proportion of routers that will want the multicast. PIM dense mode (PIM-DM) uses a flood-and-prune algorithm like DVMRP and suffers from the same scalability problem. PIM sparse mode (PIM-SM) has become the dominant multicast routing protocol and is the focus of our discussion here. The "protocol independent" aspect of PIM, by the way, refers to the fact that, unlike earlier protocols such as DVMRP, PIM does not depend on any particular sort of unicast routing—it can be used with any unicast routing protocol, as we will see below.

In PIM-SM, routers explicitly join the multicast distribution tree using PIM protocol messages known as Join messages. Note the contrast to DVMRP's approach of creating a broadcast tree first and then pruning the uninterested routers. The question that arises is where to send those Join messages because, after all, any host (and any number of hosts) could send to the multicast group. To address this, PIM-SM assigns to each group a special router known as the rendezvous point (RP). In general, a number of routers in a domain are configured to be candidate RPs, and PIM-SM defines a set of procedures by which all the routers in a domain can agree on the router to use as the RP for a given group. These procedures are rather complex, as they must deal with a wide variety of scenarios, such as the failure of a candidate RP and the partitioning of a domain into two separate networks due to a number of link or node failures. For the rest of this discussion, we assume that all routers in a domain know the unicast IP address of the RP for a given group.

A multicast forwarding tree is built as a result of routers sending Join messages to the RP. PIM-SM allows two types of trees to be constructed: a shared tree, which may be used by all senders, and a source-specific tree, which may be used only by a specific sending host. The normal mode of operation creates the shared tree first, followed by one or more source-specific trees if there is enough traffic to warrant it. Because building trees installs state in the routers along the tree, it is important that the default is to have only one tree for a group, not one for every sender to a group.

When a router sends a Join message toward the RP for a group G, it is sent using normal IP unicast transmission. This is illustrated in Figure 110(a), in which router R4 is sending a Join to the rendezvous point for some group. The initial Join message is "wildcarded"; that is, it applies to all senders. A Join message clearly must pass through some sequence of routers before reaching the RP (e.g., R2). Each router along the path looks at the Join and creates a forwarding table entry for the shared tree, called a (*, G) entry (where * means "all senders"). To create the forwarding table entry, it looks at the interface on which the Join arrived and marks that interface as one on which it should forward data packets for this group. It then determines which interface it will use to forward the Join toward the RP. This will be the only acceptable interface for incoming packets sent to this group. It then forwards the Join toward the RP. Eventually, the message arrives at the RP, completing the construction of the tree branch. The shared tree thus constructed is shown as a solid line from the RP to R4 in Figure 110(a).

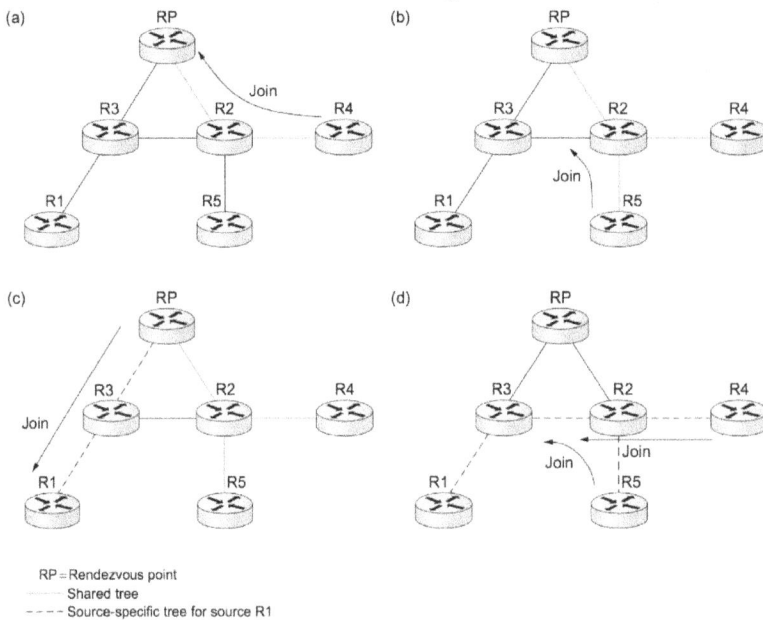

Figure 110. PIM operation: (a) R4 sends a Join message to RP and joins shared tree; (b) R5 joins shared tree; (c) RP builds source-specific tree to R1 by sending a Join message to R1; (d) R4 and R5 build source-specific tree to R1 by sending Join messages to R1.

As more routers send Joins toward the RP, they cause new branches to be added to the tree, as illustrated in Figure 110(b). Note that, in this case, the Join only needs to travel to R2, which can add the new branch to the tree simply by adding a new outgoing interface to the forwarding table entry created for this group. R2 need not forward the Join on to the RP. Note also that the end result of this process is to build a tree whose root is the RP.

At this point, suppose a host wishes to send a message to the group. To do so, it constructs a packet with the appropriate multicast group address as its destination and sends it to a router on its local network known as the designated router (DR). Suppose the DR is R1 in Figure 110. There is no state for this multicast group between R1 and the RP at this point, so instead of simply forwarding the multicast packet, R1 tunnels it to the RP. That is, R1 encapsulates the multicast packet inside a PIM Register message that it sends to the unicast IP address of the RP. Just like an IP tunnel endpoint, the RP receives the packet addressed to it, looks at the payload of the Register message, and finds inside an IP packet addressed to the multicast address of this group. The RP, of course, does know what to do with such a packet—it sends it out onto the shared tree of which the RP is the root. In the example of Figure 110, this means that the RP sends the packet on to R2, which is able to forward it on to R4 and R5. The complete delivery of a packet from R1 to R4 and R5 is shown in Figure 111. We see the tunneled packet travel from R1 to the RP with an extra IP header containing the unicast address of RP, and then the multicast packet addressed to G making its way along the shared tree to R4 and R5.

At this point, we might be tempted to declare success, since all hosts can send to all receivers this way. However, there is some bandwidth inefficiency and processing cost in the encapsulation and decapsulation of packets on the way to the RP, so the RP forces knowledge about this group into the intervening routers so tunneling can be avoided. It sends a Join message toward the sending host (Figure 110(c)). As this Join travels toward the host, it causes the routers along the path (R3) to learn about the group, so that it will be possible for the DR to send the packet to the group as native (i.e., not tunneled) multicast packets.

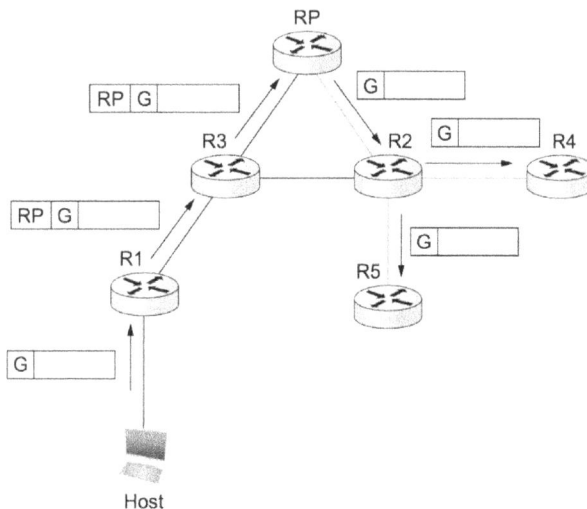

Figure 111. Delivery of a packet along a shared tree. R1 tunnels the packet to the RP, which forwards it along the shared tree to R4 and R5.

An important detail to note at this stage is that the Join message sent by the RP to the sending host is specific to that sender, whereas the previous ones sent by R4 and R5 applied to all senders. Thus, the effect of the new Join is to create sender-specific state in the routers between the identified source and the RP. This is referred to as (S, G) state, since it applies to one sender to one group, and contrasts with the (*, G) state that was installed between the receivers and the RP that applies to all senders. Thus, in Figure 110(c), we see a source-specific route from R1 to the RP (indicated by the dashed line) and a tree that is valid for all senders from the RP to the receivers (indicated by the solid line).

The next possible optimization is to replace the entire shared tree with a source-specific tree. This is desirable because the path from sender to receiver via the RP might be significantly longer than the shortest possible path. This again is likely to be triggered by a high data rate being observed from some sender. In this case, the router at the downstream end of the tree—say, R4 in our example—sends a source-specific Join toward the source. As it follows the shortest path toward the source, the routers along the way create (S, G) state for this tree, and the result is a tree that has its root at the source, rather than the RP. Assuming both R4 and R5 made the switch to the source-specific tree, we would end up with the tree shown in Figure 110(d). Note that this tree no longer involves the RP at all. We have removed the shared tree from this picture to simplify the diagram, but in reality all routers with receivers for a group must stay on the shared tree in case new senders show up.

We can now see why PIM is protocol independent. All of its mechanisms for building and maintaining trees take advantage of unicast routing without depending on any particular unicast routing protocol. The formation of trees is entirely determined by the paths that Join messages follow, which is determined by the choice of shortest paths made by unicast routing. Thus, to be precise, PIM is "unicast routing protocol independent," as compared to DVMRP. Note that PIM is very much bound up with the Internet Protocol—it is not protocol independent in terms of network-layer protocols.

The design of PIM-SM again illustrates the challenges in building scalable networks and how scalability is sometimes pitted against some sort of optimality. The shared tree is certainly more scalable than a source-specific tree, in the sense that it reduces the total state in routers to be on the order of the number of groups rather than the number of senders times the number of groups. However, the source-specific tree is likely to be necessary to achieve efficient routing and effective use of link bandwidth.

INTERDOMAIN MULTICAST (MSDP)

PIM-SM has some significant shortcomings when it comes to interdomain multicast. In particular, the existence of a single RP for a group goes against the principle that domains are autonomous. For a given multicast group, all the participating domains would be dependent on the domain where the RP is located. Furthermore, if there is a particular multicast group for which a sender and some receivers shared a single domain, the multicast traffic would still have to be routed initially from the sender to those receivers via whatever domain has the RP for that multicast group. Consequently, the PIM-SM protocol is typically not used across domains, only within a domain.

To extend multicast across domains using PIM-SM, the Multicast Source Discovery Protocol (MSDP) was devised. MSDP is used to connect different domains—each running PIM-SM internally, with its own RPs—by connecting the RPs of the different domains. Each RP has one or more MSDP peer RPs in other domains. Each pair of MSDP peers is connected by a TCP connection over which the MSDP protocol runs. Together, all the MSDP peers for a given multicast group form a loose mesh that is used as a broadcast network. MSDP messages are broadcast through the mesh of peer RPs using the Reverse Path Broadcast algorithm that we discussed in the context of DVMRP.

What information does MSDP broadcast through the mesh of RPs? Not group membership information; when a host joins a group, the furthest that information will flow is its own domain's RP. Instead, it is source—multicast sender—information. Each RP knows the sources in its own domain because it receives a Register message whenever a new source arises. Each RP periodically uses MSDP to broadcast Source Active messages to its peers, giving the IP address of the source, the multicast group address, and the IP address of the originating RP.

If an MSDP peer RP that receives one of these broadcasts has active receivers for that multicast group, it sends a source-specific Join, on that RP's own behalf, to the source host, as shown in Figure 112(a). The Join message builds a branch of the source-specific tree to this RP, as shown in Figure 112(b). The result is that every RP that is part of the MSDP network and has active receivers for a particular multicast group is added to the source-specific tree of the new source. When an RP receives a multicast from the source, the RP uses its shared tree to forward the multicast to the receivers in its domain.

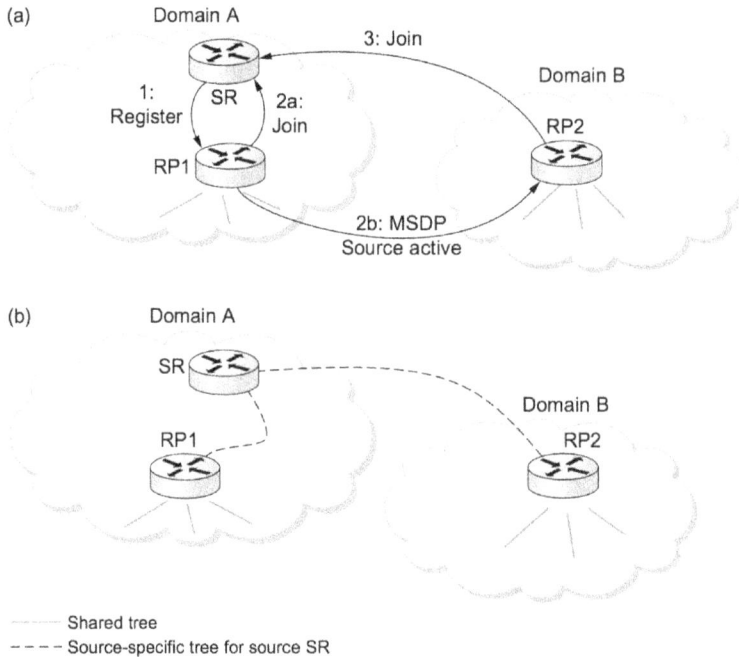

Figure 112. MSDP operation: (a) The source SR sends a Register message to its domain's RP, RP1; then RP1 sends a source-specific Join message to SR and an MSDP Source Active message to its MSDP peer in Domain B, RP2; then RP2 sends a source-specific Join message to SR. (b) As a result, RP1 and RP2 are in the source-specific tree for source SR.

SOURCE-SPECIFIC MULTICAST (PIM-SSM)

The first service model of PIM, similar to previous multicast protocols, was a concept that allowed communication between multiple senders and multiple receivers. Participants joined a collective, and any individual may transmit messages to the collective. However, it was acknowledged in the late 1990s that including a one-to-many paradigm could be beneficial. Many multicast applications often include only a single authorized sender, such as the speaker at a conference being transmitted over the Internet. PIM-SM has the capability to generate source-specific shortest path trees as an optimization strategy following the initial use of a shared tree. In the initial PIM design, this enhancement was imperceptible to hosts—solely routers participated in source-specific trees. Once the requirement for a service architecture that allows one-to-many communication was acknowledged, it was determined that the source-specific routing capabilities of PIM-SM should be made directly accessible to hosts. It was discovered that the necessary modifications primarily involved IGMP and its IPv6 equivalent, MLD, rather than PIM itself. The recently revealed functionality is currently referred to as PIM-SSM (PIM Source-Specific Multicast).

PIM-SSM introduces a new concept, the channel, which is the combination of a source address S and a group address G. The group address G looks just like a normal IP multicast address, and both IPv4 and IPv6 have allocated subranges of the multicast address space for SSM. To use PIM-SSM, a host specifies both the group and the source in an IGMP Membership Report message to its local router. That router then sends a PIM-SM source-specific Join message toward the source, thereby adding a branch to itself in the source-specific tree, just as was described above for "normal" PIM-SM, but bypassing the whole shared-tree stage. Since the tree that results is source specific, only the designated source can send packets on that tree.

The introduction of PIM-SSM has provided some significant benefits, particularly since there is relatively high demand for one-to-many multicasting:

- ⊙ Multicasts travel more directly to receivers.

- ⊙ The address of a channel is effectively a multicast group address plus a source address. Therefore, given that a certain range of multicast group addresses will be used for SSM exclusively, multiple domains can use the same multicast group address independently and without conflict, as long as they use it only with sources in their own domains.

- ⊙ Because only the specified source can send to an SSM group, there is less risk of attacks based on malicious hosts overwhelming the routers or receivers with bogus multicast traffic.

- ⊙ PIM-SSM can be used across domains exactly as it is used within a domain, without reliance on anything like MSDP.

SSM, therefore, is quite a useful addition to the multicast service model.

BIDIRECTIONAL TREES (BIDIR-PIM)

We round off our discussion of multicast with another enhancement to PIM known as Bidirectional PIM. BIDIR-PIM is a recent variant of PIM-SM that is well suited to many-to-many multicasting within a domain, especially when senders and receivers to a group may be the same, as in a multiparty videoconference, for example. As in PIM-SM, would-be receivers join groups by sending IGMP Membership Report messages (which must not be source specific), and a shared tree rooted at an RP is used to forward multicast packets to receivers. Unlike PIM-SM, however, the shared tree also has branches to the sources. That wouldn't make any sense with PIM-SM's unidirectional tree, but BIDIR-PIM's trees are bidirectional—a router that receives a multicast packet from a downstream branch can forward it both up the tree and down other branches. The route followed to deliver a packet to any particular receiver goes only as far up the tree as necessary before going down the branch to that receiver. See the multicast route from R1 to R2 in Figure 113(b) for an example. R4 forwards a multicast packet downstream to R2 at the same time that it forwards a copy of the same packet upstream to R5.

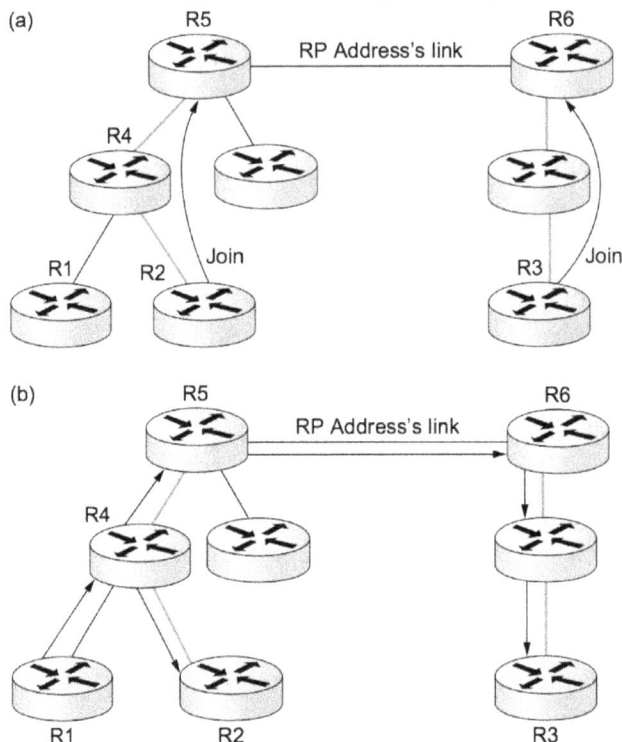

Figure 113. BIDIR-PIM operation: (a) R2 and R3 send Join messages toward the RP address that terminate when they reach a router on the RP address's link. (b) A multicast packet from R1 is forwarded upstream to the RP address's link and downstream wherever it intersects a group member branch.

A surprising aspect of BIDIR-PIM is that there need not actually be an RP. All that is needed is a routable address, which is known as an RP address even though it need not be the address of an RP or anything at all. How can this be? A Join from a receiver is forwarded toward the RP address until it reaches a router with an interface on the link where the RP address would reside, where the Join terminates. Figure 113(a) shows a Join from R2 terminating at R5, and a Join from R3 terminating at R6. The upstream forwarding of a multicast packet similarly flows toward the RP address until it reaches a router with an interface on the link where the RP address would reside, but then the router forwards the multicast packet onto that link as the final step of upstream forwarding, ensuring that all other routers on that link receive the packet. Figure 113(b) illustrates the flow of multicast traffic originating at R1.

BIDIR-PIM cannot thus far be used across domains. On the other hand, it has several advantages over PIM-SM for many-to-many multicast within a domain:

- There is no source registration process because the routers already know how to route a multicast packet toward the RP address.

- The routes are more direct than those that use PIM-SM's shared tree because they go only as far up the tree as necessary, not all the way to the RP.

- Bidirectional trees use much less state than the source-specific trees of PIM-SM because there is never any source-specific state. (On the other hand, the routes will be longer than those of source-specific trees.)

- The RP cannot be a bottleneck, and indeed no actual RP is needed.

One conclusion to draw from the fact that there are so many different approaches to multicast just within PIM is that multicast is a difficult problem space in which to find optimal solutions. You need to decide which criteria you want to optimize (bandwidth usage, router state, path length, etc.) and what sort of application you are trying to support (one-to-many, many-to-many, etc.) before you can make a choice of the "best" multicast mode for the task.

4.4 Multiprotocol Label Switching

We continue our discussion of enhancements to IP by describing an addition to the Internet architecture that is very widely used but largely hidden from end users. The enhancement, called Multiprotocol Label Switching (MPLS), combines some of the properties of virtual circuits with the flexibility and robustness of datagrams. On the one hand, MPLS is very much associated with the Internet Protocol's datagram-based architecture—it relies on IP addresses and IP routing protocols to do its job. On the other hand, MPLS-enabled routers also forward packets by examining relatively short, fixed-length labels, and these labels have local scope, just like in a virtual circuit network. It is perhaps this marriage of two seemingly opposed technologies that has caused MPLS to have a somewhat mixed reception in the Internet engineering community.

Before looking at how MPLS works, it is reasonable to ask "what is it good for?" Many claims have been made for MPLS, but there are three main things that it is used for today:

- To enable IP capabilities on devices that do not have the capability to forward IP datagrams in the normal manner

- To forward IP packets along explicit routes—precalculated routes that don't necessarily match those that normal IP routing protocols would select

- To support certain types of virtual private network services

It is worth noting that one of the original goals—improving performance—is not on the list. This has a lot to do with the advances that have been made in forwarding algorithms for IP routers in recent years and with the complex set of factors beyond header processing that determine performance.

The best way to understand how MPLS works is to look at some examples of its use. In the next three sections, we will look at examples to illustrate the three applications of MPLS mentioned above.

4.4.1 Destination-Based Forwarding

One of the earliest publications to introduce the idea of attaching labels to IP packets was a paper by Chandranmenon and Varghese that described an idea called threaded indices. A very similar idea is now implemented in MPLS-enabled routers. The following example shows how this idea works.

Consider the network in Figure 114. Each of the two routers on the far right (R3 and R4) has one connected network, with prefixes 18.1.1/24 and 18.3.3/24. The remaining routers (R1 and R2) have routing tables that indicate which outgoing interface each router would use when forwarding packets to one of those two networks.

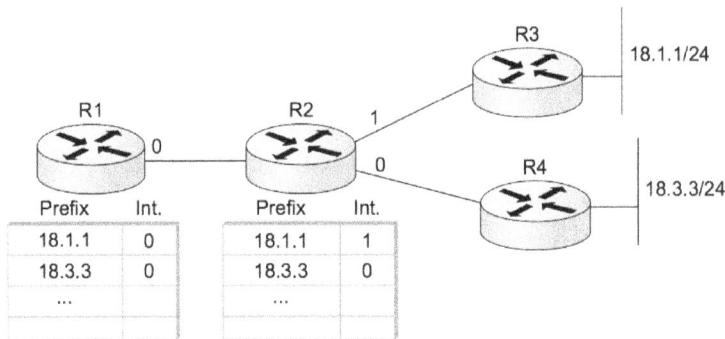

Prefix	Int.
18.1.1	0
18.3.3	0
...	

Prefix	Int.
18.1.1	1
18.3.3	0
...	

Figure 114. Routing tables in example network.

When MPLS is enabled on a router, the router allocates a label for each prefix in its routing table and advertises both the label and the prefix that it represents to its neighboring routers. This advertisement is carried in the Label Distribution Protocol. This is illustrated in Figure 115. Router R2 has allocated the label value 15 for the prefix 18.1.1 and the label value 16 for the prefix 18.3.3. These labels can be chosen at the convenience of the allocating router and can be thought of as indices into the routing table. After allocating the labels, R2 advertises the label bindings to its neighbors; in this case, we see R2 advertising a binding between the label 15 and the prefix 18.1.1 to R1. The meaning of such an advertisement is that R2 has said, in effect, "Please attach the label 15 to all packets sent to me that are destined to prefix 18.1.1." R1 stores the label in a table alongside the prefix that it represents as the remote or outgoing label for any packets that it sends to that prefix.

In Figure 115(c), we see another label advertisement from router R3 to R2 for the prefix 18.1.1, and R2 places the remote label that it learned from R3 in the appropriate place in its table.

At this point, we can look at what happens when a packet is forwarded in this network. Suppose a packet destined to the IP address 18.1.1.5 arrives from the left to router R1. R1 in this case is referred to as a Label Edge Router (LER); an LER performs a complete IP lookup on arriving IP packets and then applies labels to them as a result of the lookup. In this case, R1 would see that 18.1.1.5 matches the prefix 18.1.1 in its forwarding table and that this entry contains both an outgoing interface and a remote label value. R1 therefore attaches the remote label 15 to the packet before sending it.

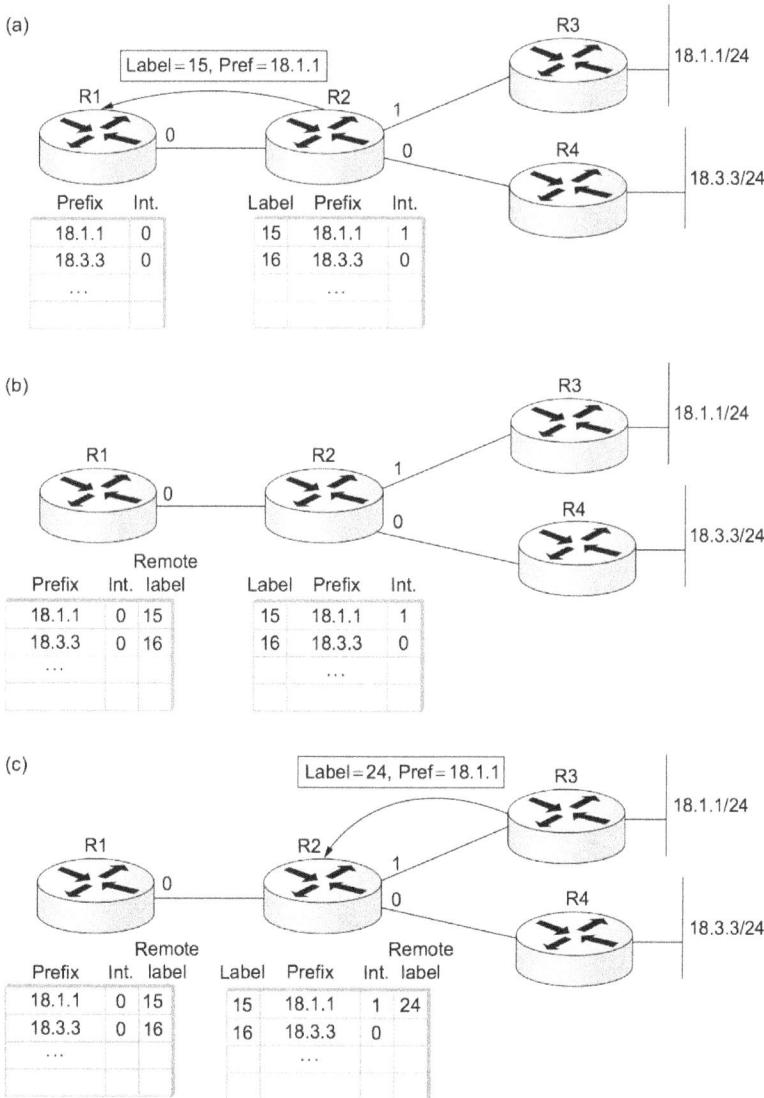

Figure 115. **(a)** R2 allocates labels and advertises bindings to R1. **(b)** R1 stores the received labels in a table. **(c)** R3 advertises another binding, and R2 stores the received label in a table.

When the packet arrives at R2, R2 looks only at the label in the packet, not the IP address. The forwarding table at R2 indicates that packets arriving with a label value of 15 should be sent out interface 1 and that they should carry the label value 24, as advertised by router R3. R2 therefore rewrites, or swaps, the label and forwards it on to R3.

What has been accomplished by all this application and swapping of labels? Observe that when R2 forwarded the packet in this example it never actually needed to examine the IP address. Instead, R2 looked only at the incoming label. Thus, we have replaced the normal IP destination address lookup with a label lookup. To understand why this is significant, it helps to recall that, although IP addresses are always the same length, IP prefixes are of variable length, and the IP destination address lookup algorithm needs to find the longest match—the longest prefix that matches the high order bits in the IP address of the packet being forwarded. By contrast, the label forwarding mechanism just described is an exact match algorithm. It is possible to implement a very simple exact match algorithm, for example, by using the label as an index into an array, where each element in the array is one line in the forwarding table.

Note that, while the forwarding algorithm has been changed from longest match to exact match, the routing algorithm can be any standard IP routing algorithm (e.g., OSPF). The path that a packet will follow in this environment is the exact same path that it would have followed if MPLS were not involved: the path chosen by the IP routing algorithms. All that has changed is the forwarding algorithm.

An important fundamental concept of MPLS is illustrated by this example. Every MPLS label is associated with a forwarding equivalence class (FEC)—a set of packets that are to receive the same forwarding treatment in a particular router. In this example, each prefix in the routing table is an FEC; that is, all packets that match the prefix 18.1.1—no matter what the low order bits of the IP address are—get forwarded along the same path. Thus, each router can allocate one label that maps to 18.1.1, and any packet that contains an IP address whose high order bits match that prefix can be forwarded using that label.

As we will see in the subsequent examples, FECs are a very powerful and flexible concept. FECs can be formed using almost any criteria; for example, all the packets corresponding to a particular customer could be considered to be in the same FEC.

Returning to the example at hand, we observe that changing the forwarding algorithm from normal IP forwarding to label swapping has an important consequence: Devices that previously didn't know how to forward IP packets can be used to forward IP traffic in an MPLS network. The most notable early application of this result was to ATM switches, which can support MPLS without any changes to their forwarding hardware. ATM switches support the label-swapping forwarding algorithm just described, and by providing these switches with IP routing protocols and a method to distribute label bindings they could be turned into Label Switching Routers (LSRs)—devices that run IP control protocols but use the label switching forwarding algorithm. More recently, the same idea has been applied to optical switches.

Before we consider the purported benefits of turning an ATM switch into an LSR, we should tie up some loose ends. We have said that labels are "attached" to packets, but where exactly are they attached? The answer depends on the type of link on which packets are carried. Two common methods for carrying labels on packets are shown in Figure 116. When IP packets are carried as complete frames, as they are on most link types including Ethernet and PPP, the label is inserted as a "shim" between the layer 2 header and the IP (or other layer 3) header, as shown in the lower part of the figure. However, if an ATM switch is to function as an MPLS LSR, then the label needs to be in a place where the switch can use it, and that means it needs to be in the ATM cell header, exactly where one would normally find the virtual circuit identifier (VCI) and virtual path identifier (VPI) fields.

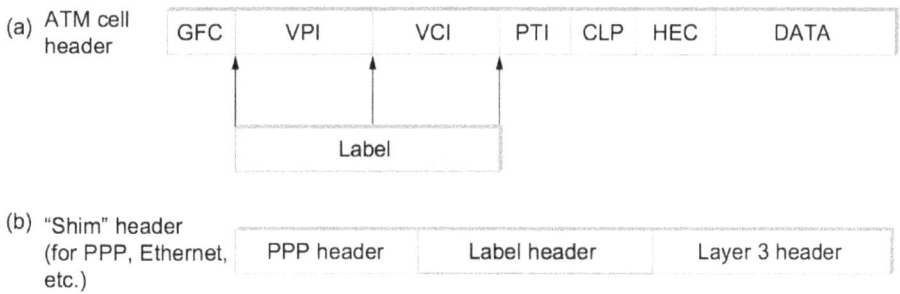

(a) ATM cell header

| GFC | VPI | VCI | PTI | CLP | HEC | DATA |

Label

(b) "Shim" header (for PPP, Ethernet, etc.)

| PPP header | Label header | Layer 3 header |

Figure 116. (a) Label on an ATM-encapsulated packet; (b) label on a frame-encapsulated packet.

Having now devised a scheme by which an ATM switch can function as an LSR, what have we gained? One thing to note is that we could now build a network that uses a mixture of conventional IP routers, label edge routers, and ATM switches functioning as LSRs, and they would all use the same routing protocols. To understand the benefits of using the same protocols, consider the alternative. In Figure 117(a), we see a set of routers interconnected by virtual circuits over an ATM network, a configuration called an overlay network. At one point in time, networks of this type were often built because commercially available ATM switches supported higher total throughput than routers. Today, networks like this are less common because routers have caught up with and even surpassed ATM switches. However, these networks still exist because of the significant installed base of ATM switches in network backbones, which in turn is partly a result of ATM's ability to support a range of capabilities such as circuit emulation and virtual circuit services.

In an overlay network, each router would potentially be connected to each of the other routers by a virtual circuit, but in this case for clarity we have just shown the circuits from R1 to all of its peer routers. R1 has five routing neighbors and needs to exchange routing protocol messages with all of them—we say that R1 has five routing adjacencies. By contrast, in Figure 117(b), the ATM switches have been replaced with LSRs. There are no longer virtual circuits interconnecting the routers. Thus, R1 has only one adjacency, with LSR1. In large networks, running MPLS on the switches leads to a significant reduction in the number of adjacencies that each router must maintain and can greatly reduce the amount of work that the routers have to do to keep each other informed of topology changes.

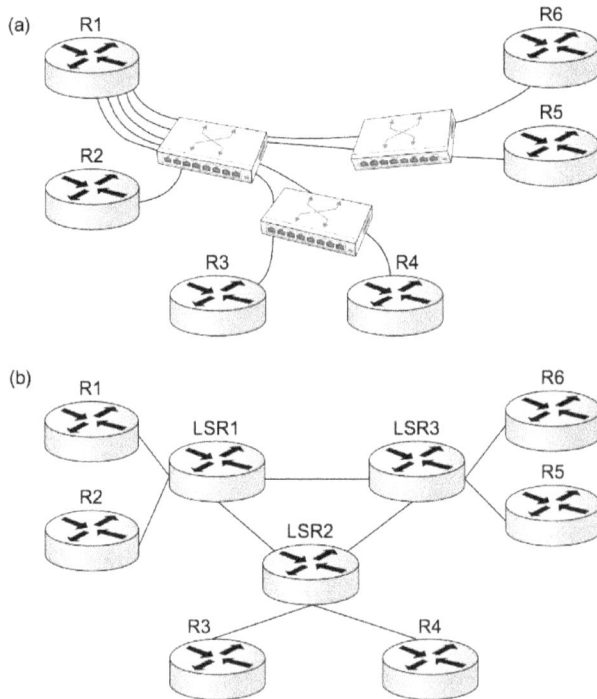

Figure 117. (a) Routers connect to each other using an overlay of virtual circuits. (b) Routers peer directly with LSRs.

A second benefit of running the same routing protocols on edge routers and on the LSRs is that the edge routers now have a full view of the topology of the network. This means that if some link or node fails inside the network, the edge routers will have a better chance of picking a good new path than if the ATM switches rerouted the affected VCs without the knowledge of the edge routers.

Note that the step of "replacing" ATM switches with LSRs is actually achieved by changing the protocols running on the switches, but typically no change to the forwarding hardware is needed; that is, an ATM switch can often be converted to an MPLS LSR by upgrading only its software. Furthermore, an MPLS LSR might continue to support standard ATM capabilities at the same time as it runs the MPLS control protocols, in what is referred to as "ships in the night" mode.

The idea of running IP control protocols on devices that are unable to forward IP packets natively has been extended to Wavelength Division Multiplexing (WDM) and Time Division Multiplexing (TDM) networks (e.g., SONET). This is known as Generalized MPLS (GMPLS). Part of the motivation for GMPLS was to provide routers with topological knowledge of an optical network, just as in the ATM case. Even more important was the fact that there were no standard protocols for controlling optical devices, so MPLS proved to be a natural fit for that job.

4.4.2 Explicit Routing

IP has a source routing option, but it is not widely used for several reasons, including the fact that only a limited number of hops can be specified and because it is usual processed outside the "fast path" on most routers.

MPLS provides a convenient way to add capabilities similar to source-routing to IP networks, although the capability is more often referred to as explicit routing rather than source routing. One reason for the distinction is that it usually isn't the real source of the packet that picks the route. More often it is one of the routers inside a service provider's network. Figure 118 shows an example of how the explicit routing capability of MPLS might be applied. This sort of network is often called a fish network because of its shape (the routers R1 and R2 form the tail; R7 is at the head).

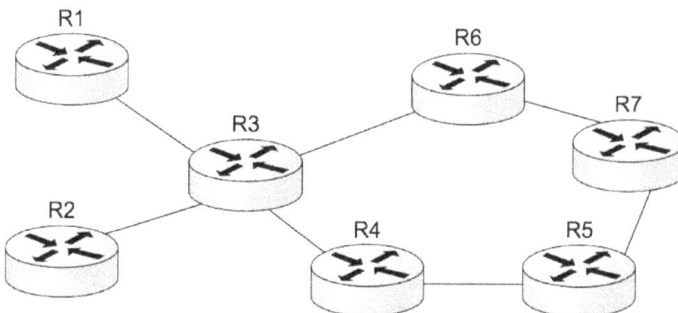

Figure 118. A network requiring explicit routing.

Suppose that the operator of the network in Figure 118 has determined that any traffic flowing from R1 to R7 should follow the path R1-R3-R6-R7 and that any traffic going from R2 to R7 should follow the path R2-R3-R4-R5-R7. One reason for such a choice would be to make good use of the capacity available along the two distinct paths from R3 to R7. We can think of the R1-to-R7 traffic as constituting one forwarding equivalence class, and the R2-to-R7 traffic constitutes a second FEC. Forwarding traffic in these two classes along different paths is difficult with normal IP routing, because R3 doesn't normally look at where traffic came from in making its forwarding decisions.

Because MPLS uses label swapping to forward packets, it is easy enough to achieve the desired routing if the routers are MPLS enabled. If R1 and R2 attach distinct labels to packets before sending them to R3—thus identifying them as being in different FECs—then R3 can forward packets from R1 and R2 along different paths. The question that then arises is how do all the routers in the network agree on what labels to use and how to forward packets with particular labels? Clearly, we can't use the same procedures as described in the preceding section to distribute labels, because those procedures establish labels that cause packets to follow the normal paths picked by IP routing, which is exactly what we are trying to avoid. Instead, a new mechanism is needed. It turns out that the protocol used for this task is the Resource Reservation Protocol (RSVP). For now it suffices to say that it is possible to send an RSVP message along an explicitly specified path (e.g., R1-R3-R6-R7) and use it to set up label forwarding table entries all along that path. This is very similar to the process of establishing a virtual circuit.

One of the applications of explicit routing is traffic engineering, which refers to the task of ensuring that sufficient resources are available in a network to meet the demands placed on it. Controlling exactly which paths the traffic flows on is an important part of traffic engineering. Explicit routing can also help to make networks more resilient in the face of failure, using a capability called fast reroute. For example, it is possible to precalculate a path from router A to router B that explicitly avoids a certain link L. In the event that link L fails, router A could send all traffic destined to B down the precalculated path. The combination of precalculation of the backup path and the explicit routing of packets along the path means that A doesn't need to wait for routing protocol packets to make their way across the network or for routing algorithms to be executed by various other nodes in the network. In certain circumstances, this can significantly reduce the time taken to reroute packets around a point of failure.

One final point to note about explicit routing is that explicit routes need not be calculated by a network operator as in the above example. Routers can use various algorithms to calculate explicit routes automatically. The most common of these is constrained shortest path first (CSPF), which is a link-state algorithm, but which also takes various constraints into account. For example, if it was required to find a path from R1 to R7 that could carry an offered load of 100 Mbps, we could say that the constraint is that each link must have at least 100 Mbps of available capacity. CSPF addresses this sort of problem.

4.4.3 Virtual Private Networks and Tunnels

One way to build virtual private networks (VPNs) is to use tunnels. It turns out that MPLS can be thought of as a way to build tunnels, and this makes it suitable for building VPNs of various types.

The simplest form of MPLS VPN to understand is a layer 2 VPN. In this type of VPN, MPLS is used to tunnel layer 2 data (such as Ethernet frames or ATM cells) across a network of MPLS-enabled routers. One reason for tunnels is to provide some sort of network service (such as multicast) that is not supported by some routers in the network. The same logic applies here: IP routers are not ATM switches, so you cannot provide an ATM virtual circuit service across a network of conventional routers. However, if you had a pair of routers interconnected by a tunnel, they could send ATM cells across the tunnel and emulate an ATM circuit. The term for this technique within the IETF is pseudowire emulation. Figure 119 illustrates the idea.

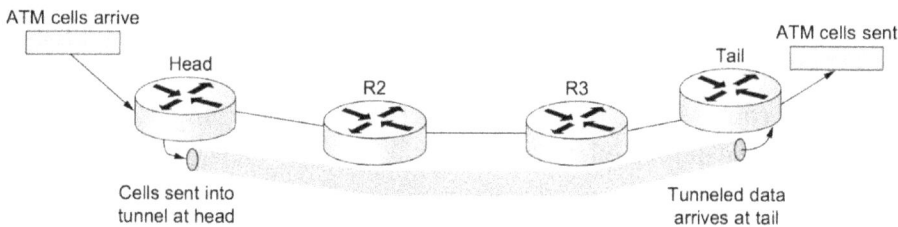

Figure 119. An ATM circuit is emulated by a tunnel.

We have already seen how IP tunnels are built: The router at the entrance of the tunnel wraps the data to be tunneled in an IP header (the tunnel header), which represents the address of the router at the far end of the tunnel and sends the data like any other IP packet. The receiving router receives the packet with its own address in the header, strips the tunnel header, and finds the data that was tunneled, which it then processes. Exactly what it does with that data depends on what it is. For example, if it were another IP packet, it would then be forwarded on like a normal IP packet. However, it need not be an IP packet, as long as the receiving router knows what to do with non-IP packets. We'll return to the issue of how to handle non-IP data in a moment.

An MPLS tunnel is not too different from an IP tunnel, except that the tunnel header consists of an MPLS header rather than an IP header. Looking back to our first example, in Figure 115, we saw that router R1 attached a label (15) to every packet that it sent towards prefix 18.1.1. Such a packet would then follow the path R1-R2-R3, with each router in the path examining only the MPLS label. Thus, we observe that there was no requirement that R1 only send IP packets along this path—any data could be wrapped up in the MPLS header and it would follow the same path, because the intervening routers never look beyond the MPLS header. In this regard, an MPLS header is just like an IP tunnel header (except only 4 bytes long instead of 20 bytes). The only issue with sending non-IP traffic along a tunnel, MPLS or otherwise, is what to do with non-IP traffic when it reaches the end of the tunnel. The general solution is to carry some sort of demultiplexing identifier in the tunnel payload that tells the router at the end of the tunnel what to do. It turns out that an MPLS label is a perfect fit for such an identifier. An example will make this clear.

Let's assume we want to tunnel ATM cells from one router to another across a network of MPLS-enabled routers, as in Figure 119. Further, we assume that the goal is to emulate an ATM virtual circuit; that is, cells arrive at the entrance, or head, of the tunnel on a certain input port with a certain VCI and should leave the tail end of the tunnel on a certain output port and potentially different VCI. This can be accomplished by configuring the head and tail routers as follows:

⊙ The head router needs to be configured with the incoming port, the incoming VCI, the demultiplexing label for this emulated circuit, and the address of the tunnel end router.

⊙ The tail router needs to be configured with the outgoing port, the outgoing VCI, and the demultiplexing label.

Once the routers are provided with this information, we can see how an ATM cell would be forwarded. Figure 120 illustrates the steps.

⊙ An ATM cell arrives on the designated input port with the appropriate VCI value (101 in this example).

⊙ The head router attaches the demultiplexing label that identifies the emulated circuit.

⊙ The head router then attaches a second label, which is the tunnel label that will get the packet to the tail router. This label is learned by mechanisms just like those described elsewhere in this section.

⊙ Routers between the head and tail forward the packet using only the tunnel label.

⊙ The tail router removes the tunnel label, finds the demultiplexing label, and recognizes the emulated circuit.

⊙ The tail router modifies the ATM VCI to the correct value (202 in this case) and sends it out the correct port.

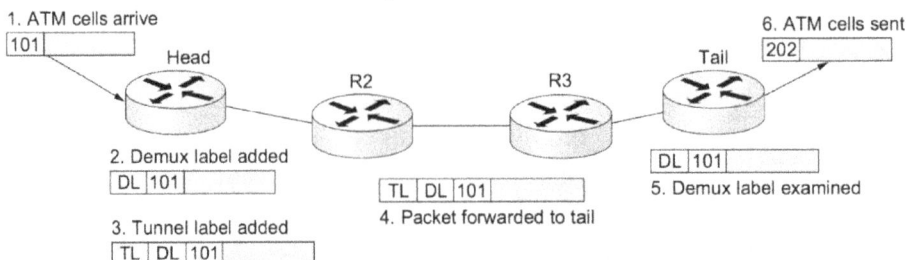

Figure 120. Forward ATM cells along a tunnel.

One item in this example that might be surprising is that the packet has two labels attached to it. This is one of the interesting features of MPLS—labels may be stacked on a packet to any depth. This provides some useful scaling capabilities. In this example, it allows a single tunnel to carry a potentially large number of emulated circuits.

The same techniques described here can be applied to emulate many other layer 2 services, including Frame Relay and Ethernet. It is worth noting that virtually identical capabilities can be provided using IP tunnels; the main advantage of MPLS here is the shorter tunnel header.

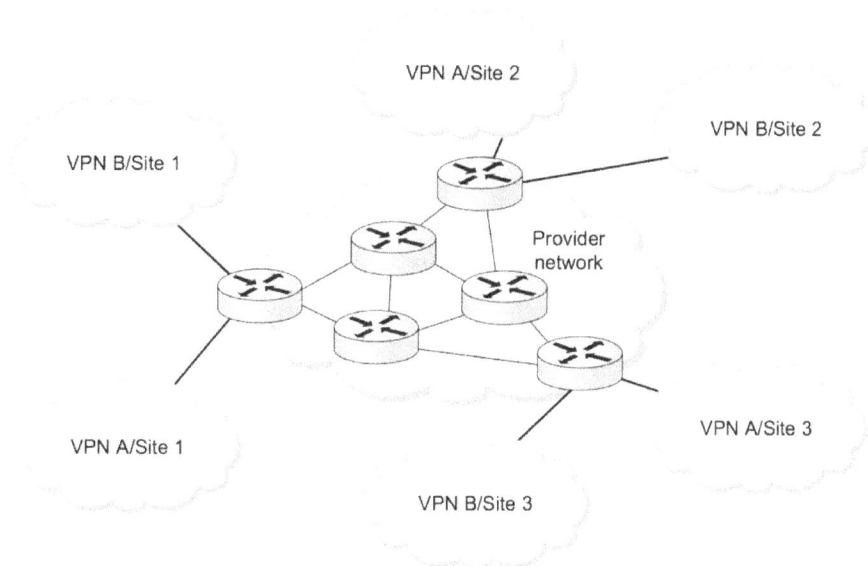

Figure 121. Example of a layer 3 VPN. Customers A and B each obtain a virtually private IP service from a single provider.

Before MPLS was used to tunnel layer 2 services, it was also being used to support layer 3 VPNs. We won't go into the details of layer 3 VPNs, which are quite complex, but we will note that they represent one of the most popular uses of MPLS today. Layer 3 VPNs also use stacks of MPLS labels to tunnel packets across an IP network. However, the packets that are tunneled are themselves IP packets—hence, the name layer 3 VPNs. In a layer 3 VPN, a single service provider operates a network of MPLS-enabled routers and provides a "virtually private" IP network service to any number of distinct customers. That is, each customer of the provider has some number of sites, and the service provider creates the illusion for each customer that there are no other customers on the network. The customer sees an IP network interconnecting his own sites and no other sites. This means that each customer is isolated from all other customers in terms of both routing and addressing. Customer A can't sent packets directly to customer B, and vice versa. Customer A can even use IP addresses that have also been used by customer B. The basic idea is illustrated in Figure 121. As in layer 2 VPNs, MPLS is used to tunnel packets from one site to another; however, the configuration of the tunnels is performed automatically by some fairly elaborate use of BGP, which is beyond the scope of this book.

Customer A in fact usually can send data to customer B in some restricted way. Most likely, both customer A and customer B have some connection to the global Internet, and thus it is probably possible for customer A to send email messages, for example, to the mail server inside customer B's network. The "privacy" offered by a VPN prevents customer A from having unrestricted access to all the machines and subnets inside customer B's network.

In summary, MPLS is a rather versatile tool that has been applied to a wide range of different networking problems. It combines the label-swapping forwarding mechanism that is normally associated with virtual circuit networks with the routing and control protocols of IP datagram networks to produce a class of network that is somewhere between the two conventional extremes. This extends the capabilities of IP networks to enable, among other things, more precise control of routing and the support of a range of VPN services.

4.5 Routing Among Mobile Devices

It probably should not be a great surprise to learn that mobile devices present some challenges for the Internet architecture. The Internet was designed in an era when computers were large, immobile devices, and, while the Internet's designers probably had some notion that mobile devices might appear in the future, it's fair to assume it was not a top priority to accommodate them. Today, of course, mobile computers are everywhere, notably in the form of laptops and smartphones, and increasingly in other forms, such as drones. In this section, we will look at some of the challenges posed by the appearance of mobile devices and some of the current approaches to accommodating them.

4.5.1 Challenges for Mobile Networking

It is easy enough today to turn up in a wireless hotspot, connect to the Internet using 802.11 or some other wireless networking protocol, and obtain pretty good Internet service. One key enabling technology that made the hotspot feasible is DHCP. You can settle in at a coffee shop, open your laptop, obtain an IP address for your laptop, and get your laptop talking to a default router and a Domain Name System (DNS) server, and for a broad class of applications you have everything you need.

If we look a little more closely, however, it's clear that for some application scenarios, just getting a new IP address every time you move—which is what DHCP does for you—isn't always enough. Suppose you are using your laptop or smartphone for a Voice over IP telephone call, and while talking on the phone you move from one hotspot to another, or even switch from Wi-Fi to the cellular network for your Internet connection.

Clearly, when you move from one access network to another, you need to get a new IP address—one that corresponds to the new network. But, the computer or telephone at the other end of your conversation doesn't immediately know where you have moved or what your new IP address is. Consequently, in the absence of some other mechanism, packets would continue to be sent to the address where you used to be, not where you are now. This problem is illustrated in Figure 122; as the mobile node moves from the 802.11 network in Figure 122(a) to the cellular network in Figure 122(b), somehow packets from the correspondent node need to find their way to the new network and then on to the mobile node.

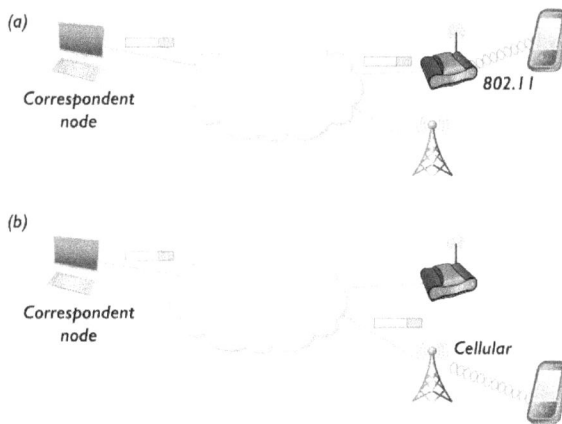

Figure 122. Forwarding packets from a correspondent node to a mobile node.

There are many different ways to tackle the problem just described, and we will look at some of them below. Assuming that there is some way to redirect packets so that they come to your new address rather than your old address, the next immediately apparent problems relate to security. For example, if there is a mechanism by which I can say, "My new IP address is X," how do I prevent some attacker from making such a statement without my permission, thus enabling him to either receive my packets, or to redirect my packets to some unwitting third party? Thus, we see that security and mobility are quite closely related.

One issue that the above discussion highlights is the fact that IP addresses actually serve two tasks. They are used as an identifier of an endpoint, and they are also used to locate the endpoint. Think of the identifier as a long-lived name for the endpoint, and the locator as some possibly more temporary information about how to route packets to the endpoint. As long as devices do not move, or do not move often, using a single address for both jobs seem pretty reasonable. But once devices start to move, you would rather like to have an identifier that does not change as you move—this is sometimes called an Endpoint Identifier or Host Identifier—and a separate locator. This idea of separating locators from identifiers has been around for a long time, and most of the approaches to handling mobility described below provide such a separation in some form.

The assumption that IP addresses don't change shows up in many different places. For example, transport protocols like TCP have historically made assumptions about the IP address staying constant for the life of a connection, so one approach could be to redesign transport protocols so they can operate with changing end-point addresses.

But rather than try to change TCP, a common alternative is for the application to periodically re-establish the TCP connection in case the client's IP address has changed. As strange as this sounds, if the application is HTTP-based (e.g., a web browser like Chrome or a streaming application like Netflix) then that is exactly what happens. In other words, the strategy is for the application to work around situations where the user's IP address may have changed, instead of trying to maintain the appearance that it does not change.

While we are all familiar with endpoints that move, it is worth noting that routers can also move. This is certainly less common today than endpoint mobility, but there are plenty of environments where a mobile router might make sense. One example might be an emergency response team trying to deploy a network after some natural disaster has knocked out all the fixed infrastructure. There are additional considerations when all the nodes in a network, not just the endpoints, are mobile, a topic we will discuss later in this section.

Before we start to look at some of the approaches to supporting mobile devices, a couple of points of clarification. It is common to find that people confuse wireless networks with mobility. After all, mobility and wireless often are found together for obvious reasons. But wireless communication is really about getting data from A to B without a wire, while mobility is about dealing with what happens when a node moves around as it communicates. Certainly many nodes that use wireless communication channels are not mobile, and sometimes mobile nodes will use wired communication (although this is less common).

Finally, in this chapter we are mostly interested in what we might call network-layer mobility. That is, we are interested in how to deal with nodes that move from one network to another. Moving from one access point to another in the same 802.11 network can be handled by mechanisms specific to 802.11, and cellular networks also have ways to handle mobility, of course, but in large heterogeneous systems like the Internet we need to support mobility more broadly across networks.

4.5.2 Routing to Mobile Hosts (Mobile IP)

Mobile IP is the primary mechanism in today's Internet architecture to tackle the problem of routing packets to mobile hosts. It introduces a few new capabilities but does not require any change from non-mobile hosts or most routers—thus making it incrementally deployable.

The mobile host is assumed to have a permanent IP address, called its home address, which has a network prefix equal to that of its home network. This is the address that will be used by other hosts when they initially send packets to the mobile host; because it does not change, it can be used by long-lived applications as the host roams. We can think of this as the long-lived identifier of the host.

When the host moves to a new foreign network away from its home network, it typically acquires a new address on that network using some means such as DHCP. This address is going to change every time the host roams to a new network, so we can think of this as being more like the locator for the host, but it is important to note that the host does not lose its permanent home address when it acquires a new address on the foreign network. This home address is critical to its ability to sustain communications as it moves, as we'll see below.

Because DHCP was developed around the same time as Mobile IP, the original Mobile IP standards did not require DHCP, but DHCP is ubiquitous today.

While the majority of routers remain unchanged, mobility support does require some new functionality in at least one router, known as the home agent of the mobile node. This router is located on the home network of the mobile host. In some cases, a second router with enhanced functionality, the foreign agent, is also required. This router is located on a network to which the mobile node attaches itself when it is away from its home network. We will consider first the operation of Mobile IP when a foreign agent is used. An example network with both home and foreign agents is shown in Figure 123.

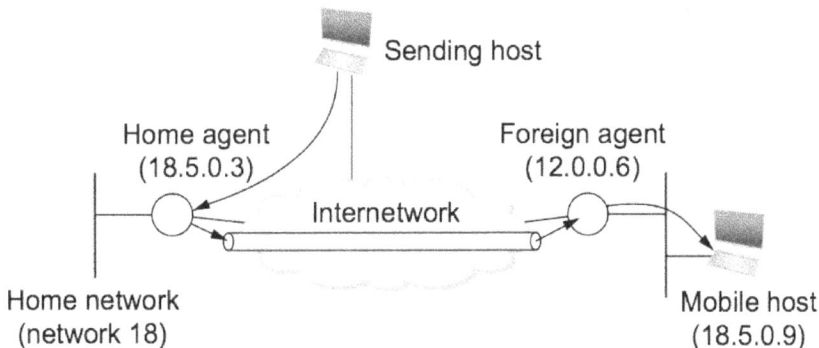

Figure 123. Mobile host and mobility agents.

Both home and foreign agents periodically announce their presence on the networks to which they are attached using agent advertisement messages. A mobile host may also solicit an advertisement when it attaches to a new network. The advertisement by the home agent enables a mobile host to learn the address of its home agent before it leaves its home network. When the mobile host attaches to a foreign network, it hears an advertisement from a foreign agent and registers with the agent, providing the address of its home agent. The foreign agent then contacts the home agent, providing a care-of address. This is usually the IP address of the foreign agent.

At this point, we can see that any host that tries to send a packet to the mobile host will send it with a destination address equal to the home address of that node. Normal IP forwarding will cause that packet to arrive on the home network of the mobile node on which the home agent is sitting. Thus, we can divide the problem of delivering the packet to the mobile node into three parts:

- How does the home agent intercept a packet that is destined for the mobile node?
- How does the home agent then deliver the packet to the foreign agent?
- How does the foreign agent deliver the packet to the mobile node?

The first problem might look easy if you just look at Figure 123, in which the home agent is clearly the only path between the sending host and the home network and thus must receive packets that are destined to the mobile node. But what if the sending (correspondent) node were on network 18, or what if there were another router connected to network 18 that tried to deliver the packet without its passing through the home agent? To address this problem, the home agent actually impersonates the mobile node, using a technique called proxy ARP. This works just like Address Resolution Protocol (ARP), except that the home agent inserts the IP address of the mobile node, rather than its own, in the ARP messages. It uses its own hardware address, so that all the nodes on the same network learn to associate the hardware address of the home agent with the IP address of the mobile node. One subtle aspect of this process is the fact that ARP information may be cached in other nodes on the network. To make sure that these caches are invalidated in a timely way, the home agent issues an ARP message as soon as the mobile node registers with a foreign agent. Because the ARP message is not a response to a normal ARP request, it is termed a gratuitous ARP.

The second problem is the delivery of the intercepted packet to the foreign agent. Here we use the tunneling technique described elsewhere. The home agent simply wraps the packet inside an IP header that is destined for the foreign agent and transmits it into the internetwork. All the intervening routers just see an IP packet destined for the IP address of the foreign agent. Another way of looking at this is that an IP tunnel is established between the home agent and the foreign agent, and the home agent just drops packets destined for the mobile node into that tunnel.

When a packet finally arrives at the foreign agent, it strips the extra IP header and finds inside an IP packet destined for the home address of the mobile node. Clearly the foreign agent cannot treat this like any old IP packet because this would cause it to send it back to the home network. Instead, it has to recognize the address as that of a registered mobile node. It then delivers the packet to the hardware address of the mobile node (e.g., its Ethernet address), which was learned as part of the registration process.

One observation that can be made about these procedures is that it is possible for the foreign agent and the mobile node to be in the same box; that is, a mobile node can perform the foreign agent function itself. To make this work, however, the mobile node must be able to dynamically acquire an IP address that is located in the address space of the foreign network (e.g., using DHCP). This address will then be used as the care-of address. In our example, this address would have a network number of 12. This approach has the desirable feature of allowing mobile nodes to attach to networks that don't have foreign agents; thus, mobility can be achieved with only the addition of a home agent and some new software on the mobile node (assuming DHCP is used on the foreign network).

What about traffic in the other direction (i.e., from mobile node to fixed node)? This turns out to be much easier. The mobile node just puts the IP address of the fixed node in the destination field of its IP packets while putting its permanent address in the source field, and the packets are forwarded to the fixed node using normal means. Of course, if both nodes in a conversation are mobile, then the procedures described above are used in each direction.

ROUTE OPTIMIZATION IN MOBILE IP

Ther e is one significant drawback to the above approach: The route from the correspondent node to the mobile node can be significantly suboptimal. One of the most extreme examples is when a mobile node and the correspondent node are on the same network, but the home network for the mobile node is on the far side of the Internet. The sending correspondent node addresses all packets to the home network; they traverse the Internet to reach the home agent, which then tunnels them back across the Internet to reach the foreign agent. Clearly, it would be nice if the correspondent node could find out that the mobile node is actually on the same network and deliver the packet directly. In the more general case, the goal is to deliver packets as directly as possible from correspondent node to mobile node without passing through a home agent. This is sometimes referred to as the triangle routing problem since the path from correspondent to mobile node via home agent takes two sides of a triangle, rather than the third side that is the direct path.

The basic idea behind the solution to triangle routing is to let the correspondent node know the care-of address of the mobile node. The correspondent node can then create its own tunnel to the foreign agent. This is treated as an optimization of the process just described. If the sender has been equipped with the necessary software to learn the care-of address and create its own tunnel, then the route can be optimized; if not, packets just follow the suboptimal route.

When a home agent sees a packet destined for one of the mobile nodes that it supports, it can deduce that the sender is not using the optimal route. Therefore, it sends a "binding update" message back to the source, in addition to forwarding the data packet to the foreign agent. The source, if capable, uses this binding update to create an entry in a binding cache, which consists of a list of mappings from mobile node addresses to care-of addresses. The next time this source has a data packet to send to that mobile node, it will find the binding in the cache and can tunnel the packet directly to the foreign agent.

There is an obvious problem with this scheme, which is that the binding cache may become out-of-date if the mobile host moves to a new network. If an out-of-date cache entry is used, the foreign agent will receive tunneled packets for a mobile node that is no longer registered on its network. In this case, it sends a binding warning message back to the sender to tell it to stop using this cache entry. This scheme works only in the case where the foreign agent is not the mobile node itself, however. For this reason, cache entries need to be deleted after some period of time; the exact amount is specified in the binding update message.

As noted above, mobile routing provides some interesting security challenges, which are clearer now that we have seen how Mobile IP works. For example, an attacker wishing to intercept the packets destined to some other node in an internetwork could contact the home agent for that node and announce itself as the new foreign agent for the node. Thus, it is clear that some authentication mechanisms are required.

Mobility in IPv6

There are a handful of significant differences between mobility support in IPv4 and IPv6. Most importantly, it was possible to build mobility support into the standards for IPv6 pretty much from the beginning, thus alleviating a number of incremental deployment problems. (It may be more correct to say that IPv6 is one big incremental deployment problem, which, once solved, will deliver mobility support as part of the package.)

Since all IPv6-capable hosts can acquire an address whenever they are attached to a foreign network (using several mechanisms defined as part of the core v6 specifications), Mobile IPv6 does away with the foreign agent and includes the necessary capabilities to act as a foreign agent in every host.

One other interesting aspect of IPv6 that comes into play with Mobile IP is its inclusion of a flexible set of extension headers, as described elsewhere in this chapter. This is used in the optimized routing scenario described above. Rather than tunneling a packet to the mobile node at its care-of address, an IPv6 node can send an IP packet to the care-of address with the home address contained in a routing header. This header is ignored by all the intermediate nodes, but it enables the mobile node to treat the packet as if it were sent to the home address, thus enabling it to continue presenting higher layer protocols with the illusion that its IP address is fixed. Using an extension header rather than a tunnel is more efficient from the perspective of both bandwidth consumption and processing.

Finally, we note that many open issues remain in mobile networking. Managing the power consumption of mobile devices is increasingly important, so that smaller devices with limited battery power can be built. There is also the problem of ad hoc mobile networks—enabling a group of mobile nodes to form a network in the absence of any fixed nodes—which has some special challenges. A particularly challenging class of mobile networks is sensor networks. Sensors typically are small, inexpensive, and often battery powered, meaning that issues of very low power consumption and limited processing capability must also be considered. Furthermore, since wireless communications and mobility typically go hand in hand, the continual advances in wireless technologies keep on producing new challenges and opportunities for mobile networking.

PERSPECTIVE: THE CLOUD IS EATING THE INTERNET

The Cloud and the Internet have a mutually beneficial relationship. In the past, they were clearly separate, but nowadays the distinction between them is becoming more blurred. The Internet enables seamless connectivity between any two hosts, such as a client laptop and a remote server machine, while the cloud encompasses multiple expansive datacenters that offer an efficient and economical means to power, cool, and operate numerous server machines. End-users establish a connection to the closest datacenter via the Internet using the same method as connecting to a server in a remote machine room. This accurately depicts the link between the Internet and the Cloud during the initial stages of commercial cloud providers such as Amazon, Microsoft, and Google. As an illustration, Amazon's cloud in 2009 consisted of two datacenters, located on the east and west coasts of the United States. Currently, each of the leading cloud providers manages multiple datacenters situated worldwide. It is not unexpected that these datacenters are strategically positioned near Internet Exchange Points (IXP), which offer extensive access to the rest of the Internet. There are more than 150 Internet Exchange Points (IXPs) globally. Although not every cloud provider duplicates a complete datacenter near each IXP (as many of these sites are shared facilities), it is reasonable to assume that the most frequently accessed content in the cloud, such as popular Netflix movies, YouTube videos, and Facebook photos, could be distributed to all these locations.

There are two consequences to this wide dispersion of the cloud. One is that the end-to-end path from client to server doesn't necessarily traverse the entire Internet. A user is likely to find the content he or she wants to access has been replicated at a nearby IXP—which is usually just one AS hop away—as opposed to being on the far side of the globe. The second consequence is that the major cloud providers do not use the public Internet to interconnect their distributed datacenters. It is common for cloud providers to keep their content synchronized across distributed datacenters, but they typically do this over a private backbone. This allows them to take advantage of whatever optimizations they want without needing to fully inter-operate with anyone else.

In other words, while the figures in Section 4.1 fairly represents the Internet's overall shape, and BGP makes it possible to connect any pair of hosts, in practice most users interact with applications running in the Cloud, which looks more like Figure 124. (One important detail that the figure does not convey is that Cloud providers do not typically build a WAN by laying their own fiber, but they instead lease fiber from service providers, meaning that the private cloud backbone and the service provider backbones often share the same physical infrastructure.)

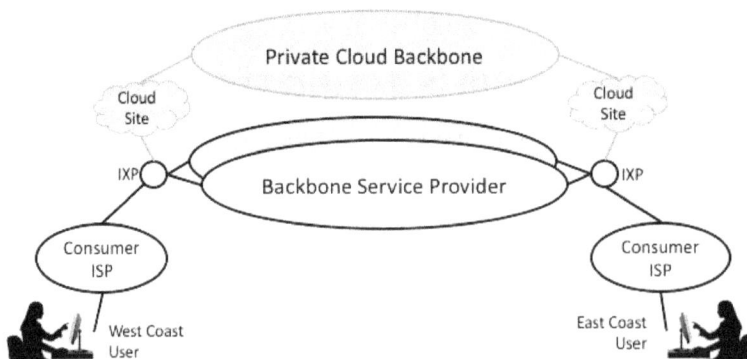

Figure 124. Cloud is widely distributed throughout the Internet with private backbones.

It is important to understand that although we can duplicate data across several places in the cloud, we now lack the capability to duplicate human beings. When users who are spread out desire to communicate with each other, such as during a video conference call, the multicast tree is deployed throughout the cloud. To clarify, multicast is not usually implemented in the routers of the service provider backbones, as mentioned in Section 4.3. Instead, it is implemented in server processes that are dispersed among a specific subset of the 150+ locations that act as the primary interconnection points of the Internet. An overlay is the term used to describe a multicast tree generated in this manner. We will revisit this concept in Section 9.4.

Broader Perspective

To continue reading about the cloudification of the Internet, see Perspective: HTTP is the New Narrow Waist.

To learn more about the Cloud's distributed footprint, we recommend How the Internet Travels Across the Ocean, New York Times, March 2019.

www.ingramcontent.com/pod-product-compliance
Lightning Source LLC
Chambersburg PA
CBHW082004190326
41458CB00010B/3073